D1739883

THE COMPLEAT ASTROLOGER'S
SUN-SIGNS GUIDE

Edited and designed by
Mitchell Beazley Publishers Limited,
14-15 Manette Street, London W1V 5LB

© Mitchell Beazley Publishers Limited 1973

All rights reserved

ISBN 0 85533 019 8

Printed and bound in The Netherlands

THE COMPLEAT ASTROLOGER'S
SUN-SIGNS GUIDE

Mitchell Beazley

Original material by
Derek and Julia Parker which has
appeared in other publications has
been re-edited for this convenient
single volume.

They and the publishers
acknowledge the contributions of
the following artists:
Donna Brown, Graham Brownridge,
Carol Binch, Bryony Dahl, Barry
Evans, Andrew Farmer, Harry Hants,
Chris McKewan, Ian Miller, Brian
Palmer, William Rankin, Justin Todd,
Paul Webb.
Other illustrations were supplied by
the Bodleian Library, Oxford, British
Museum, Bob Cundy, C. M. Dixon,
Michael Holford, Mansell Collection,
Picturepoint, Science Museum,
London, and Roger Viollet.

Astrological Organizations:
The American Federation of
Astrologers (Robert W. Cooper,
Executive Secretary), 6 Library Court,
Capitol Hill, Washington D.C. 20003.

The Astrological Association,
36, Tweedy Road, Bromley,
Kent BR1 3PP, England.
The Faculty of Astrological Studies
(Mrs. Heidi Langman, D.F.Astrol.S.),
Orchard House,
Ideford,
Newton Abbott, Devon, England.

CONTENTS

INTRODUCTION

Astrology is fun—and that is what this book is about.

Until less than a century ago (and astrology has been used for at least fifty centuries), the subject was a serious one, and was taken seriously. Astrology was a part of medicine and politics, it provided the early equivalent of psycho-analysis, it was very much in the scientific tradition. And, astrologers claim, it still is.

But in the 1920s a well-known astrologer, John Naylor, was invited to write an astrological column for a popular newspaper—the first 'What the Stars

Foretell' column. He knew perfectly well that the stars do not foretell anything, for not only have the stars nothing to do with astrology, but the true astrologer will not 'foretell' an event; he will only suggest that such-and-such an event is likely to happen. And he will only decide that after studying the full Birth Chart of his client: a map of the planets' positions at the *moment* of birth, and from the *place* of birth. Everyone has a different Birth Chart from everyone else, unless they are born in the same hospital within a few minutes of another baby.

Obviously, John Naylor could not write a popular astrology column based on a separate Birth Chart for each of his readers!—he had to find a way of simplifying the system. And he did so by choosing to write about the twelve 'Sun-signs'. Everyone knows the sign of the Zodiac the Sun was in when he was born, because it depends simply on the *date* of birth. Naylor wrote about what was likely to happen for those born with the Sun in Leo, or Sagittarius, or Libra; and very soon (for his column was very popular, and was copied throughout the world) readers were calling themselves 'Leos' or 'Sagittarians' or 'Librans'—something that had never happened before, in all astrology's long history.

This use of the Sun-sign is still the easiest way of writing about astrology for a large audience. Like every aspect of a Birth Chart or 'horoscope', the Sun-sign certainly has its effect; anyone born with the Sun in Gemini will recognize certain characteristics in the Gemini pages of this book. But do not forget that the Sun-sign is only one part of the Birth Chart, and not necessarily the most important part. If you read in this book the chapter on Aries, and find that it does not fit you well although your Sun-sign *is* Aries, it may be

because you had another sign 'rising' at birth—that is, another sign was on the eastern horizon at the time you were born— and that Sign has given you its characteristics. Or you may have several planets in, say Leo, which give you the characteristics of *that* Sign. And there are other possible reasons, which could only be discovered if your complete Birth Chart was calculated, with all the planets in position in all the astrological signs and houses. But that is not to say that you can't read a Sun-sign book for fun. Sometimes the description of 'your' sign, or parts of it, will fit you like a glove (if you happened to be born at sunrise, your Sun-sign and Ascendant—the rising sign—will be the same, so you will find the description particularly accurate).

Here are the main characteristics of 'your' Sun-sign: fit them, like a jigsaw, to your own character, and see how well they suit you and your friends. But please always remember that this book is *for fun only*: you would be very unwise to make any major decision, or be worried by anything told you either here or in the magazines or newspapers, on the basis of your Sun-sign alone! If, later, you want to set up your own Birth Chart, or have it calculated for you, you will be all the more amazed at the accuracy of astrology.

Derek Parker   Julia Parker.

THE ORIGINS,
MEANING AND POWER
OF ASTROLOGY

THE DAWN OF ASTROLOGY

*Man's First Responses to
Celestial Influence*

When the Moon passes across the face of the Sun in a total solar eclipse, even we in the 1970s feel disquiet, a moment of tension. Today the Sun and Moon undoubtedly have a strong physical effect on our lives, and that effect must have been much more strongly sensed in prehistoric times.

For early man, life was often savage and uncomfortable, his struggle to live was assailed by storms, merciless heat, famine, disease, drought. He had, moreover, to beat off attacks on his livestock from wild animals and to withstand the blows that his equally wild human neighbours aimed at his own life. As he hunted, fished, simply attempted to keep himself warm and well fed, he noticed the warmth of the Sun above him and the gradually increased cold as winter came on; the alternation of light and dark and the rhythmic motions of the sea on the shore. His attention was naturally drawn to those bodies in the sky that were constantly on the move against an apparently still background. Those bodies were the Sun, Moon and planets, and they were especially sharp to the eye in Mesopotamian latitudes where the atmosphere was clear and bright and where civilization—and astrology—began.

POWER TO THE PLANETS

The stars and planets offered early man a mirror. In them he saw an upper world that not only reflected his own predicament but—once he could interpret its secrets—would positively guide him through difficult times, avert disasters and set him on the right roads to peace and prosperity.

Almost as far back as records survive we find the notion of the Sun, Moon and planets as personalities, either commanding human life or intervening in it. The Sun and Moon formed a family group with Mercury and Venus (to call them by the well-known names that the Romans later gave them). Mercury and Venus then acquired the reputation of being respectively good and evil. Mars, Jupiter and Saturn made up a rival family with Jupiter at its head; and because Jupiter, as the leader, could only be good, the other two were thought to be evil.

Soon the planets took on more or less fixed characteristics: Mercury, the quick, cunning, fox-like planet-god, became associated with a shrewd kind of wisdom (he also became, incidentally, bisexual); Mars was the ruler of violence and war; Jupiter a king-like ruler of men; Saturn a somewhat cruel, morose god. The Sun, Jupiter and Saturn were particularly active by day, and the Moon, Mars and Venus by night. Men born under their influence, when they occupied certain positions in the sky, were in due course credited with a set of planetary characteristics unique to their time and place of birth.

ANCIENT WATCHTOWERS

The Great Quest Begins to Harness the Upper World

Left and *below*: The Caracol observatory at Chichen Itza, Mexico, where Mayan astrologers studied the planets. Below, on the wedding day of a Mayan city-chief, astrologers watch a favourable star enter their forked stick.

Right: Menhirs or great stones at Carnac, France, once linked with powerful Sun cults.

Far right: At Giza, Egypt, the corridors of the pyramids served as tubes for sighting the stars.

Even the ancients were concerned not only with the positions of the planets as related to the observer's viewpoint on earth, but also with the angular relationships that they appeared to form with each other. The early astronomer-astrologers reasoned that if the planets were to be regarded as human and as sharing human emotions, then they could be expected to have certain effects on each other. Venus and Mercury, for example, would be able to argue with the Sun, and to modify his judgments; neighbours must have some influence on the royal family, and at the same time would tend to quarrel among themselves, taking sides or even making a solitary stand for good or evil.

MOUNDS AND MEGALITHS

However, before the meaning behind the positions taken up by the various planets could be interpreted, it was obviously essential to be able to pinpoint those positions with great accuracy. For detailed work of this kind two principal methods were devised—megaliths and mounds. The huge stones brought to megalithic sites at Stonehenge, Carnac and elsewhere were positioned with almost miraculous precision to record the progressive movements through the year of

various celestial bodies. The 'mound' principle was applied in all kinds of towers, pyramids and other monumental structures offering a broader sweep of horizon; these sometimes contained sloping corridors or specially angled windows that could act as sighting devices. The appearances of particular planets in these apertures were carefully recorded, and from that information celestial maps and calendars were compiled.

It is astonishing indeed to find just how many large-scale structures all over the world, in India, China, Europe, the Middle East and America, were either built as observatories or watchtowers or were in some way adapted to the study of events in the heavens—and principally those occurring around the annual route of the Sun, as viewed from Earth. Around this path, which we now call the ecliptic, lay the region of the Zodiac, that central band of sky containing the star groups from which are derived the twelve astrological signs, which run from Aries to Pisces.

Below: One of the ziggurats or watchtowers of Ur; from these huge structures, Babylonian astrologers first observed that the revolving heavens moved to a pattern, in which lay the key to man's understanding of his earthly world.

ORIGINS OF THE ZODIAC

The Star-gods Take Their Appointed Places

In a Babylonian text, written in about 700 BC, reference is made to the Zodiac belt, and fifteen constellations are described as lying within it. In time the number of 'chief constellations' was reduced to twelve and the Zodiac belt was divided into twelve sections of 30° each. The Sun, which passed through the Zodiac once a year, was then seen to 'dwell' in turn in each sign of the Zodiac for a period of thirty days.

The creatures chosen to represent the constellations were taken from the everyday world of early civilizations in the Mediterranean region, and notably those of Babylonia (including Chaldea) and Assyria. There are seven bestial signs—Aries the Ram, Taurus the Bull, Cancer the Crab, Leo the Lion, Scorpio the Scorpion, Capricorn the Goat (or Sea-goat) and Pisces the Fishes. Four signs are 'human'—Gemini the Twins, Virgo the Virgin, Sagittarius the Archer and Aquarius the Water Carrier. (Although half horse, Sagittarius is judged to be human because of the human *activity*—firing a bow— with which he is associated.) Libra the Scales is neither bestial nor human but is considered to be a 'humane' sign, concerned with justice.

THE HOUSES

As the Earth turned on its axis once in every twenty-four hours so the Sun, Moon and planets were seen by the Chaldeans and other early observers to rise and set within this pattern, the entire sky shifting through one Zodiacal sign (or 30°) every two hours. In conjunction with this daily movement astrologers developed a system of Houses. From the line of the observer's horizon, the celestial globe was divided into twelve sections. Each section represented an area of life, as follows: 1 Life; 2 Poverty/riches; 3 Brothers/sisters; 4 Parents; 5 Children; 6 Health; 7 Husband/wife; 8 Death; 9 Religion; 10 Aspirations; 11 Friendship; 12 Family. The planets were then described in terms of the signs and houses they occupied at the moment of birth and their influence was gauged accordingly.

In their work of documenting the motions of the planets the first astrologers of Babylonia and Assyria saw that events in the sky repeated themselves, and the first tables of planetary movements were drawn up. The earliest recorded ephemerides, as they are called, date from the reign of King Assurbanipal (668–625 BC).

The future the astrologers foretold was usually not that of an individual but of the State. They were quite clear that the heavens and the Earth were interrelated, but they had no evidence that an individual could claim particular planetary influences—except one man, the King, who was seen as the embodiment of the State, and whose birth-time was used for State forecasts. These noted the approach and assessed the likely effects of major events such as famine, war and pestilence.

The Fishes, from a wall painting at Knossos, Crete, the centre of a Bronze Age civilization. In astrology Pisceans often feel driven—like the symbolic fishes— in two directions at the same time.

One of the first Sagittarians—a mythical Centaur, half-man, half-horse, shown trampling a rival to death; from the Elgin Marbles.

Egyptian gods weigh the dead; in Babylonian religion Libra was linked with the judgment of souls.

Above: From Sumeria, a compelling image for primitive Capricornians of a he-goat made of gold and lapis-lazuli. In time Capricorn was established as a fish-tailed goat, known to the ancient Babylonians as Ea, the 'antelope of the subterranean ocean', and as Kusarikku, the fish-ram.

In every culture the bull was taken up as a symbol of strength, and often of creative energy; this head represents the bull-god of Knossos, Crete.

Left: At Karnak, Egypt, where this avenue of figures is situated, the ram-headed sphinx was considered to be a symbol of power, mystery and wisdom.

CLASSICAL ASTROLOGY

*Ancient Egypt, Greece and Rome—A New Age
of Horoscopes for All*

The Egyptians were celebrated scientists and enthusiastic observers of the heavens, producing star charts as long ago as the fifth millenium BC. Their preoccupation with calendar-making and mathematics considerably helped the advance of astrology; the astrological functions of the great pyramids are still being researched today. One of the most famous of the astrologer-kings was Rameses II, 'Ozymandias, King of Kings', whose tomb at his death in *c* 1223 BC was richly decorated with astrological symbols. He it also was who fixed the four cardinal signs—Aries, Libra, Cancer and Capricorn. And from the temple of Denderah a relief, dated at about 30 BC, shows the first pictorial representation of the Zodiac to have survived: more precisely, two Zodiacs are featured, one within the other, principally supported by four standing female figures.

From Egypt too came a group of manuscripts collected under the name of 'Hermes Trismegistus', the founder of a medico-astrological cult. Many of its ingredients were also purely magical, and it is the first concrete example of astrology being linked with the occult; one of the most interesting ideas contained in the manuscripts is that correspondences exist between the great outer world (the macrocosm) and man the microcosm.

ASTROLOGY REACHES THE PEOPLE

The Greeks took to astrology with great enthusiasm, as witness a great number of surviving documents and monuments decorated with astrological symbols. It is from the time of Antiochus of Commene (about 30 BC) that the earliest horoscopes from Greek literary sources survive; from the next five centuries or so, about 180 individual horoscopes have come down to us. The Greeks' great contribution to astrology was in fact to rationalize and popularize it, making birth charts available to all and not just the preserve of the ruler— as representative of the State.

By 280 BC, the Babylonian astrologer Berosus, whose works appeared in Greek libraries, had been able to set up a highly successful school of astrology on the island of Cos, and astrologers were already setting out and rationalizing in textbooks the sum total of all they knew for posterity. This burst of study culminated in the first modern astrological text, the *Tetrabiblos*, attributed to the great astronomer, mathematician and geographer, Claudius Ptolemy. He was born in Greece in about AD 120, and was one of the major thinkers of his time. His work as a geographer and mathematician was thorough and revolutionary, and his *Syntaxis* survived for 1,400 years as the most comprehensive source of Greek astronomical ideas. The *Tetrabiblos* is an extraordinary book, as well argued as many modern textbooks (and better than some); many of its general principles are still accepted today.

SLAVES OF DESTINY: IMPERIAL ROME

During the first two centuries after Christ, astrological activity centred on Imperial Rome. In those days, as soon as it became

Right: The Roman Emperor Augustus (ruled 27 BC– AD 14) bravely risked publishing his horoscope—so revealing the death date predicted for him—and he had a silver coin struck which bore his sign—Capricorn. The sea-goat is shown guiding a small globe, included to symbolize Rome's power in the world.

clear that a man was a candidate for the emperor's throne, astrologers gathered around him. Naturally, the emperors tended to snap up the most convincing, most lucid, most persuasive astrologers available, and then kept them busy around the hub of power—if only to discourage pretenders to the throne. They looked on any attempt by someone else to consult an astrologer as extremely suspect, and as probably indicating a plot to seize power.

Tiberius (reigned AD 14–37) was of all the Roman emperors perhaps the most slavishly addicted to astrology. His accession and 'lofty destiny' had been predicted at his birth, and right until the end of his life—particularly during his retirement at Capri, when his excesses made him one of the most despised, hated and feared of men—he was surrounded by what Juvenal called his 'herd of Chaldeans'.

Claudius I (emperor AD 41–54) was old-fashioned in his ideas and preferred divination by bird-flight (augury) to astrology; indeed, he banned astrologers from the country—although the ban was not very successfully enforced. Later, a noble Roman was caught consulting an astrologer to inquire when Claudius would die—and was himself rewarded with a sudden and violent end.

Nero (AD 54–68), although on the whole disinclined to favour any religion, was excessively superstitious, and was encouraged by his astrologers to perpetrate a number of atrocities. Bilbilus, his official astrologer, advised him to divert the evil effects of a comet by slaughtering the heads of most of the great families of Rome.

THE EMPRESS AND THE GLADIATOR

Later emperors, if occasionally protesting their derisive opinion of old-fashioned superstitions, were careful to keep an astrologer about the house. Vespasian officially exiled all astrologers, but retained the most notable of them to serve him personally. His son Titus consulted foreign astrologers and was a firm believer. Domitian was utterly reliant on his astrologers. He dismissed and even murdered noblemen found in possession of the Imperial horoscope, and carefully studied the birth charts of those he thought might have an eye on the throne. Towards the end of his reign, his fears increased. One of his last acts—on the morning of his death— was to order the execution of an astrologer who had been specially summoned from Germany to interpret a series of menacing omens—and whose answers had obviously been too close to the truth!

Hadrian (AD 117–138) held a sort of *soirée* on the first day of each year, at which he would predict events in the coming year in considerable detail, finally including the hour of his own death. The last of the great emperors, Marcus Aurelius (AD 160–180), consulted astrologers about the association of his wife Faustina with a gladiator, whose muscles she had evidently been admiring from less than a stadium's length away; this same emperor seems also to have kept 'an Egyptian magician' (probably an astrologer) at court.

Above: The Egyptian Zodiac (c. 30 BC) from Denderah. This is the earliest known representation of a Zodiac.

Left: Augustus' ruling planet was Saturn. The Saturnalia devoted to the worship of the planet-god was among the liveliest of Roman festivals: presents were exchanged and slaves attended by their masters.

ASTROLOGY IN THE MIDDLE AGES

A Science of Monks and Noblemen

Astrology has always flourished in a civilized setting. After the fall of Rome and the onset of the Dark Ages the science suffered an eclipse. In the monasteries, however, some interest survived and serious study continued in the Middle East, where Albumasar (805–85), a celebrated Arab astrologer, wrote that 'Only by observing the great diversity of planetary motions can we comprehend the unnumbered varieties of change in this world.'

Gradually, as Europe crept once more towards the light, astrology began to return to man's consciousness – not only as a means of prediction, but as a means of revealing and explaining. Successive Christian philosophers and writers began to rediscover its virtues. One of the results of this new alliance was that various religions were put under the protection of the planets: Judaism was ruled by Saturn; Islam (being both warlike and sensual) by Venus and Mars; Christianity by Mercury – dominant when in Virgo, the sign of the Virgin Mary.

Among the important thinkers who upheld the astrological theory were Albertus Magnus (c 1193–1280), a German philosopher and experimental scientist. He believed that the stars could not influence the soul but that they could certainly exert control over the body, and through it reach the human will. Albertus' pupil Thomas Aquinas (1225–74) carried on the debate and went even further than his master, when he made his declaration that 'The celestial bodies are the cause of all that takes place in the sublunar world.'

ASTROLOGY BECOMES A SOCIAL SUCCESS

By the fourteenth century, astrology was firmly established in the universities, supported by theology on the one hand and science on the other. In many noble families the horoscopes of newly-born children were drawn up as a matter of course, and their lives were sometimes dominated by the resulting biographical notes, prepared before they could even walk. There are examples of the horoscopes of favourite horses, and even of pet dogs. Astrology was rapidly becoming all-pervasive, its literature ranging from popular 'Moon books' to serious consideration by both Dante and Chaucer.

Right: These illustrations from a medieval French Book of Hours, set round an early sun dial, show how each sign of the Zodiac was associated with a monthly occupation on the land.

CANCER THE CRAB
Approximately 21 June – 22 July. The traditional occupation of this Zodiacal month is cutting grass for haymaking. The labourer uses a scythe; at his belt hangs a sharpening stone.

GEMINI THE TWINS
22 May – 20 June. Hunting with hawks and falcons was a favourite seasonal

LEO THE LION
23 July – 22 August. This was the time to harvest the wheat, done by hand with a small reaping hook; the wheat was then gathered in sheaves and piled in stooks to dry.

VIRGO THE VIRGIN
23 August – 22 September. In the month of the Virgin, when the wheat had dried it was spread out and threshed – also by hand – to separate the grain from the straw.

LIBRA THE SCALES
23 September – 22 October. After the grape harvest the grapes were placed in wide, shallow barrels, and crushed by the vineyard workers to extract the juice.

SCORPIO THE SCORPION
23 October – 21 November. Sowing for the next

occupation among the landowning classes in the spacious days of the fifteenth century.

TAURUS THE BULL
20 April–21 May. Fertility was once more in the air and people gathered branches and flowers to decorate their streets and houses for the May Day festivities.

ARIES THE RAM
21 March–19 April. In the Zodiacal month of the Ram an important task was to clear away old vines, and trees and bushes were pruned in preparation for the new season.

PISCES THE FISHES
20 February–20 March. A time for keeping warm: usually the harsh weather made farming difficult, work slowed and people tended to pass the days relaxing indoors.

AQUARIUS THE WATERBEARER
20 January–19 February. Next came the feasting, an activity watched over in many medieval calendars by two-faced Janus, the ancient Italian god of the month of January.

season often took place under the sign of Scorpio, especially in areas having a clay soil.

SAGITTARIUS THE ARCHER
22 November–21 December. Country people at this time of year knocked down their acorns and sweet chestnuts to fatten their pigs, who had not long to go.

CAPRICORN THE GOAT
22 December–19 January. The pigs and other animals were slaughtered when fodder for them grew scarce, and their carcasses were salted to make the meat last longer.

THE ZODIAC AND THE BODY

How the Twelve Signs Rule our Anatomy

Hugh of St Victor (c 1096–1141), whose philosophy and mysticism were highly influential in the twelfth century, stressed the value of *natural astrology*, which 'deals with the influence of the stars upon our bodily complexions, which vary according to the state of our celestial sphere, as in health and sickness, good and bad weather, fertility and drought'. Even before his time connections were made between the signs of the Zodiac and specific parts of the human body. In the ancient library of Hermes Trismegistus, for example, there appears the notion of correspondences between the macrocosm—the universe—and man: 'The macrocosm embraces the twelve Zodiacal signs and so does man, from his head (the Ram) to his feet, which correspond to the Fishes.'

In recent years astrologers have taken this ancient lore and considered it in the light of modern medical advances. From their researches they have established links between the twelve signs and the glandular and nervous system. These may also be seen to work through what is known as polarity, or the sympathy of opposites. Thus Arian headaches may be related to a kidney condition, the latter falling under the influence of Libra, the opposite sign to Aries. In the captions on these pages the polarity sign appears second.

ARIES/LIBRA
Arians tend to have headaches more readily than most, for Aries rules the head; they may also be headstrong, suffering from sudden rushes of anger.

TAURUS/SCORPIO
Taureans are vulnerable to colds and chills, for Taurus rules the throat and neck; it is advisable to keep the throat protected during cold weather.

CANCER/CAPRICORN
Cancerians traditionally tend to worry more than most, and since Cancer rules the stomach their tensions may provoke stomach upsets or even ulcers.

VIRGO/PISCES
Virgo rules the nervous system and intestines, and Virgoans (like Cancerians) tend to suffer from slight stomach upsets, often of a digestive type; many Virgoans are vegetarians, and anyway should watch their diet.

GEMINI/SAGITTARIUS
Geminians may tend to break collar-bones and arms, which are ruled by this sign; they may also find that colds fly immediately to their chests and lungs, and should guard those areas.

SAGITTARIUS/GEMINI

Sagittarians need exercise and the women of this sign should take special care, for they put on weight very easily around the hips and thighs. Sagittarius also rules the liver.

AQUARIUS/LEO

Aquarians playing rough games should watch their shins and ankles; but Aquarius also rules the circulation, and circulatory difficulties (varicose veins, hardening of the arteries) may arise in old age.

PISCES/VIRGO

Anything wrong with a Piscean's feet immediately irritates him; and Piscean feet are often slightly misshapen. Pisceans should also remember that they do not react well to drugs.

LEO/AQUARIUS

Leo's strong association with the heart can in late years mean weakness in that organ, especially if Leo subjects pursue their appetite for the high life and so put too much strain on their hearts.

LIBRA/ARIES

The sign's connection with the kidneys is such that any emotional upset can immediately cause a stomach upset, too; a good reason for controlling the temper!

SCORPIO/TAURUS

Scorpio's association with the sexual organs can lead to impotence in males; more usually the effect is psychological, and Scorpios may be stimulated to violent emotions as well as actions.

CAPRICORN/CANCER

The knees and teeth are emphasized by this sign; dental decay can occur, as can a stiffening of the joints—indeed Capricorn sometimes limits movement by rheumatism.

THE PLANETS AND THE BODY

How the Ten Planets Influence our Glandular System

An important set of correspondences has long existed between specific body areas and the planets. These were used chiefly for medical purposes. Originally they applied to the Sun, Moon and the other five known planets; later they were of course revised to include Uranus, Neptune and Pluto—once the natures of these 'modern' planets could be properly assessed.

A seventeenth-century book, the *Astrological Judgment of Diseases* by Nicholas Culpeper (1616–54), though many astrologers today would not agree with its conclusions, is interesting for its detailed lists of the parts of the body ruled by planets and signs, the diseases ruled by signs and notes on their diagnosis. Culpeper also devised astrological tests to discover whether a patient was faking symptoms, and he sets out a well-reasoned procedure for cure. This includes consideration of the planet governing the disease; side by side with this astrological commentary run purely medical notes dealing with pulse readings, conditions of the blood and urine, and so on.

Since Culpeper, modern medical progress has uncovered a more significant zone of influence—that between the planets and the endocrine glands. These small but vital glands release hormones into the blood and control a great diversity of body functions, from the way we breathe to the expression of our sexual needs.

MERCURY
The brain and nervous system as a whole is ruled by Mercury, which also exerts influence on the way we breathe.

VENUS
The parathyroids, which control the calcium level of the body fluids, are ruled by Venus, which traditionally is connected with the throat, kidneys and lumbar region.

THE SUN
The Sun is particularly associated with the thymus, though it also rules (traditionally) the heart, back and spinal column.

JUPITER
Jupiter's concern is with the liver and its cleansing work; but it also affects the pituitary gland, which regulates hormone growth and production, and governs our physical growth.

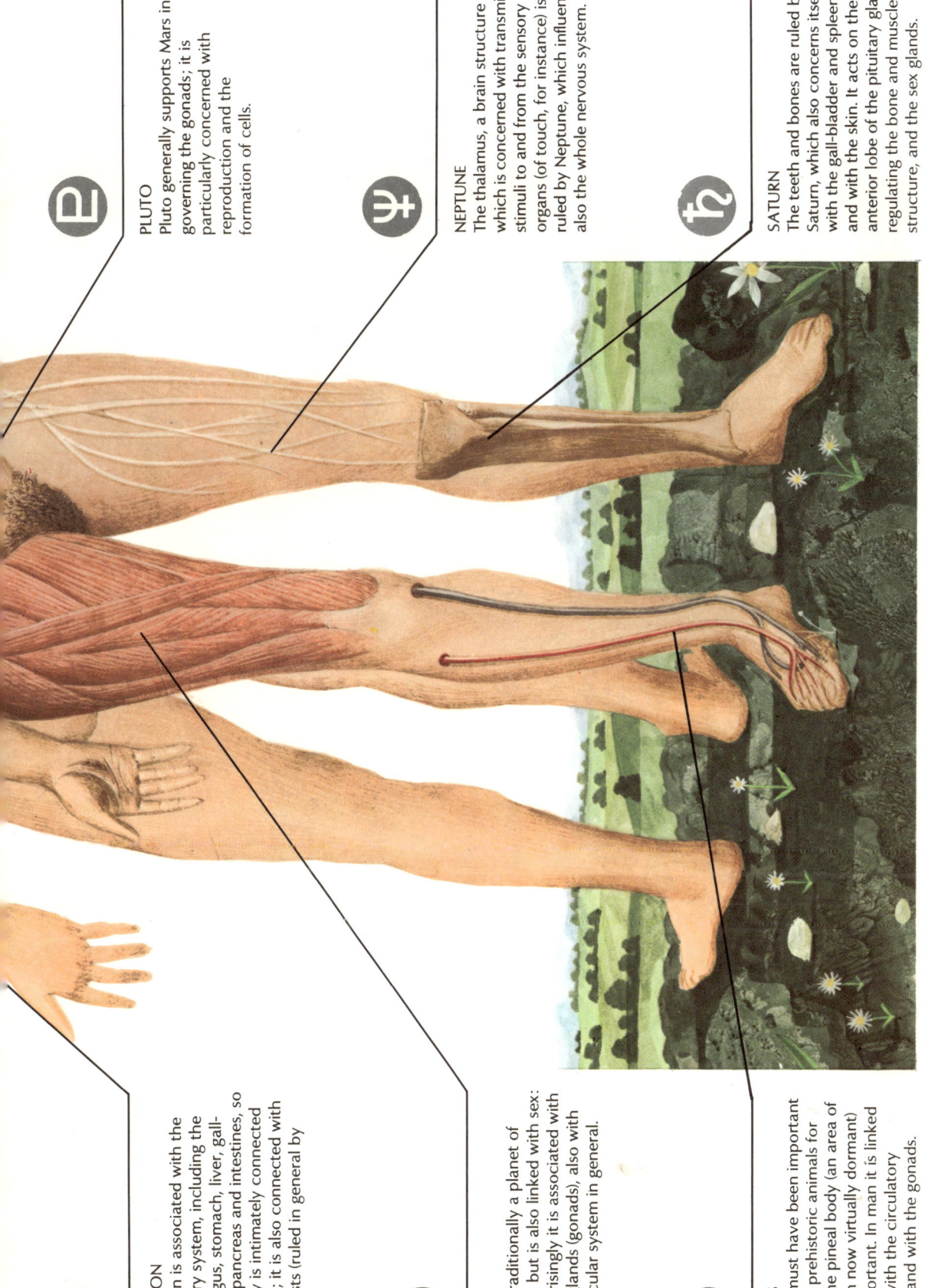

PLUTO
Pluto generally supports Mars in governing the gonads; it is particularly concerned with reproduction and the formation of cells.

NEPTUNE
The thalamus, a brain structure which is concerned with transmitting stimuli to and from the sensory organs (of touch, for instance) is ruled by Neptune, which influences also the whole nervous system.

SATURN
The teeth and bones are ruled by Saturn, which also concerns itself with the gall-bladder and spleen, and with the skin. It acts on the anterior lobe of the pituitary gland, regulating the bone and muscle structure, and the sex glands.

THE MOON
The Moon is associated with the alimentary system, including the oesophagus, stomach, liver, gall-bladder, pancreas and intestines, so obviously is intimately connected with diet; it is also connected with the breasts (ruled in general by Cancer).

MARS
Mars is traditionally a planet of violence, but is also linked with sex: not surprisingly it is associated with the sex glands (gonads), also with the muscular system in general.

URANUS
Uranus must have been important to those prehistoric animals for whom the pineal body (an area of the brain now virtually dormant) was important. In man it is linked mainly with the circulatory system, and with the gonads.

THE SCIENTIFIC REVOLUTION

Copernicus Reshapes the Universe

The influence of astrologers in the sixteenth and seventeenth centuries was at its weightiest in the courts of Europe. Astrology was found to be intellectually stimulating as well as practically useful for the conduct of war and peace, and in politics and private life. Some of the royal advisers were astronomer-astrologers, some had an equal interest in the occult or in alchemy. And so, while Elizabeth I of England summoned the visionary Dr Dee and heard his advice, Catherine de Medici in France was advised by Nostradamus, and Christian IV of Denmark, Sigismund III of Poland (and Sweden) and Frederick of Bohemia all had astrologers attached to their courts.

THE GREAT ASTRONOMERS

One event that caused a great stir was the publication in 1543 by Copernicus, the Polish church official and astronomer, of his new theory of the universe. In it he demolished the sacred idea, held by scientists since Ptolemy's day (c AD 120–180), that the Sun, Moon and planets all revolved around the Earth. Copernicus proposed instead that the Sun lay at the centre. People were horrified, the Church banned his work and it remained on the Papal Index until 1835. But astrological theory was little affected by Copernicus–even when his findings were later confirmed by Johannes Kepler (1571–1630); the reason is that astrology is concerned with the positions of the planets *as seen from* Earth; for purposes of calculation it was not unreasonable to maintain the Earth at the centre of the universe.

The great astronomers of the period were attached to the courts of various European rulers, and invariably were also astrologers. Indeed Tycho Brahe (1546–1601) in his *De disciplinus mathematicus* states that 'those who deny the influence of the planets violate clear evidence which for educated people of sound judgment it is not suitable to contradict'. And Kepler, who was Brahe's successor as Imperial Mathematician at the court of the Holy Roman Emperor, wrote in *De stella nova:* 'Nothing exists nor happens in the visible sky that is not sensed in some hidden moment by the faculties of Earth and Nature.'

It would be wrong to assume that all thinking men of this period believed completely in astrology as a means of accurate prediction. This would be an over-statement. The general attitude was nearer that of Francis Bacon (1561–1626). 'I am certain,' he wrote, 'that the celestial bodies have in them certain influences besides heat and light.' His cautious view underlines the growing scientific spirit among intelligent men of the day.

Left: In these star maps drawn by G. C. Eimmart the constellations of the Zodiac are grouped along the ecliptic, or path of the Sun, at the base of each hemisphere. Around the main charts diagrams explain the phases of the Moon (*bottom left*), the seasons (*bottom right*) and the tides (*top right*); the others describe three different universal systems. In that of Ptolemy (*top centre*) the Earth lies at the centre of the universe, while Copernicus (*bottom centre*) placed the Sun at the core of his system; and Tycho Brahe (*top left*) put the Earth in the centre but made the planets orbit the Sun.

25

A TABLE of the principal AFFECTIONS of the PLANETS.

Jan. 1st 1794.
Published as the Act directs by
W. & S. Jones.

ANNO 1794	Mean distances from the Sun in English Miles	Periodical revolutions round the Sun	Diurnal rotations upon their Axes	Diameters in English miles the Sun being 883.217	Greatest elongation of inferior & Parallax of superior planets
MERCURY	37.000.000	87 d. 23 h. 15 ½ m.	* * *	3.222	28° 20'
VENUS	68.000.000	224 d. 16 h. 49 ½ m.	23 h. 22 m.	7.687	47° 48'
EARTH	95.000.000	365 d. 6 h. 9 ½ m.	23 h. 56 m. 0 4 f.	7.964	
MARS	144.000.000	686 d. 23 h. 30 ½ m.	24 h. 39 m. 22 f.	4.189	47° 24'
JUPITER	490.000.000	4332 d. 8 h. 51 m.	9 h. 56 m.	89.170	n. 5'
SATURN	900.000.000	10761 d. 14 h. 36 ½ m.		79.042	6° 29'

JEFFREY'S Satellites.

Distances Miles	Revolutions
150.000	1 d. 21 h. 19 m.
200.000	2 d. 17 h. 25 m.
390.000	4 d. 12 h. 35 m.
700.000	15 d. 22 h. 4 m.
2.000.000	29 d. 7 h. 40 m.

D.......d for the NEW PORTABLE ORRERY L.. W. 40

...and Made and Sold by W. & S. JONES
30 Holborn
LONDON

THE SOLAR SYSTEM

DECEMBER
JANUARY
FEBRUARY
MARCH
APRIL
MAY
JUNE

♒ Aquarius
♓ Pisces
♈ Aries
♉ Taurus
♊ Gemini
♋ Cancer
♑ Capricornus
♒ Aquarius
Sagittarius

SOUTH
NORTH
EAST
WEST

THE MECHANICAL COSMOS
Rational Science and the Rebirth of Astrology

Towards the end of the seventeenth century astrology fell from general favour. Some people assume that the publication in 1687 of Isaac Newton's *Principia* began this process. On the contrary, astrological practices had begun to deteriorate some years before that date. There had always been dishonest practitioners on the edge of the subject, ready to take advantage of the over-credulous. Now they multiplied as they saw that the middle classes, gradually becoming more educated, offered a rich ground for speculators who claimed impossible powers of prediction.

The seventeenth century was, above all, the age of science and rationalism. Since the first telescopic observations, made by Harriott, Galileo and Marius in about 1609–10, there was a general dedication to scientific truths. A rift occurred between astrology, which depends not only on mathematics but on intuition and sensitivity as well, and those areas of knowledge in which it was permissible to verify new theories only by empirical means. Ironically however, Isaac Newton himself, the man whose book finally opened the modern phase of astronomy, never lost his profound regard for the hidden truths of astrology.

ASTROLOGY TURNS THE CORNER

During the nineteenth century there were few astrologers with a serious interest in their craft, and where astrology flourished it was usually debased by occultism. Astrological magazines such as *The Prophetic Messenger* published predictions and information about magic talismans and 'animal magnetism', and were far from being serious astrological publications. But, towards the end of the century, astrology began to revive under the aegis of Madame Blavatsky and the Theosophists. Later William Frederick Allan (1860–1917) under the nom-de-plume of 'Alan Leo' became the first important popular astrologer of the twentieth century; although the mass-produced horoscopes he sent out to the public at large were of little value, his textbooks on astrology were responsibly written and are still read for their instructional value in the 1970s.

In the USA the first popular astrologer of importance was Evangeline Adams (1865–1930), whose remarkable predictions brought her fame and a dedicated following. She is best remembered for her radio series, which did much to publicize the benefits of astrology. In more recent years Dane Rudhyar (1895–   ) has sought to bring astrology to a high academic level, investing it with a language by which 'man can discover the pattern of order which reveals both his individuality and his destiny'. In Europe, meanwhile, many people were swayed by the astrological essays of C. G. Jung (1875–1961).

Today, of course, astrology is becoming an essential part of our culture and is making a widely respected contribution in many fields, including those of business, psychiatry, science, education, and the law. Astrology has done more than come in out of the cold. It is now a major source of warmth to many thousands of people.

Above is an orrery, a mechanical device that demonstrates the relative motions of the celestial bodies. This example was made in 1794 and shows the Sun in the centre: around it turn Mercury (white disk), Venus, the Earth and the Moon.

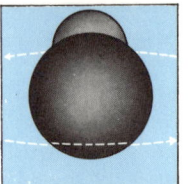

Above: The Trifid Nebula in Sagittarius. Modern research suggests that the rhythms of bodies remote in space may be linked by a complex system of harmonies to man's own activity cycles such as our heartbeats and brain rhythms.

Left: The light-curve diagram below shows how emissions from the double star Algol vary every 2½ days. Scientists are now considering whether such cosmic activities may affect our lives on Earth.

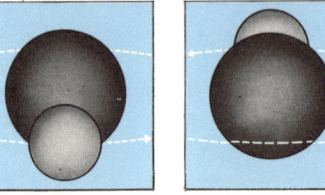
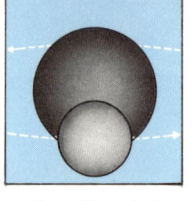

The changing cosmic intensity of the double star Algol: its brightness decreases (1 and 3) when the fainter star eclipses its partner; but when (2 and 4) the brighter member is to the fore the combined body emits more light.

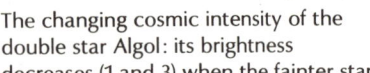

THE NEW ASTROLOGY

Exploring the Frontiers of Cosmic Energy

Today, in the celebrated words of the great psychologist C. G. Jung, astrology 'knocks at the doors of the universities, from which it was banished some three hundred years ago'. Every year astrologers meet at international conferences to exchange information and discuss new developments which link astrology with all manner of scientific disciplines. Doctors, for example, find astrology useful: in Czechoslovakia, Dr. Eugen Jonas has been experimenting in the prediction of the sex of unborn children, and has also produced impressive evidence to show that fertility in women fluctuates with the motions of the Sun and Moon.

Meteorologists are becoming more and more aware of the effect the planets have on terrestrial weather—producing statistics to show that the Moon influences rainfall, Mercury the temperature, and the planetary cycles the general year-to-year weather picture. Dr. R. Tomaschek, Chairman of the World Geophysical Council, found the position of Uranus significant in the cases of 134 earthquakes which he studied.

TOWARDS ANCIENT BELIEFS

In Renaissance times, every educated man believed in astrology—that the planets, while not dictating what he *must* do, inclined him to certain actions or attitudes. After three hundred years during which belief tended to swing away, more and more people are now beginning to come to the conclusion that the astrologers are probably right. And science is beginning, slowly, to support the view. As Sir Bernard Lovell, the English astronomer, put it some years ago, 'It almost seems as though we are moving through a series of scientific fantasies to a proof of ancient beliefs.'

In Russia, astrology, like religion, is officially denigrated; in India, perhaps men rely on it too much. In the Western countries in general, public opinion is turning more and more towards the belief that, as Jung wrote, 'whatever is born or done this moment, has the qualities of this moment of time'.

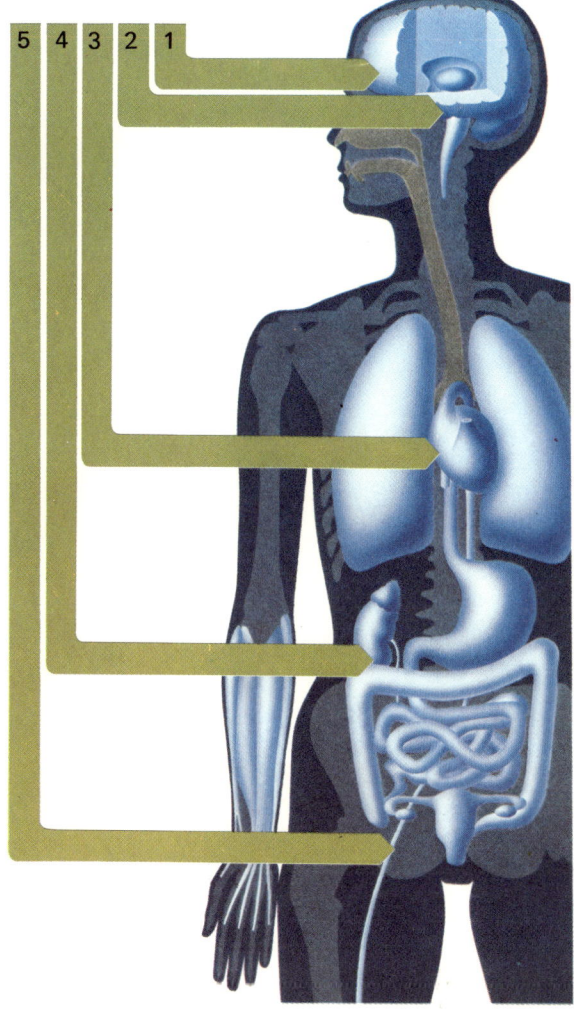

Above: Some of the human activity cycles that may correspond to broader cosmic functions. Beta rhythms (1) affect our sense of judgment; alpha rhythms (2) are most active during sleep; the others shown here relate to the heart (3), the kidneys (4) and the ovaries (5).

Left: We now know that extra-terrestrial powers, especially from the Sun and Moon, affect all kinds of plant and animal behaviour, from oysters and birds to man himself. This diagram shows F. A. Brown Jr's discovery that flatworms (*planetaria*) are directed by lunar phases: at the new Moon (black disk) they turn about 10° to the left on leaving their enclosures; at the time of the full Moon (white disk) they turn to the right by the same amount.

Dr Eugen Jonas wrote that women became fertile at times dictated by the Sun and Moon; and that

at conception the Moon in a positive (plus) sign meant the child would be a boy; negative meant a girl.

HOW ASTROLOGY WORKS
The Mechanics of Celestial Knowledge

To early man the celestial bodies—chiefly the Sun—were forces to be reckoned with: they had the power to intervene in his life. On the other hand he was reluctant to concede that any external body was more important than the Earth itself, around which the rest of the universe was seen to revolve.

AN EARTH-CENTRED VIEW OF THE UNIVERSE

The celestial sphere, opposite, demonstrates both these ancient attitudes. Today we all know that really the Sun not the Earth lies at the centre of the universe, but modern astrologers, like their ancestors, are principally concerned with the positions of the planets *as seen from* Earth, and so the convention can be retained.

The celestial sphere shows how we might look out from Earth at the universe beyond. There in the sky are the Sun, Moon and planets, all moving within the Zodiacal band against the starry background. This, in astrology, is divided into twelve equal segments (the signs) which serve as reference points for charting the positions taken up by the planets in their various orbits.

KEY
A Path of ecliptic
B The fixed Zodiac
C Earth
N/S Poles of the celestial equator

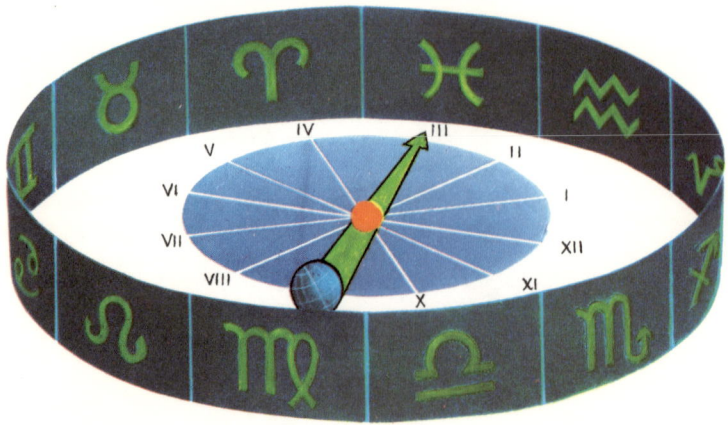

Above: The Sun through the year. Although it is really the Earth that turns round the Sun once a year, to us on Earth it seems to be the Sun that moves. Behind the Sun the fixed signs of the Zodiac—each of which occupies a 30° segment of the band—change from month to month; the Sun is seen, for example, against Pisces during March, the third month of the year.

Below: In addition to the Sun nine other significant astrological bodies—planets—occupy our Solar System. Except for Pluto these always remain within the area of the Zodiac. They are shown below with their ancient glyphs or symbols: these represent, from left to right, Neptune, Saturn, Mars, Venus, the Sun, Mercury, the Moon (next to the Sun in importance), Jupiter, Uranus and Pluto.

Above: The Earth is seen at the centre of a hollow sphere, encircled by the ecliptic—the apparent annual path of the Sun as viewed from Earth. The ecliptic is contained within a specific band of sky known as the Zodiac.

THE PLANETS

Their Scale, Orbital Paths and Range of Influence

Many who are discovering astrology for the first time may not realize that the Sun, although of the first importance, is not the only active force in the heavens. In serious astrology a subject's Birth Chart is calculated for his or her birth date, time and place, and interpreted according to the positions of *all* the planets. Anyone wishing, incidentally, to see which signs of the Zodiac were occupied by all the planets at his or her birth should consult an ephemeris, or table of planetary positions, for the year of birth.

These positions are determined by precise factors. Although to the ancient Babylonians the planets were known as 'wanderers' or 'goats' because they seemed to move erratically across the sky—in contrast to the 'fixed' stars that were so far away as to seem unmoving—in fact the planets are held by gravity to a fairly regular course around the Sun.

The Sun is the major body of the Solar System, in which we live. In size it is enormous: it has a diameter of 865,000 miles and its volume is more than a million times greater than the Earth's. Gravity of course works by mass rather than size: the greater the mass the greater the pull one body exerts on another. At times this can cause one planet physically to influence another, setting up 'perturbations' or irregular movements. This was precisely what led to the discovery of Pluto in 1930, as we shall see.

THE ASTROLOGER'S VIEW

In astrology the Sun and Moon are regarded as planets. In addition to them, eight other bodies in the Solar System are held to be astrologically significant. Those nearest to the Sun—Mercury, Venus, Mars, Jupiter and Saturn—were known in ancient times and each early acquired a set of human characteristics and was associated with such earthly phenomena as a specific metal, a precious stone, and so on. Each, furthermore, had a special relationship with at least one sign of the Zodiac. The Sun and Moon ruled one sign each and the other planets two signs each.

THE MODERN PLANETS

When Uranus, the nearest of the three modern planets, was discovered by William Herschel in 1781, astrologers had to reassess these Zodiacal relationships. After a great deal of consideration—and not a little controversy—Uranus was felt to represent the principle of sudden, disruptive change and was allied to Aquarius (which formerly had been felt to reflect certain qualities of Saturn).

A similar process followed the appearance of Neptune in 1846. This planet was linked with Pisces since they were felt to share qualities of receptivity and diffuseness. Pluto, the latest planet, is very new. It was

discovered only in 1930, when irregularities in the motions of Uranus and Neptune suggested to scientists that a third body, by its gravitational pull, was influencing their orbital pattern. Dramatically, a team led by Clyde Tombaugh at the Lowell Observatory in Arizona proved this to be the case—and the tenth planet was added to astrological lore.

Today most astrologers agree with the association of Pluto, whose keyword is 'elimination', with Scorpio. They are, all the same, very aware of the strong residual influence of Mars in that sign.

Because of their remoteness the three modern planets move very slowly through the Zodiac. Many astrologers believe that their influence is similarly 'distant', extending over entire generations rather than closely affecting individual lives as, in particular, the Sun does.

Left: The signs and their ruling planets. These are: Sun—Leo; Moon—Cancer; Mercury—Gemini, Virgo; Venus—Taurus, Libra; Mars—Aries; Jupiter—Sagittarius; Saturn—Capricorn; Uranus—Aquarius; Neptune—Pisces, and Pluto—Scorpio. The old links, i.e. before the discovery of the modern planets, are shown in white.

Right and below: The planets are seen extending outwards from the fierce heat of the Sun to the cold, remote zone occupied by Uranus, Neptune and Pluto; and in scale against part of the Sun's curvature with their glyphs (the Moon is not shown).

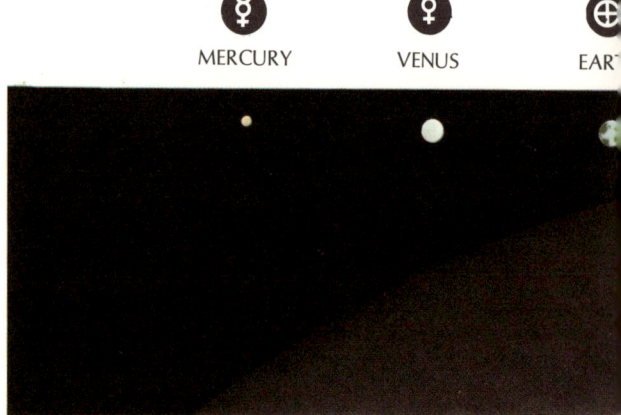

MERCURY   VENUS   EART

♂	♃		♄		♅	♆	♇
MARS	JUPITER		SATURN		URANUS	NEPTUNE	PLUTO

PLANET PEOPLE

How the Planets Can Dominate Our Lives

You probably know your Sun-sign: that you have, say, the Sun in Cancer (if you were born between 21 June–22 July); but until you either ask an astrologer to work it out, or learn to work it out for yourself, you will not know which signs of the Zodiac the other planets occupy. Quite often another planet makes its presence felt very strongly indeed on an individual's personality, showing characteristics that are different to those of the Sun sign. Here are some examples of very powerful influences by planets on people—influences which have made a vital mark on their personalities.

THE SUN
KEYWORD: POWER

Our two Sun people both, as it happens, had the Sun rising in Gemini. In Queen Victoria's case, this made her in essence a very 'queenly' person—almost adding an element of Leo to her personality

(the Sun rules Leo). The second Sun person is Richard Wagner: the huge scale of his operas and of his whole artistic expression are characteristic of what astrologers would call 'a prominent Sun'. Being in Gemini, it gave him considerable duality—he wrote the libretti as well as the music of his operas.

THE MOON
KEYWORDS: RESPONSE, FLUCTUATION

The significance of the Moon in a Birth Chart is second only to that of the Sun; and when it is in its own sign (Cancer), or in certain other special positions, its characteristics can be almost over-whelmingly powerful. Lord Byron had a very powerful Moon in Cancer—and this made personal relationships difficult for him. The famous conductor Arturo Toscanini also had a prominent Moon; it represented for him the general public, and his fame, as well as his dealings with his orchestra as a whole.

MERCURY
KEYWORD: COMMUNICATION

Among the characteristics of Aquarius are originality, eccentricity, inventive-ness: Jules Verne had Mercury in this sign, in the area of his Chart influencing his career. Mercury represents the

mind, writing and communication, and all the originality and futuristic qualities of Aquarius were combined with those of Mercury in Verne's science fiction.

VENUS
KEYWORD: HARMONY

The Venus in Isadora Duncan's Chart was very powerful. It was in Aries, which is a very assertive sign; those with important planets in it are usually

highly sexed. The romantic side of Venus was very strong in Isadora, and many of her real needs were also Venus-influenced—her need, for example, to be loved, and to give both love and affection.

SATURN
KEYWORD: LIMITATION

Saturn in George Gershwin's Chart was in Sagittarius when he was born, and fell in the area of his Chart concerned with his health. It undoubtedly under-mined his physical strength; Gershwin died at the relatively early age of thirty-nine, two years after completing the opera, *Porgy and Bess*. The Saturn in Pablo Picasso's Chart is also interesting —it is in Taurus, and its influence is particularly strong in the work Picasso did at the time of the Spanish Civil War: the important painting *Guernica* is a striking example, as are some of the passionately expressive sculptures that he created.

JUPITER
KEYWORD: EXPANSION

Albert Einstein had a marvellous Jupiter in his Birth Chart: it fell in Aquarius, the humanitarian sign. Jupiter was also in the area of his Chart ruling the mind in its most advanced and broadest capacity. Jupiter worked in a different way for the notorious spy Mata Hari. She had the planet rising in the secretive, emotional water sign, Scorpio, and her Jupiter principle of expansiveness only came decisively to the fore when, facing the firing-squad, she thanked the officer commanding her execution.

MARS

KEYWORDS: ENERGY, INITIATIVE
Horatio Viscount Nelson had a very prominent Mars in his Birth Chart. It was rising in Scorpio when he was born. This gave him fantastic powers of endurance, an abundance of emotional energy and bravery. Vincent van Gogh also had an important Mars, but in his case it was in the less intense sign, Pisces. Sacrifice is very much a part of the Piscean influence, and the fact that van Gogh cut off his ear could easily be related to this planet's influence, for Mars is a violent planet and can lead people to take impulsive action under pressure.

THE MODERN PLANETS

The three modern planets—Uranus, Neptune and Pluto—are so far away that they travel very slowly along the ecliptic. Whereas the Sun moves once through the Zodiac or 360° in a year, Uranus moves approximately 4°, Neptune 2° and Pluto 1°. Thus Uranus takes seven years to pass through one sign of the Zodiac (30°), while Neptune takes fourteen years and Pluto—because it has an eccentric orbit—anything from thirteen to thirty-two years. The modern planets will therefore occupy similar positions in the Birth Charts of people born over an extended period; and for this reason their influences are believed to be over generations more than individuals—unless, of course, one of these planets is sensitively placed in a Chart. This could be because it is 'in aspect' (having a specific angular relationship) with another planet or group of planets; in which case the modern planet must be assessed together with the aspected planet(s) and their combined effect carefully weighed.

URANUS

KEYWORD: SUDDEN CHANGE
Franklin D. Roosevelt had Uranus accentuated in his Chart; as with Gershwin's Saturn, it fell in the area of the Chart concerning health. Uranus is related to paralysis, which crippled Roosevelt for most of his active political career. Karl Marx was also a Uranian person: in him the Uranian qualities of radicalism and humanitarianism were very powerfully expressed. His whole life centred around these ideals.

NEPTUNE

KEYWORD: CLOUDINESS
The influence of the planet Neptune is various: at its best it can make a true and inspired actor, poet or artist, but under other circumstances it can lead to suicidal tendencies. Marilyn Monroe had all the splendid attributes of Neptune (which include glamour as well as artistic ability) but the negative side of the planet's influence proved tragically strong. Neptune was extremely powerfully placed in her Chart and was astrologically 'afflicted'—meaning that other planets occupied difficult relationships to it, making her liable at times to commit extreme actions.

PLUTO

KEYWORD: ELIMINATION
Pluto's influence is generally believed by astrologers to be disruptive: it can play havoc in many ways with the unconscious, while at its best it can help people to make fresh starts in life, or to live through drastic periods of upheaval, coming through well or badly according to the planet's position in the Chart and its relationships to other planets. The Pluto in Marlene Dietrich's Chart falls in the area concerned with overseas countries and, many believe has brought about her worldwide fame. Another very interesting Pluto person is Greta Garbo. The influence of her Pluto has been the reverse of Dietrich's case, for it falls in the area of her Chart relating to seclusion and withdrawal. Garbo disappeared from the public eye in 1941, and has stayed in seclusion ever since. Some have affirmed that Pluto played a key part in this drastic change.

THE USES OF ASTROLOGY

Eight ways to Deepen Your Experience of Life

'But how can astrology help *me*?' The question is a very natural one—especially if you have never had the experience of reading a full astrological report. The answer is that if your full Birth Chart is consulted by a professional astrologer there will be no area of your everyday life in which he or she cannot be of help to you. Here are just a few.

KNOWING YOURSELF

You may think that you know as much about yourself as you want to! But astrology can reveal, in advance, the days when you may be feeling strangely impatient, the days when your temper may be snappy, the days when you will be feeling particularly relaxed. It can tell you some of the things your best friends might hesitate to reveal: that you can be selfish or that your eating habits may bring a weight problem.

CAREERS

If you are just leaving school or college, an astrologer can provide a list of careers in which you may be interested; or if you feel restless, and want a change of occupation, you can learn from him whether in fact it is a good time for such a change, and the direction in in which you might like to lead your life. And of course you can ask an astrologer about careers for your children.

CHILDREN

Career advice is only one area of work an astrologer can do for children: even with very young children, he can tell you when they may go through that worrying stage of infant illnesses—mumps, chickenpox, and so on. He can suggest what sort of school would best suit *your* child's temperament; and which parent is best suited to dealing with the different areas of the child's personality. The child may, for example, turn to his mother in times of difficulty but perhaps he enjoys the company of his father more when the family goes out for the day.

SEX AND LOVE

In synastry, a term for the comparison of Birth Charts, the astrologer assesses just how suited two people

are to each other. Not that he will tell you not to marry the girl! But he can point out that while you like peace and quiet, she really feels at her best at a noisy party; that while you tend to throw your money around, she prefers to save it. After that it's up to you to decide. However, in every marriage there are difficult times and an astrologer will not only see such problem periods approaching, he will also be able to say whether a permanent break is likely or just a temporary hitch.

BUSINESS

Many businessmen now consult astrologers about the best time to make heavy investments, to sell overseas, to make a takeover bid . . . and an astrologer will be able to warn a businessman of a period when he may be particularly under stress, and would do better to take some time off.

HEALTH

Some of the most valuable work an astrologer can do is in warning clients of periods when their health may be a little low, when they may tend to catch cold, or feel run-down and should take a tonic. Using traditional astrology, it is also possible to warn which areas of the body may be weak, and should be specially watched and checked by a doctor—and at what times this is likely to happen.

WEATHER

Ask an astrologer what the weather is going to be like in California or New South Wales, Algiers or Boston, during the third week in May. A practised astrological weather forecaster will be much more accurate than a meteorologist (some astrologers have records of 87% accuracy in this field).

FOR THE FUN OF IT!

Astrology is fun, too; use it to choose the colour of gift wrapping paper, or to choose the gift inside; use it to make up a dinner-table of guests, or to choose a pet. And always remember that it is nothing to do with 'fate': you still have free will. Astrology doesn't tell you what *will* happen, what you *must* do. It's like a weather-forecast: if rain is likely, you can always stay indoors!

Astrologers are often asked to interpret the birth data of couples planning to marry. Either singly or compared, the Charts can reveal much about character and compatibility that many prefer to know *before* the shoes and rice. After that it's up to them—and to love—to make the most of each other.

YOU AND YOUR ASTROLOGER

First Steps in Complete Astro-analysis

Consulting an astrologer is a fascinating and revealing experience for anyone. Whether you are in need of help—perhaps with a difficult emotional or career problem—or whether you simply want to find out more about yourself and your psychological motivation you will, after the consultation or the arrival of a written report, be in a much better position to face life with greater confidence.

The first thing an astrologer must do before he can help you is to take your birth date, time and place. From these he calculates the positions of all the planets in their various signs of the Zodiac and houses (see page 14) for that given moment and location. He in fact makes a map of the sky, one which is very individual to *you*; no two people can have the same Birth Chart (as the map is called) unless they were born at precisely the same moment in the same hospital or street—for the whole celestial picture changes every four minutes for every location on earth.

First contact with an astrologer often comes when a fresh approach is needed to an emotional problem, perhaps some kind of marital deadlock.

If you do, incidentally, meet someone who was born within the same hour and in the same area as yourself—and whose chart is very similar if not identical to yours—you may be astounded by the similarities between your life and that of your 'astrological twin'. You may well share personal mannerisms and pursue the same careers and pastimes—you may even marry each other, it has been known!

From the Birth Chart the astrologer is able to build up a picture of you—your motivation, your potential, how you react in emotional relationships, and so on. As you grow older, so your Birth Chart grows older with you, and by studying the positions of the planets for, say, eighteen days after you were born (known as 'progressing' the Chart) the astrologer is able to assess the trends which were working in your life when you were eighteen years old. He also studies the planets as

they appear in the sky at the present time, and relates their positions to the positions they occupied at the time of your birth.

People unhappy in their work find impartial advice hard to come by and many turn to astrology for expert and impartial guidance on how best to use their real talents.

Do not expect your astrologer to tell you that you will fall in love with a beautiful blonde on 26 October, and marry her three weeks later! Serious astrologers do not predict events: they are not fortune-tellers. They assess the trends working in their clients' lives, and will say such things as: 'You may live through a blissfully happy and romantic period', or, 'There is indication of an important period of change, likely to concern your career'; *never* 'This (or that) *will* happen'.

Remember, too, that it takes a good astrologer many days to study and fully interpret a Birth and Progressed Chart; if he offers a too-rapid service, the quality of his service may well be found wanting. No, wait until you are in a position to consult a reputable astrologer; you will be all the more satisfied with the results, and richer in knowledge of yourself.

Responsible astrologers advise on trends but make no firm predictions. They cannot foresee death but they can help a client's health by anticipating moments of stress.

You have read how for 5,000 years astrologers have observed the planets' effect on man's life. The Sun has its own influence: see how, in the various signs of the Zodiac, it affects you and your friends at work and play.

ARIES
21 MARCH – 19 APRIL

As the Sun begins its journey through the Zodiac, it first enters the sign of Aries the pioneer, the agitator, the most assertive and aggressive of all the signs. Aries' ruling planet is Mars, the warrior god. The colour of Aries is bright red, as befits the sign of Mars, the red planet! The Arian metal is iron—the material of swords and other weapons: but of ploughshares, too, when the Martian energy of Aries is tamed and well directed. The gem most sympathetic to this sign is the diamond. Its splendour and piercing brilliance are quintessentially Arian. The Arian's element, fire, endows him with directness and ardour. His quality is cardinal —meaning that by nature he is outgoing, and ever-ready to express and assert himself.

YOUR SUN-SIGN CHARACTER

The Zodiacal Self Revealed

The Arian's most striking characteristics are his natural enthusiasm and his simple, straightforward approach to life. For him, as for her, life is black or white, yes or no. Arians are born leaders—not so much because they want to inspire others to look up to them, as because they want to be out in front, to be 'there' before anyone else. This uncomplicated driving force represents the essence of their whole being, and it is expressed in many ways.

'Me first' is an oft-heard cry among Arians, who at their worst can be intolerably selfish. This is because—in their need to be first—they put themselves and their feelings before all else. Invitations to dinner will be accepted with enthusiasm, only for the host to receive a last-minute phone-call from his Arian guest saying that 'something has cropped up'—that he has to work late, or that someone is ill, that he is sorry but he cannot make it. In reality, someone else has invited him out, and the new date promises to be more exciting or interesting than the first!

Faced with this kind of selfishness others can either tolerate it or complain. At all events it is easy enough to tell when an Arian is making up excuses or telling lies—he simply cannot do it convincingly, probably because basically he is too straightforward!

The Arian's response is positive, and he usually gets things done even if at times he shows scant concern for detail. Sometimes, though, he may need a more careful person supporting him, to pick up the bits and pieces he leaves behind him in an untidy trail.

QUICK TO ANGER, QUICK TO REPENT

The Arian's lack of diplomacy is something he should try to deal with, otherwise he may find himself upsetting one person too many, and as a result losing some important, 'out-front' position; and he would not like that. He is quick to lose his temper, and should try to take a deep breath instead. Luckily he is uncomplicated—and so is his temper; he will bear no malice, and all will quickly be over. If one has to have a temper, this is probably the best kind to have! What is past, to the Arian, *is* past. He will realize that it was his natural impulsiveness which made him give way to anger in the first place. He will inwardly repent, telling himself that this must never happen again; and he will *try* not to let it happen again.

Having to sit still for long periods does not come naturally to Arians, and trying to develop patience is rather a Herculean task for them. The best approach is to find a compelling interest; once deeply involved in something, they will find that the hours will have fled before they know it, and patience will have quietly taken root amid the general enthusiasm. The latter mood, it is to be hoped, will not be too short-lived!

ARIES IN ACTION

Mind and Body: You and Your Life Style

There is no doubting the Arian's enterprise and his pioneering spirit. These qualities are to be found somewhere in every Arian, and will inevitably find expression in some way. His enterprise very often takes the form of trying to make extra money through some sideline activity: however successful the Arian may be from the financial point of view, many never cease to find a special pleasure in the challenge—and perhaps the thrill—of earning an extra bonus to the monthly pay-cheque.

Arians are an enterprising species all round, and hate to let the grass grow under their feet. This applies both in small ways and in important projects that concern their whole progress in life. When working within a large organization, for instance, Arians will hasten to make their presence felt, and will use their enterprising spirit to carry them along. They may reveal at times a touch of ruthlessness, which they must consciously try to keep under reasonable control if they are not to mar the lively, likeable and enthusiastic qualities that most people admire in them.

DISREGARD FOR DANGER

The Arian has a marked disregard for danger, and tends —especially in youth—to be foolhardy. He will eventually, in most cases, grow out of this; but he is accident-prone and still liable to cut and burn himself. He will like to drive his car fast—perhaps very fast. It would be unwise to try to dissuade him from this, since it is yet another expression of his essential 'me-first' tendency; it would be more practical if, instead, he could be encouraged to take an advanced driver's course.

The Arian badly needs freedom. He will not function at all well or happily if he feels restricted, or if his own individual style is cramped. For him, limiting conditions are impossible to bear; to be told he cannot do this or that, perhaps because it is against some set of rules, is worse for the Arian than a blow on the head. Others must respect this vital need for freedom. On the other hand the Arian himself should try not to let his love of liberty spoil the happiness of others. In the family, above all, he must learn to carry his share of the burdens and, for instance, take his turn with the baby—even if his heart is at the ball game!

If he is given his head in a specific situation, say at work, he will deal with problems that arise in his own individual way, and the less interference he has from others, the better. More than most other people, he is at his best working out his own salvation; and the quick Arian temper may well erupt if others interfere or try to tell him what to do, regardless in some cases of how good their advice may be. This is a prickly area, and others should proceed with caution.

The Arian is usually physically strong, but Aries rules

the head and too often he will get headaches; indeed he may wake up with one and then find – however many pills he takes – that it is still with him at bedtime. Sometimes the Arian's headache is caused by a slight kidney upset, and if he suffers at all regularly in this way he should seek medical advice.

The Arian's physical build is often rather stringy, and he should try to keep it that way. If he plays sport this should take care of itself, but if not he should try doing a set of exercises for a few minutes every day. He will not find the routine easy; after a few weeks his enthusiasm is bound to wane!

FAST THINKERS

Arians are often quick thinkers, and it is right for them to take snap decisions. They have a high energy level and dislike wasting time – so they never stay at a crossroads for long, whatever is at stake. There is another side to this, however. Quite often Arians have so many ideas going round in their heads at the same time that they become entangled – and then take some sorting out!

Arians may therefore reveal a certain amount of mental confusion. This, obviously, tends to cloud issues for them, but as a characteristic it can be rather endearing, and may soften some of their more harshly assertive habits. An Arian can be forgetful over small matters; he tends to find in his coat pocket a letter his best friend asked him to post two weeks ago. He may forget to turn off lights, or forget people's names when introducing them. These are all 'human' weaknesses and add a new dimension to the customary image of the purposeful, straightforward Arian.

SATIRICAL HUMOUR

The Arian's sense of humour tends to be satirical, yet not without warmth; he is good, for example, at puncturing group tensions with some well-chosen, generally offbeat comment which helps others to relax. The Arian's mind mostly progresses by leaps and bounds: the flow of his thought patterns is seldom very even, and though he usually reaches a conclusion without undue trouble, he will tend not to know *how* he reached it until afterwards. The art of planning in advance may not be a strong point: this may well require a special effort from him.

Arians do not worry a great deal. They appreciate that it is simply not possible to *get* anywhere by worrying; one must *act*, and this is what they do. They can absorb facts quickly, and are among the few people able to sit up all night studying on the eve of an examination – and profit by it. If they do this, however, they may well have to cope with an all-too-familiar headache on the following day.

EMOTIONAL RELATIONSHIPS

Couples: How You Compare in Friendship, Love and Marriage

ARIES IN LOVE

Arians in love are extremely passionate. They are highly sensual and become impatient if their advances are not answered with the same freedom and speed that they themselves are not afraid to venture. Because of their impatience they may also seem inexpert in the gentler arts of love. They make their approach with the subtlety of a cavalry charge, and the object of their affection may well at this stage be put off—especially if he or she had been at all uncertain beforehand.

There is little doubt that the Arian motto in love is 'Faint heart never won fair lady'. But if the lady is taken aback by the quick development of the affair, she may be thoroughly charmed and won over by the habit that many Arians have of presenting their loved ones

with small gifts. All in all Arians are very generous, and this charming characteristic will add pleasure and an element of surprise to many a date.

FRIENDS AND HOW TO KEEP THEM

Friendship with an Arian is a lively experience, for his enthusiasm is thoroughly infectious. He will always be the one to suggest outings, but then leaves his friends to make the arrangements—booking theatre seats for instance. But he does not commit himself too far in advance, for after all—as we saw earlier—something more interesting could well crop up! Although the Arian friend will fight battles on behalf of others, he may also be given to making scenes. So, if he forms a friendship with someone more sensitive than himself,

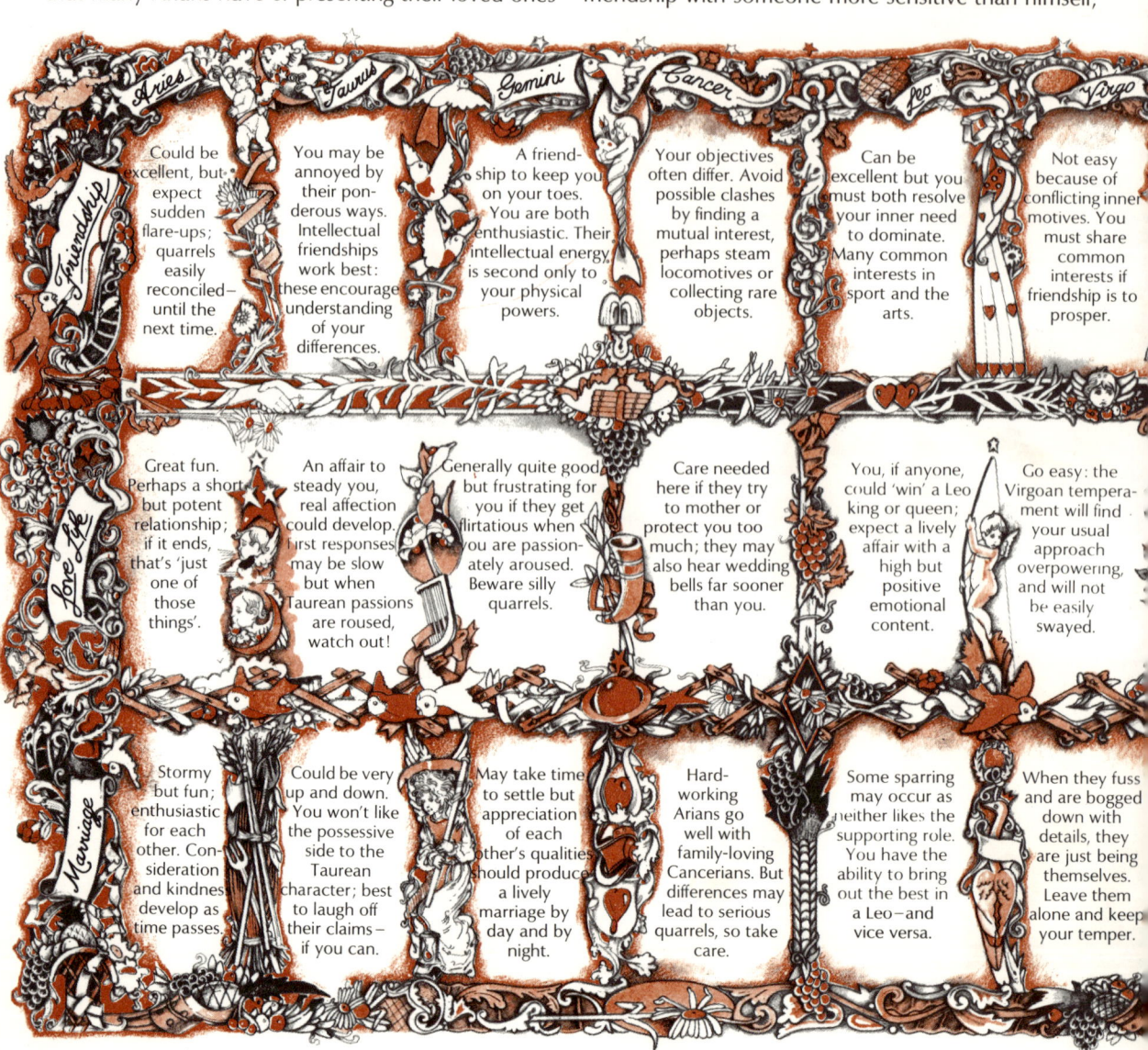

Aries | Taurus | Gemini | Cancer | Leo | Virgo

Friendship
- **Aries:** Could be excellent, but expect sudden flare-ups; quarrels easily reconciled—until the next time.
- **Taurus:** You may be annoyed by their ponderous ways. Intellectual friendships work best: these encourage understanding of your differences.
- **Gemini:** A friendship to keep you on your toes. You are both enthusiastic. Their intellectual energy is second only to your physical powers.
- **Cancer:** Your objectives often differ. Avoid possible clashes by finding a mutual interest, perhaps steam locomotives or collecting rare objects.
- **Leo:** Can be excellent but you must both resolve your inner need to dominate. Many common interests in sport and the arts.
- **Virgo:** Not easy because of conflicting inner motives. You must share common interests if friendship is to prosper.

Love Life
- **Aries:** Great fun. Perhaps a short but potent relationship; if it ends, that's 'just one of those things'.
- **Taurus:** An affair to steady you, real affection could develop. First responses may be slow but when Taurean passions are roused, watch out!
- **Gemini:** Generally quite good, but frustrating for you if they get flirtatious when you are passionately aroused. Beware silly quarrels.
- **Cancer:** Care needed here if they try to mother or protect you too much; they may also hear wedding bells far sooner than you.
- **Leo:** You, if anyone, could 'win' a Leo king or queen; expect a lively affair with a high but positive emotional content.
- **Virgo:** Go easy: the Virgoan temperament will find your usual approach overpowering, and will not be easily swayed.

Marriage
- **Aries:** Stormy but fun; enthusiastic for each other. Consideration and kindness develop as time passes.
- **Taurus:** Could be very up and down. You won't like the possessive side to the Taurean character; best to laugh off their claims—if you can.
- **Gemini:** May take time to settle but appreciation of each other's qualities should produce a lively marriage by day and by night.
- **Cancer:** Hard-working Arians go well with family-loving Cancerians. But differences may lead to serious quarrels, so take care.
- **Leo:** Some sparring may occur as neither likes the supporting role. You have the ability to bring out the best in a Leo—and vice versa.
- **Virgo:** When they fuss and are bogged down with details, they are just being themselves. Leave them alone and keep your temper.

he must try to curb those sudden flare-ups; his friend could be highly distressed by his behaviour.

LIFE AFTER MARRIAGE

In marriage many Arians develop splendid characteristics that even they did not suspect they had. There is much in their nature which really needs to relate deeply, seriously and permanently to a partner. It is even true to say that marriage 'makes' many an Arian – more so than with most other signs of the Zodiac. Once he is married the Arian will have good reason at long last to do something about his 'me-first' tendency, and will make a conscious effort not to be selfish. What he may now want is not to be first himself but that he and his family should be. This is, excellent, for

he is a fighter and will fight for his family to ensure its comfort, safety and prosperity.

Aries needs a partner who shows enthusiasm, a fighting spirit and a sense of fun. As well as a satisfactory love life, Aries needs someone to come home to who will calm and reassure him; underneath all that lively fire and bravery there is a delightfully childlike quality, which is refreshing to others but which also indicates the Arian's need for a soothing partner.

Below: Use this Friends and Lovers Sun-sign chart to check how Aries is likely to make out with others in friendship, love and marriage. Relationships are listed from left to right, Aries to Aries, Aries to Taurus, etc., and from top to bottom in friendship, love and marriage.

Libra	Scorpio	Sagittarius	Capricorn	Aquarius	Pisces	
An attraction of opposites – very good for friendships. Perhaps you can spur the lazier type of Libran into action.	A friendship to weather many storms, but remember you are emotional in different ways and likely to fall out at times.	Very good, the more you get to know them the better and more rewarding your friendship. They will usually fall in line with you.	Often only good if you share a joint ambition, or plan a business partnership. You tend to prefer warmer people.	Good, Aquarians are the best friends in the world; your warmth and enthusiasm will be welcomed and they will enjoy helping you.	An unusual combination, but you may succeed in giving a dreamy Piscean some sense of purpose.	Friendship
Don't expect a sudden conquest, it's not because they can't or won't but – to begin with at least – because a Libran must have time.	A very passionate, uneven affair likely, you are both highly potent. The course of love will not run smooth. Expect peaks and troughs.	Sagittarians will give you a run for your money; don't pursue too much, for the more you chase the more they will hunt elsewhere.	Be careful, they are not really for you. Make sure their ardour is real, that they are pursuing you, not their own ambitions.	First break down their distant glamour – it won't be all that easy. They like a delicate refined approach which you may find difficult.	If you can cope with a gushing weepy mortal, fine. But don't expect the way to be smooth.	Love Life
Very good, Libra is likely to refine your animal tendencies, and you can inspire some much-needed exuberance in them.	Don't rush into it despite your affinity for Scorpio. You are both very emotional; jealousy can occur. Proceed with caution.	They like freedom and should stimulate your intellectual interests. Squabbles could occur about using the family car.	Fine for ambitious Arians but if you are the less go-ahead type take care, they may not give you a moment's peace.	Good, Aquarians like their freedom, as you do. You should see eye to eye. Compared to them, you may seem surprisingly conventional.	Intellectual links may deepen the relationship. Be patient, you are two very different people.	Marriage

PARENTS AND CHILDREN

The Zodiac Family Portrait

THE ARIAN FATHER

If there is a father in the world who will choose an elaborate model train set for his small son at Christmas and then not let the poor child near it, it is Aries! He himself loves this side of parenthood, and is particularly delighted when his child is old enough to take to ball games or able to join in father's interests. He will, though, find it puzzling if one of his children turns out to be a shy, quiet type who hates sport and wants to sit at home quietly reading on a Saturday afternoon! But Aries must try to be understanding, and not force his children into activities that simply do not suit their characters or temperaments.

The Arian father may find it hard to accept that his son wants to fish, or read poetry; but he must try to do so. He could harm the child by insisting on dragging him to the sports stadium; and this could harm their relationship, too. Much wiser if Aries takes an interest in the child's own choice of pastime—he might even find it more attractive than at first it seemed.

THE ARIAN MOTHER

The Arian mother has a strong personality and will fight tooth and nail for her children's rights. If one of her children has been treated unjustly at school, she will waste no time rushing to the head teacher's office to make her opinions felt. In a way, the Arian mother is a natural boy's mother; she won't mind boys running all over the house with dirty shoes on—at least, inwardly she won't mind though she will shout and make them mop up the mess themselves; this she sees as part of their training. Towards a daughter she will act in much the same way: if girls want to be boisterous, she will be equally tolerant.

The Arian mother is naturally ambitious for her children, and perhaps rather 'pushy'. She will fix up extra skating lessons, for example, so that when the time comes her child is well placed to win glory for the family. In other words, she will say: 'My girl *will* win first place' and 'My boy *will* be top of his class'. This is fine, but like the Arian father she must learn to develop a tactful approach. It is important that she does not frighten her children into making a great effort in subjects which only interest *her*, and not them.

THE ARIAN CHILD

The Arian child is usually a rather bouncy, exuberant creature, who must be kept busy so that his energy is burned up in a lively, positive way. He will not be patient, and perhaps the worst punishment for him is to be told to sit still and be quiet! This just does not suit him a bit—he would much rather be out in the garden leading the attack on the enemy's secret hide-out. The Arian girl will be out there too with the best of the boys, shooting her way past bandits and leading small brothers to safety!

School reports in some subjects are bound to contain the all-too-familiar phrase, 'Is lazy, could do better if he tried'. But the truth of the matter is that young Aries isn't lazy, his trouble is that he is bored; he cannot stir up enthusiasm for anything that he considers unimportant or dull. Both boys and girls of the sign should be in their element on the sports field, and can do well in any area where they are given their heads to express their true pioneering spirit. They will feel deflated if they are denied this freedom. Adventure is something that Arians of all ages require, almost of right since enterprise and liberty lie at the heart of their motivation. Parents may not have an easy time trying to curb the tendency to be selfish, but it will help if the Arian child can be given a little responsibility—perhaps to help with younger brothers and sisters—for if he fails at something it is better to correct him in the light of practical experience than to offer explanations in the abstract.

The Arian child's exercise books will not be shining examples of neatness, but the content of essays and stories will be lively and amusing, and an understanding teacher will forgive his untidiness. All the same, a careful and tidy approach to life should be encouraged both in school work and in the home: newly tidied drawers or a well written 'thank-you' letter should be amply rewarded.

While Arian children need firm control and guidance, their abundant energy must be channelled, and if it is possible to choose a school where there is an accent on adventure and pioneering, so much the better.

49

CAREERS AND PASTIMES

A Sun-sign Guide to Work and Play

CAREERS

The Arian will not be happy working in peace and quiet, away from the rest of humanity; neither will he like a dull routine job of work that is too predictable. He will thrive in a noisy, crowded atmosphere where there is plenty going on. A busy machine-shop, a factory floor (perhaps where automobiles are being assembled), or some form of industry will all be environments in which the Arian will be extremely happy. Because he has plenty of push, he will probably work his way into a position of some responsibility; then he will thrive even more, for he will be expressing his assertive qualities to the full. Many Arians become ardent trade unionists, and this could well be an area in which they will make their presence felt.

MECHANICS AND HAIRDRESSERS
Arians are mechanically minded, and could specialize as motor mechanics, or generally in doing the kind of work that calls for someone who doesn't mind getting his hands dirty. An equivalent job for Arian girls with the same characteristics might be that of filling-station attendant; they could well enjoy this work. The Arian's pioneering spirit may lead him to join the army; and if he can accept the discipline, he will find much in army life to suit him. The thrills of driving a tank, of target practice, of combat generally—these are in essence very Arian.

Aries rules the head, and this may induce in many Arian girls a flair for hairdressing or millinery. Millinery, though not a large profession, suits the Arian girl, since she delights in quick results and the sort of sewing that millinery entails is excellent for her: a few large stitches here and there can give a splendid effect, and her comparatively small reserves of patience need scarcely be tested at all!

PIONEERS OF SCIENCE AND THE MIND
If an Arian has a scientific bent, which is quite likely, he or she will best express it in some form of research; it is good for an Arian to break new ground in one way

or another. The pioneering spirit makes them explorers, and whether they find themselves in a remote part of Java or exploring the construction of an atomic nucleus, they will be happy.

The urge to explore can be turned inwards, and psychology and psychiatry are both Arian professions. If the Arian can keep up his enthusiasm for his subject during the arduous years of study and training, these are excellent directions for him to take.

Many Arians are professional sportsmen, and if in his youth Aries shows a talent for sport he should be given all possible encouragement to enable him to become a professional; typical Arian sports are motor racing, football and boxing. The Arian's love of speed and danger will also attract him to ice hockey, skiing and speed skating; these, like the other sports mentioned, should be encouraged in youth.

To sum up the Arian career, it is fair to say that it may involve working with metal; if inclined to a medical career, the Arian may specialize in surgery—elsewhere, he may be a butcher! And if he writes for a living, his work will tend to be satirical.

PASTIMES

The Arian will either spend his spare time working hard at a favourite hobby or he will go in for complete relaxation. There are no half measures. He will love carving, and could excel in metalwork. He is also good at 'do-it-yourself', and will spend a great deal of time at weekends servicing his own car.

Many Arians become professional sportsmen, and many others will be involved in some sort of sporting activity in an amateur way. In addition to the sports mentioned earlier as full-time careers, Arians enjoy motor-cycle scrambling and judo—the latter is particularly good for the Arian girl.

If the Arian is musical he will like to hear his favourite pieces good and loud. If he plays, he will tend to choose a noisy instrument such as the drums, or perhaps the trumpet.

AT HOME

A Sun-sign Guide to Home Décor

Arian homes have a glow about them. They glow with the colour red, which tends to be present, if not dominant, in every decorative scheme. The rooms are warm and cheering; but as the Arian loves warmth, they often become overheated and usually need ventilating at least once during the evening.

Although the Arian likes new things, he will furnish his home with an eye to permanence, for he is not restless as far as furniture is concerned, and will not choose tables and chairs that will date quickly, or look fragile and likely to fall apart. The furniture will be functional, plain, and fairly solid. Coverings are more than likely to be in tweed or some other tough fabric; Arians like natural texture patterns or stripes rather than ornate or fussy designs. Favourite colours are shades of red, especially scarlet; for a change Aries may also use touches of pleasant pale blue.

Wrought ironwork is a feature of many Arian homes: if the Arian girl has a patio to furnish she will undoubtedly favour wrought-iron chairs and tables.

As the Arian is highly sensual, he will have an opulent bedroom, seductively lit, and with lamps giving a warm sensual glow to the room as a whole. The Arian workroom will be a law unto itself, crammed with every conceivable tool or piece of equipment, apparently in complete disorder but not to the owner; he knows where everything is—or most of the time he does!

Arians usually love weapons, and often collect pistols and swords; as part of the decoration of a room, it is quite common to find framed prints or drawings of spears, shields and swords, or some antique weapon, perhaps a pistol, proudly displayed. Arians also love engines (especially steam locomotives) and pictures of them adorn many Arian rooms.

The Arian has a distinctive taste in pictures: he will draw great sensual pleasure from the heavy nudes of Rubens; the aggressive beauty of Goya's etchings will appeal to him, as will the Renaissance battle paintings of Uccello and the true-to-life scenes from the Moulin Rouge portrayed by Toulouse-Lautrec. Van Gogh was an Arian, and reproductions of his paintings are favourite subjects in the Arian living-room.

Visitors to an Arian home will be enthusiastically welcomed. They may not be in for a very relaxing evening, but at least they will not be bored. However, if the Arian decides to play his latest LP, he should remember that while he likes the sound level high, his guests may not want to be blown out of their chairs by the opening chord!

DINNER WITH ARIES

Entertaining with Your Sun-sign

THE ARIAN HOST

The Arian host has a talent for arranging good dinner-parties, drawing up a balanced guest-list and planning the right menu for them. But although Arians are excellent general planners, they sometimes overlook small details. As a result the soup may have no salt in it, or a small but essential ingredient may be missing from the main course.

On another level, however, an Arian might be an admirable man to have in control of a large kitchen: he thrives in a noisy, busy atmosphere, especially when he is running things. In his own kitchen—where he has to do most of the work himself—he may be over-hasty, and his general aptitude for slightly cutting or burning himself will tend, almost inevitably, to come to the fore; so take great care, Arians, at the cooker, and when you are using that sharp knife to prepare the vegetables.

THE ARIAN GUEST

The Arian guest can be difficult. A slight mishap may plunge him into one of his fits of impatience, and he is certainly not likely to sit and quietly plough his way through a dish he doesn't like. He will make it perfectly clear that he is not going to eat it. Most days, however, his quickness, allied to his satirical wit, make him an excellent companion at the dinner-table, and if the evening goes well it may be largely due to his particular contribution. By the way, Arians can have dauntingly large appetites, so don't offer an Arian a second helping unless you have plenty!

THE SETTING

Arians like red, the colour of Mars, their ruling planet; in the dining-room bright red table-napkins will delight an Arian guest. Honeysuckle, as a table decoration, will also be much appreciated. For background music try something fairly spirited: marches played by a brass band would probably be going too far (for the other guests, anyway) but something of the order of, say, Rossini overtures would exactly suit an Arian.

WINES

France is an Arian country, which of course leaves any host with plenty of room to manoeuvre. A good burgundy with plenty of body would be ideal. Aries is also associated with Germany, but the Rhine wines may perhaps on the whole be a little light for his palate. The Arian's tastes are strong—like his physique.

An all-star evening for famous Arians of past and present would very likely include the illustrious guests in our picture (not all, incidentally, believers in astrology!). For details of the dishes on the table—every one an Arian favourite—turn to page 54.

Peter Ustinov   Gloria Swanson

Bette Davis

Joan Crawford

Lenin

Houdini

Vincent van Gogh

Charles Chaplin

RECIPES FOR ARIES

Cooking with Astrology

Using astrology to choose a menu is something many people do just for fun. Some foods are traditionally associated with certain astrological signs; but in other cases, we rely on our own researches and general experience of the way the various Sun-signs react to certain dishes. Arians generally like pungent, 'hot' flavours, and mulligatawny soup will cater for this taste—as well as containing onions, traditionally an Arian vegetable. The bright red skins of the peppers, even when blackened and charred, will appeal to the Arian eye, and the beef casserole will have just the rich, full flavour that any Arian will appreciate—even if in his heart he may yearn for a touch of curry powder!

The Arian cook who can't be bothered with long preparations of food, will find crown of lamb easy but impressive; he might find baked alaska more tricky to prepare — but the sudden change to cold ice cream after the hot crust of the meringue will be just the kind of shock to appeal to the Arian guest! Of course, cooking with astrology is just fun – but it's surprising how often the theory turns out to be accurate.

'The discovery of a new dish does more for the happiness of mankind than the discovery of a star.' J. A. Brillat-Savarin, 1825.

MULLIGATAWNY SOUP
Rather a lot of trouble to make, but how Arian! In a pan, melt some butter; add 2 onions, 1 carrot, 1 small turnip and 1 tart green apple, all peeled and/or cored as necessary, and diced. Sprinkle with 1 tablespoon curry powder and $\frac{1}{2}$ tablespoon flour; add the meat of 1 rabbit, well washed and cut small. Pour in 7 cups cold water; add a bouquet garni and season with salt and pepper. Simmer for 2 hours, skimming from time to time. Strain through a sieve, but rescue a few nice pieces of meat for garnish. Rub remaining meat and vegetables through the sieve, and return to the soup. Add a little hot milk and a squeeze of lemon before serving. For a really good filler, stir in some boiled rice.

CHARRED PEPPERS
Broil 4 sweet red peppers, turning frequently, until skin chars and blisters. Rub off under running cold water. Core and seed peppers, and soak in good French dressing (olive oil, a touch of vinegar). Serve just with the dressing, or flavour with a few pieces of fish—tunny fish, sardine, anchovy.

CROWN OF LAMB
Simple but spectacular. Have the crown made up, i.e. lamb cutlets arranged bones upwards in a circle to make the crown, the centre stuffed. Simply push a few chips of garlic into the meat; season with salt and pepper, and roast at 300°F until tender. You can always prepare a stuffing for the centre of the crown yourself, if you like.

BEEF CASSEROLE ARIAN
Braising steak cut into large chunks and rolled in a mixture of flour and paprika (proportion, say, 3:1), salt and pepper. Brown gently in butter. Transfer to a casserole with 3 cups small white mushrooms, $\frac{1}{2}$ Bermuda onion, finely chopped, and about $\frac{2}{3}$ cup beef stock. Cover tightly and cook over the lowest possible heat for anything up to 4 hours. Serve with noodles or rice, thickening the sauce with cornstarch if need be.

BAKED ALASKA
Buy (or make, if you feel so inclined) a sponge cake case. Having pre-heated oven to 450°F, put cake on a fireproof plate; moisten lightly with fruit juice—the juice from a can of fruit will do perfectly well. In the centre of the cake put a large block or heap of ice cream (plain vanilla is probably best), taken straight from the freezer. On top of this, pile the contents of a drained can of fruit (peaches, oranges or whatever). Then cover top of entire pile with a meringue, made by beating 3 to 4 egg whites to soft peak stage, beating in $\frac{3}{8}$ to $\frac{1}{4}$ cup fine sugar and, when mixture is glossy, gently folding in a further $\frac{3}{8}$ to $\frac{1}{4}$ cup sugar. (Of course, you will have to prepare the meringue before piling up the ice cream and fruit!) The meringue must meet the edge of the cake right around. Quickly transfer plate to the oven and bake for 2 to 3 minutes, or until surface of meringue just starts to brown. Serve at once. A baked alaska is marvellous made with fresh fruit when in season, and a spoonful or two of sherry or rum sprinkled over the cake base at the start will do no harm. This is without doubt one of the most spectacular dishes with which to conclude a meal; Arian diners will warm to the grandeur of its appearance as well as to the vividly contrasting tastes of meringue and ice cream: a true grand finale!

TAURUS
20 APRIL–21 MAY

Taurus is an earthy sign, dependable, firmly planted in reality.
The Taurean's ruling planet is Venus, goddess of love.
Taurean love is deep and permanent, but may be possessive.
Taurus will not be hurried—until his passion is roused, or his
bullish anger released. He will enjoy life and its comforts,
surrounded by favourite possessions and in an atmosphere
enhanced by Venusian colours—pale blues and pinks;
his precious stone, the sapphire, may be magnificently set in a
ring. The Taurean element is earth, hence his solid, reliable
nature. His quality is fixed. Within his environment his friends
can relax in security and be restored with heavy but superb
food, cooked, no doubt, in the glowing radiance of copper pots
—for copper is the metal of Taurus.

YOUR SUN-SIGN CHARACTER
The Zodiacal Self Revealed

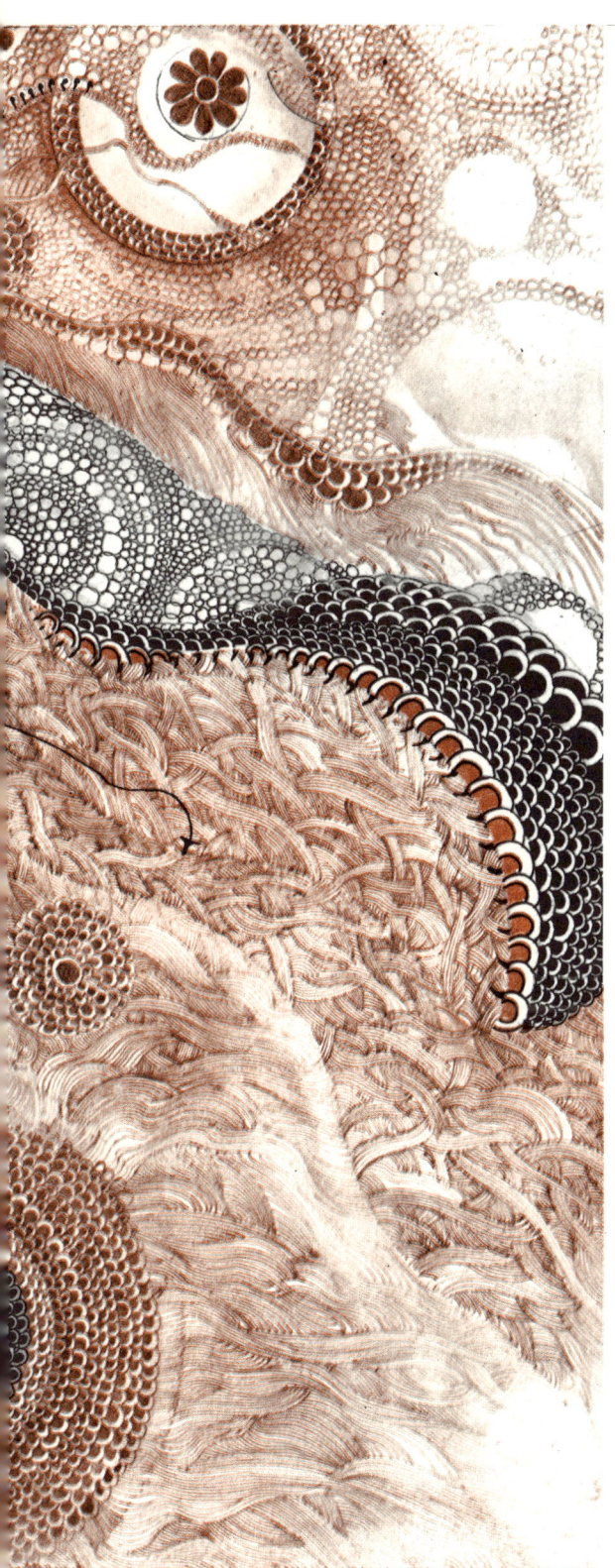

It is essential for the Taurean to have security: not only financial security, but mental security as well. This vital facet of his character will be most evident if, as a child, he suffered unwelcome changes, or was the victim of a broken marriage. He does not like change and strives always to have a regular pattern in his life. He also takes great comfort from familiar possessions. He will hang on to an old tweed jacket, or she will tend to keep the same hair-style or the same eye-shadow much longer than most. Continuity is very important to Taureans, so much so that if they are not careful opinions formed in youth will stay with them for life. The Taurean may in such cases be accused—and rightly so—of being a stick-in-the-mud.

But at least Taureans are entirely dependable—provided they are not rushed. If a favour is needed they must be given adequate notice. Change, as we have said, worries them. They must have time to get used to new ideas or alterations to their routine. For example, if they have been asked to go baby-sitting in a week's time they will want to work out how this is going to affect them in detail. Thus it becomes important for them to know that they can still watch their favourite TV programme—but in a different house. However, Taurus will be there, and on time: and his friends can go off for the evening sure in the knowledge that their child is in reliable hands.

POSSESSIVE LOVERS

The biggest Taurean fault is possessiveness, and this is directly linked to their need for security. The more they own, the more secure they feel; and their possessions act as a buffer against an insecure, ever-changing, restless outside world. All too often Taureans decide that their husband, wife or sweetheart is yet another possession—albeit the most precious: they cannot appreciate their partner's need for perhaps more freedom than they are willing to give. To counter this tendency they must always try consciously to realize that people have their own lives to lead.

Taureans lack adaptability, and their general slowness can make them seem boring to more lively people. However, they are very kind and charming; they tend also to be self-indulgent. They make excellent hosts—though at their dinner parties the accent is on food rather than conversation.

The Taurean should be allowed to plod his way through life at his own slow, steady pace. He is a creature of habit but all his habits are formed for very good practical reasons. He will waste no energy on unnecessary movement, for instance. At home his possessions will be placed at just the right distance from him, so that he can reach out for them in comfort from his favourite armchair.

TAURUS IN ACTION

Mind and Body: You and Your Life Style

Taureans have a splendid flair for business. Even in childhood they use their pocket money to the best advantage. They are excellent in business partnerships, for they have a real flair for making money, and their steadiness makes them a still more valuable asset. They are also good at controlling others, perhaps the more exuberant and go-ahead members of a business team, whose enthusiasm for rapid progress might land the company in financial difficulties. Taurus should be the one to control the flow of capital; and his less financially orientated business colleagues must respect his excellent judgment when it comes to finalizing deals or contracts that the more assertive members of the group may have captured in the first place. Finance and stability are both areas of special strength with Taurus—and in business he will not lack for opportunities to assert these excellent qualities.

WEIGHT PROBLEMS

Partly because Taureans tend to be self-indulgent, and partly because they are not generally speaking very active or quick in their movements, they are inclined to put on weight—perhaps more so than any other sign of the Zodiac. They find it extremely hard to diet: try as they may, merely 'cutting down' will not do, for they love sweet things. A Taurean on a diet may well succumb to chocolate bars. Weight can be a problem from quite an early age, and if they find it difficult to diet, they should try two weeks at a health farm now and again—perhaps increasing their visits as they approach middle age. They are generally strong, but should try to interest themselves in some form of physical exercise, which may not be easy. The Taurean's throat is vulnerable, and minor chills or colds will settle in that area.

Since ancient times Taurus has enjoyed a reputation for being the best-looking of all the signs; and there is no doubt that a great number of Taureans live up to this distinction. The men of the sign usually have marvellously deep and rather fervent eyes, and their hair often curls around their foreheads in a most attractive way. This is so of the girls too—both sexes being well endowed by Venus, the goddess of beauty and their ruling planet.

The most trying Taurean fault is his temper. It is not all that often roused, but when it is it will take a lot of calming. The Taurean temper is like a very heavy thunderstorm—one can see it gathering for some time beforehand, and when it breaks everyone around suffers. Taureans really need to accept that their anger, once roused, can be devastating, and while they may go for months on end without losing their temper, they must try very hard to learn to steady themselves when storms do break. Sometimes the cause of their

anger is jealousy, which in itself probably is rooted in possessiveness; again, the Taurean should try to see his temper as a negative characteristic and resolve to control it.

The Taurean is artistic, and many find satisfaction in creative activities. They tend to have a special feeling for music, which seems to possess a deep-seated psychological relevance for them. The Taurean usually has a large collection of LPs, and many sing very well indeed. They derive a similar satisfaction from gardening. The Taurean has an eye for beauty – whether it be in a handsome man, a pretty girl, a song, or a perfect rose.

MENTAL FIRMNESS

The Taurean thinks slowly and carefully and will not be rushed into a decision. He is not indecisive but requires time to ponder. Once his mind is made up, an element of stubbornness may then assert itself, for as the Taurean dislikes and resists change in his day-to-day life, so his mind is equally stolid. Taureans probably feel that if they have taken the trouble to come to a conclusion about something, or to have formed an opinion, then their views should be upheld and the matter should be regarded as settled. They can then return to what they consider to be the major business – their favourite routine.

It is not easy for the Taurean to grasp new or forward-looking ideas; he needs to try things himself and then must be allowed to make up his own mind in his own time. More often than not he will reject what is new, and in his liking for the familiar he may well at times find himself left behind. He should recognize this; and while it will go against much of what he feels to be right and proper, he must not ignore either present-day opinion or the opinions of those younger than himself.

A SLOW BUT CAREFUL WORKER

The Taurean mind is superb at retaining facts; but if Taurus is studying, it is vital that a specific amount of time is put aside each day, so that the curriculum is worked through systematically without fuss or bother. In this way a last-minute rush can best be avoided. When it comes to examination time, the Taurean must make quite certain that he has a good night's rest before he enters the examination room. It is no good at all for him to sit up all night trying to assimilate facts at the last minute. He will only succeed if he plods, working slowly and carefully through the syllabus. But if he takes his examinations in the knowledge that he has done just this, he will answer the questions with confidence and in a sound and constructive way, without a trace of fuss or pretension; he will do more than enough, in fact, to pass the test.

EMOTIONAL RELATIONSHIPS

Couples: How You Compare in Friendship, Love and Marriage

TAURUS IN LOVE

There is no doubt that Taureans are good-timers. They enjoy every moment of an affair, and are not the type to hold back once they have set their heart on someone. The Taurean male may begin by asking the girl out to dinner—or to a concert. He may well forget, however, to ask whether she enjoys the things he does —like heavy German food and opera!

Taureans are extremely passionate, but they are cautious by nature and will take their time. A rebuff will hurt them far more than most; and to avoid such unpleasantness they will make absolutely sure of their feelings before going ahead.

A girl considering an affair with a Taurean man can expect to be treated well; she should have the best of everything. But she must ask herself at an early stage whether she wants to put up with his possessiveness, which will soon come to the fore. As, too, he is likely to become serious rather quickly (once his mind is made up) she must either try to help him understand that he is being too possessive—if she likes him—or quickly withdraw if she doesn't.

Similarly, the man dating a Taurean girl will soon run into the same difficulties, and will have to come to terms with them. She will be pretty and charming, and this may make a difference; but her whole life will collapse around her if she is unexpectedly dropped when she thinks she is secure in her relationship.

The Taurean friend is a real friend, though he may drive more lively people mad if he becomes too set

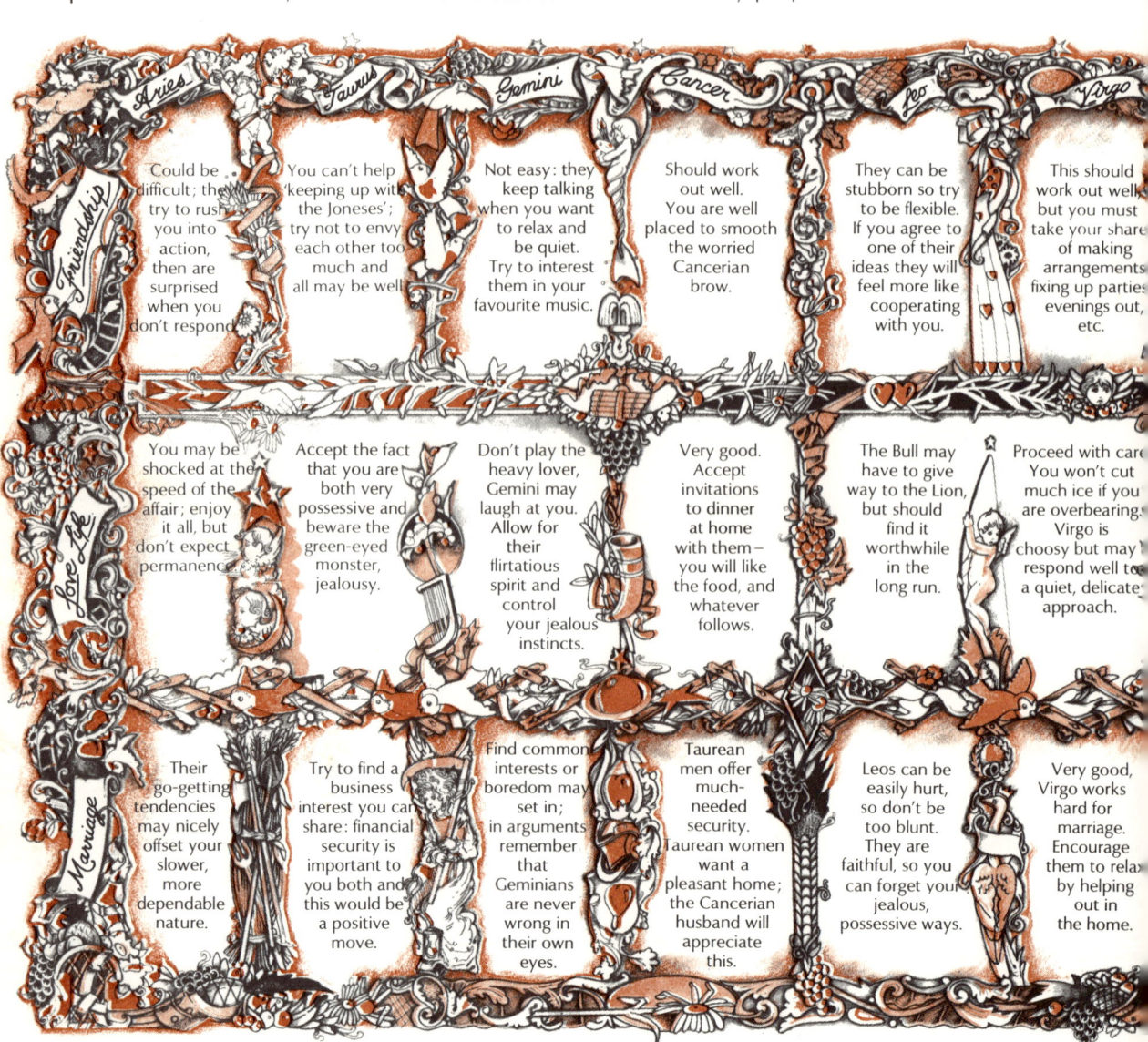

Aries | **Taurus** | **Gemini** | **Cancer** | **Leo** | **Virgo**

Friendship

Could be difficult; they try to rush you into action, then are surprised when you don't respond.

You can't help 'keeping up with the Joneses'; try not to envy each other too much and all may be well.

Not easy: they keep talking when you want to relax and be quiet. Try to interest them in your favourite music.

Should work out well. You are well placed to smooth the worried Cancerian brow.

They can be stubborn so try to be flexible. If you agree to one of their ideas they will feel more like cooperating with you.

This should work out well, but you must take your share of making arrangements fixing up parties evenings out, etc.

Love Life

You may be shocked at the speed of the affair; enjoy it all, but don't expect permanence.

Accept the fact that you are both very possessive and beware the green-eyed monster, jealousy.

Don't play the heavy lover, Gemini may laugh at you. Allow for their flirtatious spirit and control your jealous instincts.

Very good. Accept invitations to dinner at home with them—you will like the food, and whatever follows.

The Bull may have to give way to the Lion, but should find it worthwhile in the long run.

Proceed with care. You won't cut much ice if you are overbearing. Virgo is choosy but may respond well to a quiet, delicate approach.

Marriage

Their go-getting tendencies may nicely offset your slower, more dependable nature.

Try to find a business interest you can share: financial security is important to you both and this would be a positive move.

Find common interests or boredom may set in; in arguments remember that Geminians are never wrong in their own eyes.

Taurean men offer much-needed security. Taurean women want a pleasant home; the Cancerian husband will appreciate this.

Leos can be easily hurt, so don't be too blunt. They are faithful, so you can forget your jealous, possessive ways.

Very good, Virgo works hard for marriage. Encourage them to relax by helping out in the home.

in his ways. But he's a 'good sort'; he knows all the best restaurants and what the stock market is up to, and his advice will be sound—if unadventurous.

THE TAUREAN MARRIAGE
A Taurean builds his life around his marriage. He needs and thrives on the security it brings, and will try to make the marriage as permanent as he can. The Taurean wife may spend far too much on labour-saving devices: she may never be satisfied with anything but the largest washing-machine, for instance, and the whole house (where one or other of the partners is Taurean) will have an air of comfortable opulence.

A Taurean has much to give in marriage: he is dependable, straightforward and kind. But he is a creature of habit, not only needing his meals on time, but probably wanting the same menu week in and week out. Similarly, the Taurean wife will be at her happiest cooking the same meals in turn. Life must have an even pattern, a definite rhythm. The Taurean needs a partner who can and will willingly sit still listening to music or watching TV (flickers on the picture are not tolerated). At least the Taurean is soothing company—for the most part, anyway.

Below: Use this Friends and Lovers Sun-sign chart to check how Taurus is likely to make out with others in friendship, love and marriage. Relationships are listed from left to right, Taurus to Aries, Taurus to Taurus, etc., and from top to bottom in friendship, love and marriage.

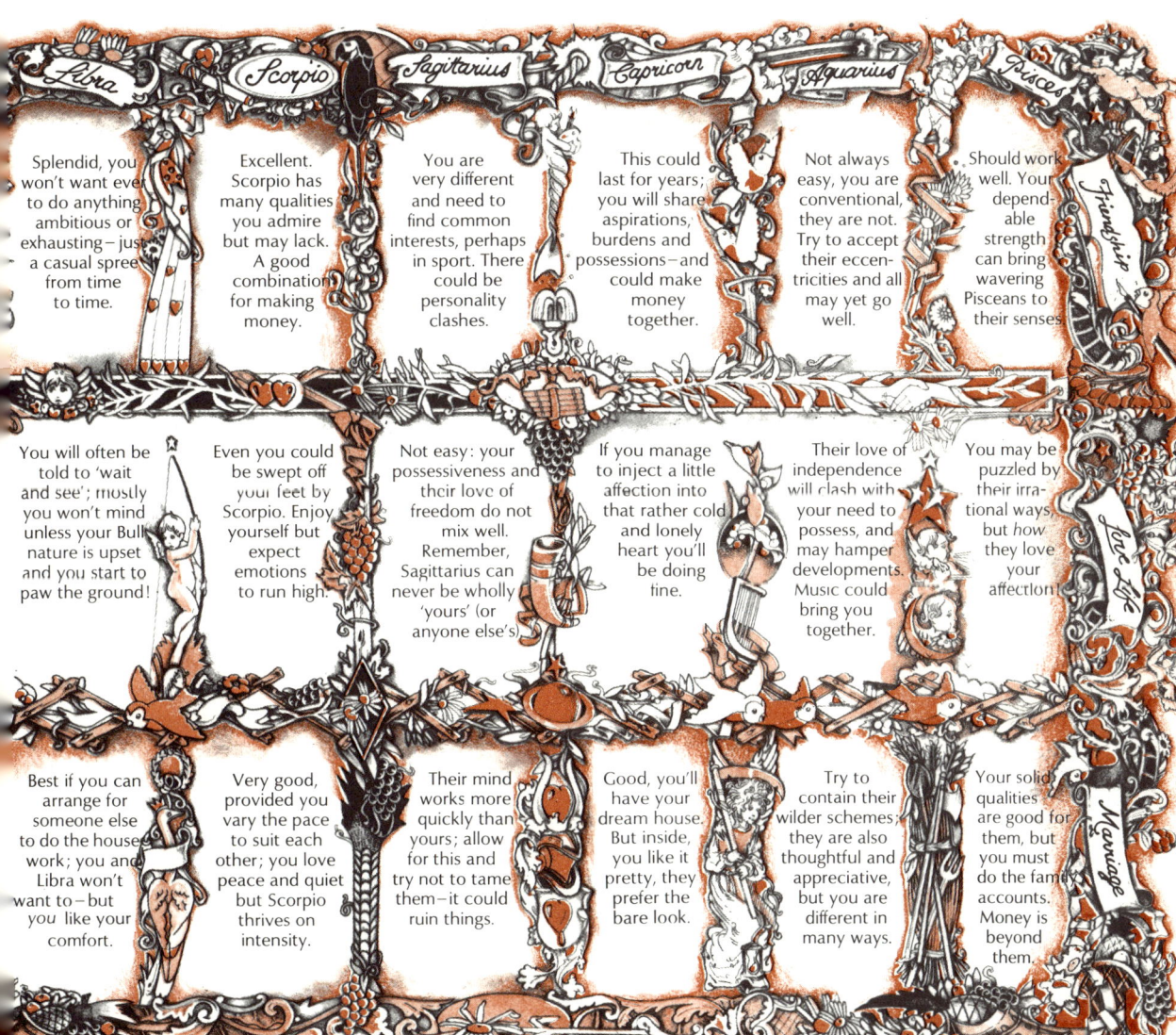

	Libra	Scorpio	Sagittarius	Capricorn	Aquarius	Pisces
Friendship	Splendid, you won't want ever to do anything ambitious or exhausting—just a casual spree from time to time.	Excellent. Scorpio has many qualities you admire but may lack. A good combination for making money.	You are very different and need to find common interests, perhaps in sport. There could be personality clashes.	This could last for years; you will share aspirations, burdens and possessions—and could make money together.	Not always easy, you are conventional, they are not. Try to accept their eccentricities and all may yet go well.	Should work well. Your dependable strength can bring wavering Pisceans to their senses.
Love Life	You will often be told to 'wait and see'; mostly you won't mind unless your Bull nature is upset and you start to paw the ground!	Even you could be swept off your feet by Scorpio. Enjoy yourself but expect emotions to run high.	Not easy: your possessiveness and their love of freedom do not mix well. Remember, Sagittarius can never be wholly 'yours' (or anyone else's).	If you manage to inject a little affection into that rather cold and lonely heart you'll be doing fine.	Their love of independence will clash with your need to possess, and may hamper developments. Music could bring you together.	You may be puzzled by their irrational ways, but *how* they love your affection!
Marriage	Best if you can arrange for someone else to do the housework; you and Libra won't want to—but *you* like your comfort.	Very good, provided you vary the pace to suit each other; you love peace and quiet but Scorpio thrives on intensity.	Their mind works more quickly than yours; allow for this and try not to tame them—it could ruin things.	Good, you'll have your dream house. But inside, you like it pretty, they prefer the bare look.	Try to contain their wilder schemes; they are also thoughtful and appreciative, but you are different in many ways.	Your solid qualities are good for them, but you must do the family accounts. Money is beyond them.

PARENTS AND CHILDREN

The Zodiac Family Portrait

THE TAUREAN FATHER

The Taurean father will be proud of his children, and perhaps his theme-song to them will be: 'You are so fortunate that I am able to give you so many opportunities that *I* never had'. Even if his own background was by no means poor, he will impress on his children that theirs is so much more comfortable.

As the children grow up, Taurus will have to take care to modernize his opinions, and try to understand what the younger generation is thinking. Because of his tendency to be staid and set in his opinions, the generation gap between him and his children could be wide, and under extreme conditions communications between them could break down. In some cases the fixity of his views will prevent him from understanding them, and they will find it hard to understand him. One special area of conflict could arise when the children want to leave home for the first time, for Taurus will be reluctant to let them go; his instinct is to resist changes. If his wife is wise, she can play a part here by saying that the children want to build their own lives and secure their own futures—as he himself has done. This is the kind of sensible argument that should, in theory at least, appeal to sound, rational Taurus.

THE TAUREAN MOTHER

The Taurean mother will do all she can to make her children behave well and look attractive. She herself is almost certain to be pretty, and her good looks will be passed on to her children. If the family is not well off, she will scrimp and save to buy attractive clothes for them. As with the Taurean father, she will not want to let go of her family—she bore the children, so they are hers; and it will be quite a battle for the children themselves to convince her that no one can actually *own* anyone.

The Taurean mother will make life fun for her children—she is excellent at giving birthday parties and special suppers. Although she will encourage her children, probably from a very early age, to take an interest in music, she may not always like the noise, for Taureans usually favour peace and quiet.

Both Taurean parents must remember that many children need answers in depth to their searching questions—even if the parents may think that they are 'too young to know'. Taureans must recognize that they are not very adaptable, and that their children may be different in many respects from themselves.

THE TAUREAN CHILD

The Taurean child must under all circumstances be allowed to develop at his own, usually rather slow rate. Do not expect him to jump from the bottom of the class to the top in one leap. He will thrive on encouragement, but he is a plodder. He must be made to feel secure, and upsets at home could cause him—much more than most children—to slip back at school.

He is conventional, and needs to be at a school where the discipline is fairly strict. The 'free expression' school is not on the whole the place for Taurus. No, he will be at his best learning facts, perhaps parrot fashion, so that they really sink in permanently. Once in his mind, they will stay there for the rest of his life. He will be quite good at heavy sports, and may excel in weight-lifting, boxing, and heavy team games. He is not enterprising, and will not show notable powers of leadership; but in a team his dependability and extra weight will be an asset. Taurean girls are excellent at making beautiful things, and will for instance sit for hours happily knitting or doing embroidery or sewing. All Taurean children must be discouraged from eating too many sweet things, for they tend like their elders to have weight problems. They must be encouraged to help with younger brothers and sisters, for jealousy can occur.

At all costs the Taurean child should be helped if he takes an interest in music. His interest may be satisfied by singing in the school choir and listening to records at home, but if he asks to learn to play the piano or, indeed, any other instrument, an effort should be made to let him have lessons, for the Taurean can excel in music—it seems to be 'his' art form.

The Taurean child's money-box will never be empty and, to help him become less possessive, he should be encouraged from time to time to give a tiny contribution to a charity; he must also learn to share his toys with his friends.

CAREERS AND PASTIMES

A Sun-sign Guide to Work and Play

The Taurean must have security in a career. Equally important is a regular routine that tells him exactly 'how he stands', so that he can plan quietly and confidently well in advance. He needs this assurance for his peace of mind. It helps him to work better if he knows that a monthly pay-cheque will arrive regularly at his bank, and that the decisions he makes will not have to be changed at a moment's notice.

FINANCE AND ARCHITECTURE

Taureans are in their element in the world of banking. They are extremely money-conscious, and it will satisfy them to work in an environment concerned with finance. But a bank is not the only career solution: they will also do well as brokers, working on the Stock Exchange, or in any finance corporation.

The solidity of the product and the idea of being constructive are factors which draw many Taureans to architecture. This is a splendid profession for them, though their need for security can make them reluctant to go it alone. A Taurean may succeed with his own business, but on the whole he will do better working for a large concern.

BEAUTY AND THE ARTS

The Taurean girl makes an excellent beautician. All Taureans have a fine appreciation of beauty, and this can be expressed very positively indeed in beauty culture. The luxury trades in general are also good, for Taureans will really 'feel' for beauty products, perfumes, jewels, furs, and so on. Taureans can themselves be outstandingly beautiful, and if the Taurean girl can keep her weight down she could be a successful fashion model. Her patience will be endless, so she will not mind waiting around for lights to be fixed! On the other hand, in the early stages she will probably find that the modelling life is not as luxurious as she may have hoped.

If the Taurean has an artistic bent, there is a high probability that it will be directed towards music. Many

Taureans are famous professional musicians, and many of these are singers. Perhaps the fact that Taurus rules the throat has a bearing on this. They should not therefore let any musical talent stagnate, and parents of Taurean children would do well to encourage them to sing or play an instrument.

MASTERS OF CLAY AND STONE

If their artistic feelings are inclined to the visual arts, Taureans would do well to concentrate on carving; sculpture is likely to be their true *métier*, and they may excel at working with a variety of materials, or at modelling in clay—rather than plaster. They love the feel of stone, especially the sense it gives them of permanence. Taurus could develop into a splendid sculptor; the possibilities of the medium are endless and full of promise. And he has the persistence to achieve complete technical mastery of it.

The Taurean likes doing things which allow him to sit still for long periods of time. He enjoys going to concerts and listening to long symphonies or large-scale choral works. The Taurean girl usually sews well and may be an embroidress. Taureans love their gardens, and will happily spend hours growing either beautiful flowers or vegetables. They may well have a greenhouse, too, and will fill this with the more exotic and colourful types of flowers, which will be a great source of pleasure to them.

Male Taureans enjoy some of the 'heavier' sports such as football, which they will probably play at school and then later follow as spectators. They need more exercise than they can usually be bothered to take, and may like to consider keeping in trim by going to a weight-lifting class. Wrestling could also appeal! They enjoy long country walks, and should try to take them whenever possible. Taurus is perhaps happier living in the country than in town, and should try to arrange this, if he can.

AT HOME

A Sun-sign Guide to Home Décor

The Taurean home is extremely comfortable. However much Taurus earns there will always be touches of luxury. The couches will be scattered with large, very soft cushions, and there will more than likely be an abundance of large floral chintzes—either as loose covers or drapes. Traditions are established and continued by Taureans, and traditional themes will dominate their taste in interior decoration. For instance, the furniture will be in good taste, but rather heavy, and there will be a traditional air about its design.

COMFORT BEFORE ELEGANCE

Taurean colours are delicate shades of blue and pink—relaxing colours. These will be very much to the fore in their schemes for interiors; perhaps pale blue walls or a warm pink carpet will be chosen. The Taurean likes to be warm, and there should be no draughts in his house; indeed, everything will be designed, above all, for comfort; even looks feature less highly in his list of priorities. Perhaps Taurean ideas on décor are best summed up by saying that a visitor coming into a Taurean house or flat will at once be able to sit down with a comfortable sigh in a calm, cushioned atmosphere.

The Taurean is usually musical, so the hi-fi will be prominent; music will be everywhere but not so loud that it will disturb a guest if it is not to his taste. There may be musical instruments in the house—a piano, perhaps, or an old mandolin (the latter for decoration).

OPULENT FLOWERS

Taureans love flowers, so expect to see large, well-arranged bowls of them. They will tend to be showy both in arrangement and kind, and will probably consist of such types as hydrangeas, large chrysanthemums and full-blown roses. Many will have been brought in from the garden: the Taurean will have a garden if he possibly can.

The Taurean is conservative in his taste, and this will be reflected in his choice of pictures: reproductions of Renoirs or Dutch flower pieces may be prominent. If he is a collector, he may specialize in small carvings, which he favours because they are permanent, and will not break as easily as, say, porcelain.

The Taurean displays his possessions well; they are extremely important to him. They are, perhaps, more an extension of himself than happens with people born under any other sign of the Zodiac. In some respects, the visitor 'sings for his supper' when a Taurean shows off his latest acquisition; he will expect it to be admired with enthusiasm and joy. This will then make his day: as a reward the visitor will be invited into the dining-room and there regaled with a vast, rich dinner!

William Shakespeare

Barbra

Queen Elizabeth II

Dame Margot Fonteyn

Ella Fitzgerald

Orson Welles

DINNER WITH TAURUS

Entertaining with Your Sun-sign

THE HOST

Largely by catering to his own love of luxury and good food, the Taurean host has a reputation for providing a good table. The only drawback to his dinner parties will be if he is feeling loquacious, and guests must then earn their meal by patiently listening as he meanders on for hours on some favourite topic.

More to his credit, however, he will greatly enjoy preparing the food—even if he takes still more pleasure in tasting it to see that all is well. He will be strongly tempted, especially if the dishes are a success, to put some aside for himself, for the next day!

The food a Taurean offers his guests will not be particularly imaginative, but it will be sound and nourishing, probably with a strong accent on meat. Taureans are on the whole great meat-eaters. Their evenings at home are well planned—for theirs is a home-loving sign—and they will be upset by any little incident which disturbs the flow of the evening.

THE GUEST

The Taurean guest will need no prompting to ask for a second helping of any dish; the greedier Taurean may even be caught helping himself, and any offer to help in the kitchen will probably not be unconnected with the idea of picking the chicken bones or seeing if there is any more custard cream! He is a slow eater and ploughs through helpings as large as he or his plate can manage, with great deliberation. Taurus will very likely be the first to start and the last to finish. His natural, patient charm will take on a still greater glow as he becomes fuller and fuller.

THE SETTING

Pinks and blues tend to dominate the table decorations —these are the colours of Venus, the Taurean's ruling planet. Roses make an appropriate centrepiece.

Taureans are often singers, and they love the human voice: this is likely to influence their choice of background music, which will range from pop to opera.

WINES

Taurus, as befits his great affinity with the dining room, likes his wine and may well imbibe large quantities of it. He tends to enjoy claret and wines that meet the general requirement of having 'body'. These he sips at no great rate, thoughtfully working his way through the bottles that his host provides.

Left: An all-star evening for famous Taureans of past and present would very likely include the illustrious guests in our picture. For details of the dishes on the table—every one a Taurean favourite—turn to page 68.

eisand

Sigmund Freud

Bing Crosby

RECIPES FOR TAURUS

Cooking with Astrology

The Taurean, however eager to get to work on the delicacies spread before him, is by nature incapable of rushing; so he will sit down deliberately at the table and survey the menu with care. Cauliflower soup, rich, thick and rather bland, will be a good start to a hearty Taurean meal, preparing the way for an opulent Tournedos Rossini, with its full flavour and heavy, satisfyingly alcoholic sauce!

But two rich courses won't satisfy the Taurean's appetite: he will demand a rich sweet as well—and chocolate gâteau, fattening and filling, with a good thick covering of cream dripping over its beautifully spongy, mouthwatering sides, will be just right for him. He will acknowledge your invitation by bringing with him a large box of succulent chocolates, also helping to eat them!

CAULIFLOWER SOUP
An easy, rather original, delicious soup: cook a small cauliflower and 2 medium-sized potatoes, peeled and sliced, in the same $2\frac{1}{2}$ cups water (or stock) until soft, adding salt and pepper to taste. Strain vegetables, mash and rub through a sieve (for once, sieve rather than blend, which tends to reduce them to a watery mush). Dilute with $2\frac{1}{2}$ cups milk and some cream for extra richness. Correct seasoning and serve, with croûtons.

AVOCADO AND APPLE SALAD
A simple idea: core and slice crisp dessert apples. Peel and slice avocados. Brush apple and avocado slices with lemon juice to prevent them going rather a strange colour. Serve with a French dressing made with lemon juice rather than vinegar.

TOURNEDOS ROSSINI
Tournedos are thick slices cut from the middle of a fillet of beef; which means that in England this dish is extremely expensive, while in America it is more delicious than anywhere else. Anyway, season tournedos (one per guest) with salt and pepper, and sear on both sides in a little butter to which you have added some olive oil to prevent it burning. Keep beef warm while you gently fry some trimmed slices of bread (one per steak) in the same fat until crisp and golden. On top of the bread, arrange slices of pâté — classically, pâté de foie gras, but otherwise any good

pâté. Lay tournedos upon this succulent bed and serve with Madeira sauce.

For the Madeira sauce, simply take beef stock made very strong and add Madeira to taste. Of course, if you can be bothered to make the stock rather than dissolve a cube, the result will be all the more delicious!

WIENER SCHNITZEL
The splendid Viennese way with veal: 1 thinly pounded veal scallop per guest; dust with flour and dip in beaten egg; then coat with breadcrumbs and chill for an hour or so if there is time. Fry in butter and oil until veal is cooked through but still very moist, about 4 minutes per side. Serve with spaghetti and tomato sauce. Or top each schnitzel with a fried egg and a garnish of anchovy fillets and capers—thus making a Schnitzel Holstein.

'My advice if you insist on slimming: Eat as much as you like—just don't swallow!' Harry Secombe.

CHOCOLATE GATEAU
Taureans dearly love a good heavy, fattening dessert, and this admirably fits the bill. Oil two $7\frac{1}{2}$-inch layer cake pans and line bases with oiled paper. Sift into a bowl: $1\frac{1}{4}$ cups cake flour, 4 tablespoons cocoa powder, $1\frac{1}{2}$ teaspoons baking powder and a pinch of salt. Stir in $\frac{3}{4}$ cup sugar and make a well in the centre. Add 2 egg yolks, 6 tablespoons oil (anything but olive) and 6 tablespoons water. Beat vigorously with a wooden spoon for at least 3 minutes. In a separate bowl, beat 2 egg whites until they form stiff peaks. Fold into chocolate batter with a metal spoon or spatula. Pour into prepared cake pans and bake in the centre of a moderate oven (350°F) for about 30 minutes. Turn out on to wire racks, peel off lining paper and cool. When cold, spread with sieved, warmed apricot jam (optional) and put layers together with whipped cream. Make a frosting with 1 packed cup confectioners' sugar, beating in $1\frac{1}{2}$ tablespoons each oil and milk, and a few drops of vanilla extract. Beat until smooth; then use to cover top and sides of gâteau. Allow frosting to set before serving.

Note: The gâteau can be given a lemon or orange flavouring by using $1\frac{1}{2}$ cups cake flour instead of the flour and cocoa mixture, and lemon or orange juice instead of water.

GEMINI
22 MAY–20 JUNE

With Gemini, the sign of the Heavenly Twins, the accent is on
duality; it is reflected on every level of his delightful personality.
He will not be content with one objective at a time in any
sphere of his life. His ruling planet is Mercury, the messenger of
the gods, who endows him with sublime communication.
He will talk for ever. He will change his mind, his loves,
his life style—his whole outlook. Gemini's element is air,
on which he thrives, since it serves to transmit his eternal
message! And his quality is mutable, for he is the restless one.
He is too changeable to like one or even two colours, but might
settle for sizzling yellow. His stone seems to be the most
placid association of the sign, for it is the cool, nebulous agate.

YOUR SUN-SIGN CHARACTER

The Zodiacal Self Revealed

Geminians must be kept busy. They need to be constantly flicking their way through the events of the day, probably uttering a sigh of relief when one task is over and they can move on to the next—to see what that has to offer by way of new, lively amusement and challenge.

Perhaps 'one task' is inaccurate, for rarely if ever does the Geminian confine himself merely to performing one task. He does many, all at the same time. He will continue to write a letter while he is answering the telephone; he will for certain read more than one book at a time, and will relax by watching TV and reading at the same time. He will also like to work with a musical background—perhaps more so than any other sign. He can be quite insatiable and many less energetic mortals can find him rather wearing; his constant duality often proves far too much for more single-minded, less energetic people.

However, his energy is not always physical: although he is usually of a fairly light build and rather wiry, he is not always as strong as some other slim types. Gemini's energy is mental—he is the sort of man who 'lives on his nerves', and is sometimes (especially when young) rather tense.

NEED FOR CONSISTENCY

One Geminian problem is restlessness: if he does not consciously check himself, he will tend to fritter his energy away, leaving a trail of unfinished tasks in his wake. This is a great pity: if he *is* inclined to fall into this trap he will waste many of his splendid qualities, for he is usually clever. He must try to develop consistency of effort, otherwise much hard work and mental energy will be wasted, and he himself will feel unfulfilled.

The Geminian is inconsistent in many ways: he will argue one line of opinion one day, then reverse his attitude and argue from exactly the opposite standpoint the next. He will swear that he has not changed his views—no, no, he never changes his mind; once he has made a decision, taken an attitude, he sticks to it. (At least, that is what he will say if challenged.) And, as he is such a fluent talker, he may even talk his listener round into thinking that they must have misheard or misunderstood him the first time! But the shrewd friend will soon learn about Gemini and his tricks, and an opponent who is a specialist in a particular subject will eventually tie the Geminian up in intellectual knots—though the Geminian will give a spirited impression of knowing a great deal about his friend's subject.

More seriously, the Geminian's tendency to be superficial can harm him in the eyes of others. He has a tendency to dismiss issues and the opinions of others, and sometimes even whole areas of life, without having given them the consideration that they deserved.

GEMINI IN ACTION

Mind and Body: You and Your Life Style

The Geminian hates to be bored. The prospect fills him with anxiety. He may also be afraid of being himself classified as boring by other people. So sometimes, in his need to escape from 'boring people', he tends to miss quite a lot in life, simply because someone he may consider 'boring' is merely living his life at a slower, steadier pace. Geminians constantly skim the surface: they will do themselves a great deal of good psychologically, if they can also discipline themselves to explore the depths of a situation.

Their urge to communicate is overwhelming. Geminians are forever talking, writing to the newspapers and trying to appear on radio and TV talk shows, whether simply as a telephone contributor or as a studio guest. They *must* communicate! Geminians are forever talking to strangers—'having a word', they call it, though it will probably amount to several hundred words! If they cannot communicate, Geminians will develop claustrophobia, which will not suit them at all (not that it is a pleasant affliction for anyone else). But Geminians cannot bear to be deprived either of a chance to air their views or of the attention this brings them. However, they have great charm and friendliness. Their company is stimulating and fun, and their general liveliness in fact makes them one of the most likeable types to be found.

TWITCHY GESTURES

His tendency to live life at a frantic pace—especially on an intellectual level—makes the Geminian liable to suffer from nervous breakdowns. His nervous system may be extremely highly strung, and the strain of a difficult period can sometimes tip the balance and his nerves will snap. The Geminian will then find himself engulfed in a period of enforced inactivity which he will of course find difficult to cope with. Long before that time his tensions will show themselves in many ways: perhaps the most noticeable is for the Geminian to be too talkative—so much so that he hardly ever takes in a word that is said to him. He is also likely to be fidgety and restless, his mind jumping forward to the next job or the next place where he has to be. If he can recognize the danger signals—such as unnecessarily criticizing his colleagues or his wife, or overdoing his usual rather twitchy gestures, or even nervously gnawing at his fingers—he will be wise to calm down and force himself to let life pass him by for a few days. In the end, this may be far better than having to miss the latest film, book, play—whatever he will miss most—for several weeks or months.

The areas of the body ruled by Gemini are the arms, shoulders and hands. Many a Geminian has suffered a broken collar-bone or arm. They are highly aware of their hands, which are frequently well-shaped and

which they may have manicured. But injuries will also gravitate to these areas of the body. The lungs, too, are Geminian, and whenever a cough settles on the chest, they should have immediate medical treatment, or a simple cough may turn into bronchitis.

A SNAPPER-UP OF TRIFLES

The Geminian has a built-in computer for a mind. He feeds it with facts, snippets of information, bits and pieces and unconsidered trifles of all sorts, which he later parades in the course of his numerous conversations and arguments—or in one of his many letters to the newspapers.

He is very quick-witted and will come to grips with a new subject at the drop of a hat. He will absorb what he wants from a printed page in a very short time. As a student, he is able to learn at great speed; before examinations he will study up to the very last minute, then impress the examiner with his performance and generally do very well. But within a few weeks what he has learned will have disappeared into thin air and been forgotten; meanwhile, the Geminian is away skimming the surface of another subject. At university he is likely to begin one subject, then change course in mid-stream; and while this may broaden his outlook, it will not give him the depth which he needs for real success (he must face the prospect that the effort of acquiring knowledge in depth may bore him).

The Geminian is clever and may sometimes resort to being cunning and artful; in extreme cases, he will turn to crime, matching his sharp wits against the police. He has precisely what it takes to make a highly professional criminal; apart from having the right sort of mind, he may also be a master of the quick getaway!

Most Geminians have a rather low emotional level—they will, for instance, enjoy a major artistic experience in an intellectual way. If they find themselves moved to tears, the chances are that they will question themselves about *their reaction* rather than the actual content of the work of art that has moved them. They are rational and may well despise a flow of emotion.

The Geminian has an excellent mind, and is of all types the least likely to allow cobwebs to grow there. He will avoid this in a variety of ways, the most common being by keeping up with the younger generation's opinions, especially their feelings on controversial matters. He will argue with young people until he is (or they are) blue in the face. The Geminian mind is itself essentially youthful. Indeed, Gemini is the most youthful sign and there is many a nonagenarian Geminian who, while keeping his mind active, will also have an eye for a pretty girl, and will peer (if a little shakily) over his wire-framed spectacles for a better look at any he sees!

EMOTIONAL RELATIONSHIPS

Couples: How You Compare in Friendship, Love and Marriage

GEMINI IN LOVE

'Constant and true' is *not* the Geminian motto when he is in love. He has a flirtatious reputation. But many a Geminian, once committed to a permanent relationship, can adapt very well to the new situation—provided his partner is intellectually stimulating, keeps herself young and attractive, and also keeps her Geminian on his toes.

The Geminian, pursuing someone he finds attractive, will try a clever approach: he will perhaps ask to borrow a record or a book, and then will begin a string of letters about the record or the book . . . what was her opinion of . . . and did she like . . . and how was . . . and how did the singer's interpretation on Band Three compare with so-and-so's later recording? This is all

part of a Geminian ploy; then one of the many letters or phone calls will include a casual invitation to dinner or a film—and the romance will be under way.

THE GEMINIAN FRIEND

It is fun to have a Geminian friend. He will be stimulating company, the type who enjoys walking around the town, looking at the shops and markets. Anyone who does not have many interests will soon acquire them when he has a Geminian friend, for the latter will constantly be pointing out items of interest, or explaining what he has just been doing or making. Through him one's whole circle of friends may widen; the Geminian himself will undoubtedly have a great many acquaintances—even if he does enjoy his books

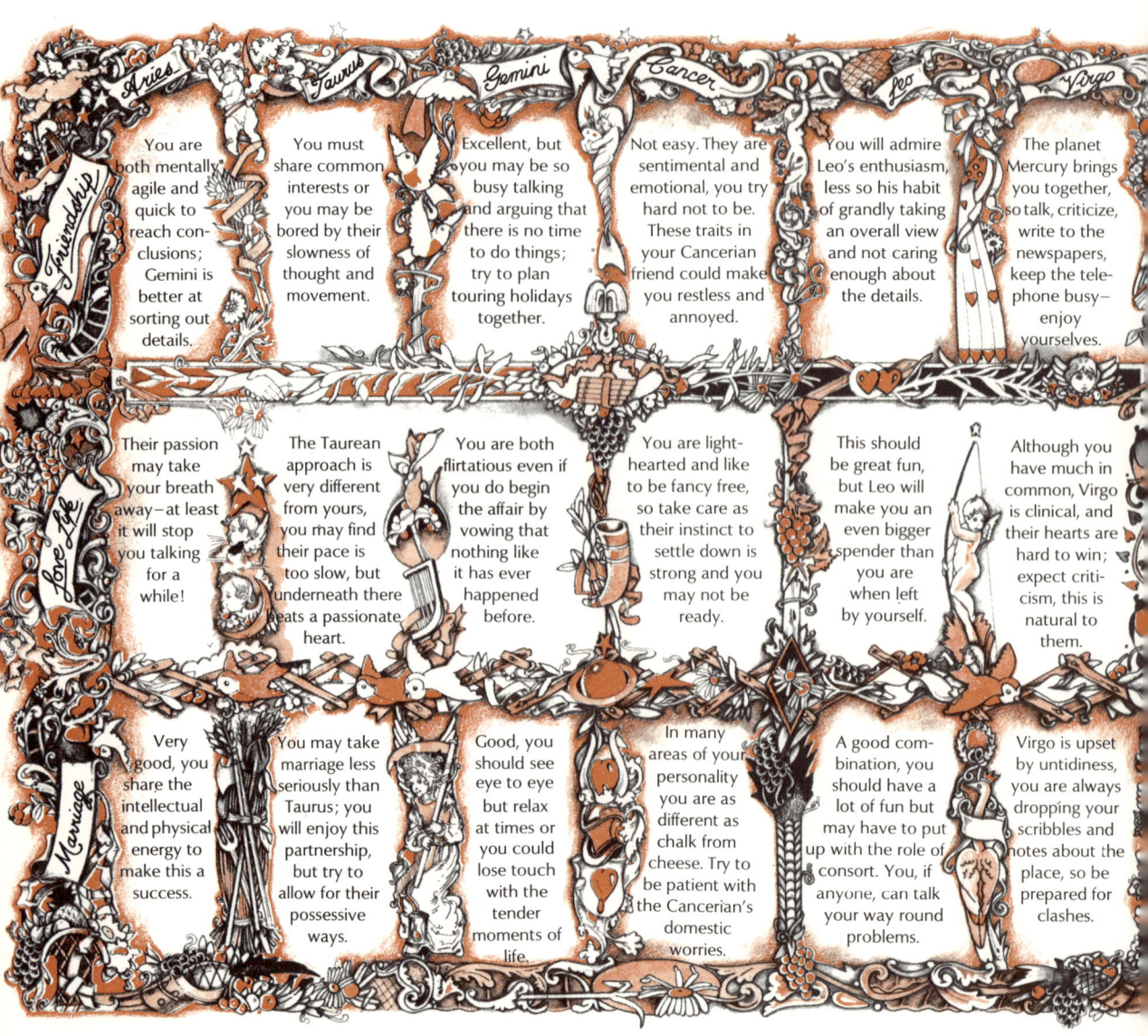

Aries · **Taurus** · **Gemini** · **Cancer** · **Leo** · **Virgo**

Friendship

Aries: You are both mentally agile and quick to reach conclusions; Gemini is better at sorting out details.

Taurus: You must share common interests or you may be bored by their slowness of thought and movement.

Gemini: Excellent, but you may be so busy talking and arguing that there is no time to do things; try to plan touring holidays together.

Cancer: Not easy. They are sentimental and emotional, you try hard not to be. These traits in your Cancerian friend could make you restless and annoyed.

Leo: You will admire Leo's enthusiasm, less so his habit of grandly taking an overall view and not caring enough about the details.

Virgo: The planet Mercury brings you together, so talk, criticize, write to the newspapers, keep the telephone busy—enjoy yourselves.

Love Life

Aries: Their passion may take your breath away—at least it will stop you talking for a while!

Taurus: The Taurean approach is very different from yours, you may find their pace is too slow, but underneath there beats a passionate heart.

Gemini: You are both flirtatious even if you do begin the affair by vowing that nothing like it has ever happened before.

Cancer: You are light-hearted and like to be fancy free, so take care as their instinct to settle down is strong and you may not be ready.

Leo: This should be great fun, but Leo will make you an even bigger spender than you are when left by yourself.

Virgo: Although you have much in common, Virgo is clinical, and their hearts are hard to win; expect criticism, this is natural to them.

Marriage

Aries: Very good, you share the intellectual and physical energy to make this a success.

Taurus: You may take marriage less seriously than Taurus; you will enjoy this partnership, but try to allow for their possessive ways.

Gemini: Good, you should see eye to eye but relax at times or you could lose touch with the tender moments of life.

Cancer: In many areas of your personality you are as different as chalk from cheese. Try to be patient with the Cancerian's domestic worries.

Leo: A good combination, you should have a lot of fun but may have to put up with the role of consort. You, if anyone, can talk your way round problems.

Virgo: Virgo is upset by untidiness, you are always dropping your scribbles and notes about the place, so be prepared for clashes.

and records quite as much as the company of others.

The Geminian is argumentative, but not generally quarrelsome; he can be extremely sarcastic, and indeed his sense of humour is often rather mocking. But even his more negative traits are usually not serious, for he is a lightweight and on the whole he does not feel so strongly about issues that he will want to lose friends because of them.

MARRIAGE – THE FACTS

In the same way that it is fun to have a Geminian friend so, generally speaking, it is fun being married to one. Geminians bring a great deal of lively friendship into marriage, and although there are moments of great passion they rightly feel that companionship within the marriage is also important for their well-being.

Many Geminians are flirtatious, and a steady and perhaps possessive partner could take their lighthearted approach too seriously, and be hurt or upset. But if the partner is young at heart and up-to-date in his or her attitude, there should be no difficulty, and the marriage will be happy. Gemini seems to embody a 'spark plug' element – a quality of stimulating his partner to lively discussion or action.

Below: Use this Friends and Lovers Sun-sign chart to check how Gemini is likely to make out with others in friendship, love and marriage. Relationships are listed from left to right, Gemini to Aries, Gemini to Taurus, etc., and from top to bottom in friendship, love and marriage.

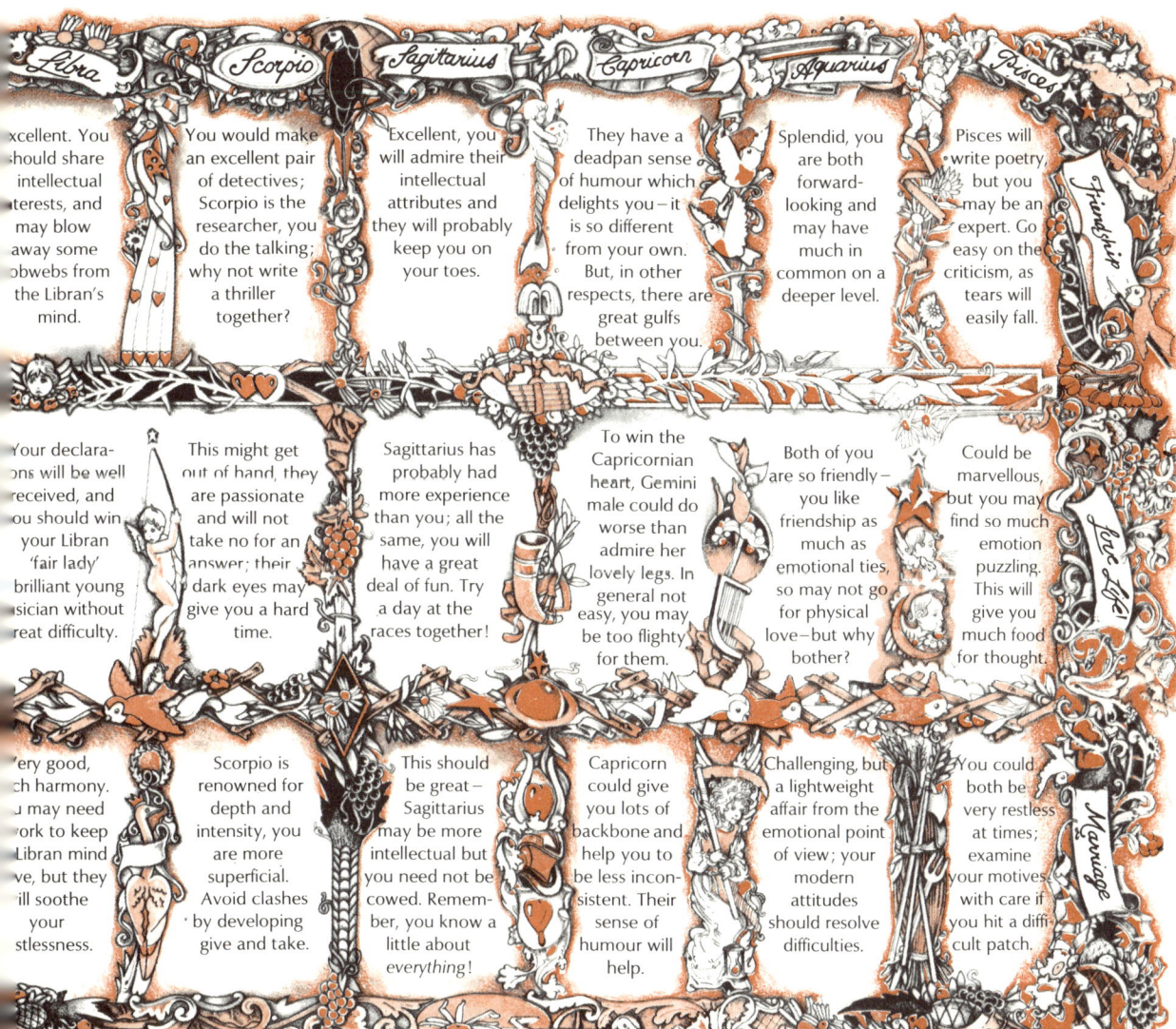

Libra / Scorpio / Sagittarius / Capricorn / Aquarius / Pisces

Friendship

xcellent. You should share intellectual terests, and may blow away some obwebs from the Libran's mind.

You would make an excellent pair of detectives; Scorpio is the researcher, you do the talking; why not write a thriller together?

Excellent, you will admire their intellectual attributes and they will probably keep you on your toes.

They have a deadpan sense of humour which delights you – it is so different from your own. But, in other respects, there are great gulfs between you.

Splendid, you are both forward-looking and may have much in common on a deeper level.

Pisces will write poetry, but you may be an expert. Go easy on the criticism, as tears will easily fall.

Love Life!

Your declara-ons will be well received, and ou should win your Libran 'fair lady' brilliant young sician without reat difficulty.

This might get out of hand, they are passionate and will not take no for an answer; their dark eyes may give you a hard time.

Sagittarius has probably had more experience than you; all the same, you will have a great deal of fun. Try a day at the races together!

To win the Capricornian heart, Gemini male could do worse than admire her lovely legs. In general not easy, you may be too flighty for them.

Both of you are so friendly – you like friendship as much as emotional ties, so may not go for physical love – but why bother?

Could be marvellous, but you may find so much emotion puzzling. This will give you much food for thought.

Marriage

ery good, ch harmony. u may need ork to keep Libran mind ve, but they ill soothe your stlessness.

Scorpio is renowned for depth and intensity, you are more superficial. Avoid clashes by developing give and take.

This should be great – Sagittarius may be more intellectual but you need not be cowed. Remem-ber, you know a little about everything!

Capricorn could give you lots of backbone and help you to be less incon-sistent. Their sense of humour will help.

Challenging, but a lightweight affair from the emotional point of view; your modern attitudes should resolve difficulties.

You could both be very restless at times; examine your motives with care if you hit a diffi-cult patch.

PARENTS AND CHILDREN
The Zodiac Family Portrait

THE GEMINIAN FATHER

The Geminian father often feels younger than his children! If the latter are not especially forward-looking, or perhaps rather serious, the Geminian's outlook on life could well be ahead of theirs. His is one of the few signs that does not usually have much trouble with the generation gap, and he will be anxious to ensure that he does not fall behind the times—especially in areas which have a direct bearing on his children's welfare and future development.

He may, however, try to interfere. He will pick up his children's schoolbooks, try to solve a problem, and all too often be forced to recognize that he is growing old, and that teaching methods must have changed since his days, for he cer-tainly didn't do it *that* way when *he* was in school! But he may be too proud to say so at the time; rather than be thought old-fashioned, he is more likely to walk off in a huff—in search of some other world to conquer.

The Geminian father can be over-critical of his children's efforts, and is too in-clined—when, for example, the child produces a paint-ing—to say, 'Yes, it's very nice, *but* . . .' This can be more than a little deflating for the child, and Geminian fathers should try to over-come this tendency.

THE GEMINIAN MOTHER

The Geminian mother is lively and stimulating. She would rather take her children round to the local bookstore than stay at home and make a pudding. After all, she will say, one can buy excellent puddings in cans, and there are *far* more interesting things to do with one's own and the children's time!

Although it is possibly dangerous to generalize about this, she is rather more likely than most to have twins. And if there have been twins in her own or her husband's family, she may find it worthwhile insuring against twins the moment she becomes pregnant—especially if she was born within an hour or two of sunrise (not forgetting daylight saving time!).

If anyone can cope with the demands of keeping up a career while the children are small, she can. Indeed, if she can possibly manage to maintain some other interest while she is bringing up the children,
she should do so, for she needs intellectual stimula-tion and may find that just being a mother is not sufficiently demanding. She is an excellent mother in many ways, and although she may not be quite as affectionate as she might be—a possible flaw that she should be aware of—she is marvellous at pro-viding stimulating books, painting equipment and plenty of activities for the children outside their school work.

THE GEMINIAN CHILD

The Geminian child will be a likeable and lively type, constantly asking questions, the answers to which he will almost inevitably turn into still more questions. He is so highly strung, that parents must watch out for tensions; these can occur even in quite young Gemi-nian children. If they do, it may not be easy to calm the child down again.

Restlessness must also be countered. It will be ex-tremely difficult for the Geminian child to sit still for any length of time; he is one of the great fidgets. This must, up to a point, be accepted; so must his natural duality. But he also tends to grow bored with his hobbies, and parents would do well to help him to be consistent in his efforts. They should also endeavour to let him ex-press his duality by giving him two or three tasks to do at the same time. But, most important of all, it must be impressed on him that he should produce finished results—a *complete* model ship, for instance, assembled and painted, and not half a ship and half the next thing.

The Geminian child is not likely to take kindly to strong discipline, but will accept it if he is persuaded that rules are made for particular reasons, and that those reasons are sensible. If rules seem silly to him, he will tend not only to speak his mind about them—something he almost never stops doing, anyway—but also to ignore them in future. He is generally bright and will do well at school. But he is not a plodder; he will prefer working in bursts when the mood takes him —which it often will do. The progress that the Gemini child makes at school will probably be erratic, with plenty of highs to balance occasional lows.

CAREERS AND PASTIMES

A Sun-sign Guide to Work and Play

CAREERS

Because Geminians are intelligent, lively and positive, the choice of careers open to them is perhaps wider than for other signs. The Geminian is very adaptable, too, and usually manages to fit into most kinds of working environment—apart, perhaps, from the quiet old-fashioned office where tradition is paramount, and where life moves at a snail's pace. That, decidedly, is not for him.

There are a great many Geminians in radio, television and journalism. They are in their element seated at a typewriter, relaying their impressions of life to the world outside; or, better still, presenting their own scripted and edited radio and television programmes. They make excellent interviewers, for they know a little about most things, and have very inquiring minds. And even if they know nothing about some remote subject, they will quickly research it to a point where they can present a scholarly image to the expert they are due to confront.

GUIDE AMONG THE RUINS

Geminians like to move around, and many work as couriers or guides: how they love taking groups of tourists around ancient ruins! Geminian guides tend to be good at their jobs, too; to maintain their interest they will slightly vary the story every time, adding new and lively comments as they go. The travelling element is also strong in Gemini, and all Geminians like driving; so they will be happy as chauffeurs.

Gemini will often have two sources of income; indeed, he will often have two jobs. He will enjoy this, although one occupation will probably dominate. Gemini is a cultivator of lucrative sidelines, which sometimes may be developed into full-time business interests. Skilled with their hands, Geminians can make excellent mechanics or craftsmen if they set their minds to it. Geminians with an artistic flair will do well to think along the lines of a specialist craft such as fabric design, rather than the more intensive forms of fine art. Book illustration might be rewarding.

TRAVELLING MAN SUPREME

The Geminian is a salesman supreme. He enjoys everything about selling and is well equipped to charm his customers with persuasive talk, usually ending up with the best of a deal. He will like, too, the travelling involved; and is more suited to the role of sales representative than he is to selling in a store.

Geminian girls will do well and be happy as telephone operators. If they want a career in a beauty salon, then that of manicurist could be attractive to them. They also make excellent secretaries, but may grow bored at the prospect of learning shorthand; dictaphone machines are much more in their line! If the Geminian girl has an opportunity to open her own shop she should seriously consider doing so. There her natural ability for salesmanship will be able to flower; if it is a clothes shop, she will enjoy buying clothes for it. If she is artistic, she will want to design and make dresses, blouses and accessories for it.

Geminians make excellent teachers at all senior levels but they may find infants rather trying; they themselves are not renowned for their patience!

PASTIMES

It is almost impossible to isolate specifically Geminian hobbies and pastimes. There is almost nothing they will not try. Even so, we can draw a few conclusions: often Gemini's car, for instance, will be a two-seater convertible and this will be the centre of his life. He will probably *start* to write a book at least once in his life and, if encouraged, may even finish it. He will also enjoy photography and amateur film-making.

The Geminian needs physical exercise, which, because of his great intellectual energy, is something he tends to ignore. Tennis will be excellent for him and he should also consider taking up fencing—a sport in which quickness of eye and dexterity of movement are important. He will enjoy dancing, and may find himself joining a modern or classical ballet class simply for the physical and intellectual challenge—rather than for emotional release or artistic expression.

AT HOME

A Sun-sign Guide to Home Décor

If Gemini has his way, his home will be untidy; tidiness to him often means no more than a crazy pile of magazines about to topple to the floor, books packed so tightly into a shelf that it is impossible for any but the deftest Geminian fingers to extract them, and scraps of paper with indecipherable telephone numbers, shopping lists or notes lying in odd corners.

HOUSE OF GADGETS

The Geminian home teems with the paraphernalia of living; gadgets abound, especially in the kitchen. The Geminian tends to go wild when choosing furniture, and will spend a great deal of money on the latest designs.

The Geminian must be careful when choosing upholstery fabrics, for he loves light, bright colours and may well choose a yellow carpet or easy-chair. This is fine—when he is newly wed—but after a few years, when they have been cared for by children's sticky fingers and the passing dog, they will look dreadful. But provided the Geminian stops to think, his choice will be in good taste: he will not like heavy or lumpy furniture, and if he is very rich the light, dainty style of the eighteenth century will most likely appeal strongly to him. Woods will be light and probably natural in any modern furniture that he chooses, and he will also like to use glass—perhaps for the tops of tables or additional mirrors about the walls.

The Geminian will avoid heavy curtains and drapes. His curtains will be drawn back as far as possible to let in plenty of light; they may thus be of rather thin silk or perhaps cotton, probably with a smallish pattern. Gemini often collects his possessions in pairs: two ornaments, two matching pictures, a set of records; this is all part of his 'twin' nature.

ART WITH A SENSE OF HUMOUR

He will choose pictures with a touch of humour: the lively faces and semi-abstracts of Klee will certainly amuse him, and so will the sunny Riviera paintings of Dufy. He may like restless but also amusing abstracts— those of Kandinsky, for instance. In a classical style, he will admire Flemish paintings of fifteenth-century life, perhaps by Van Eyck; and from a still earlier period he may choose to decorate his walls with pages from illuminated manuscripts.

Do not visit a Geminian friend in search of a *relaxing* evening! You will receive a lively welcome, and will at once have a drink thrust into your hand and be whisked into conversation Then, before you have time to finish the drink, you will be off to the dining-room to eat; then (Gemini will have finished first) back again to the living room to talk and talk. But you will have fun, Gemini will see to that.

Bob Dylan

Catherine the Great

Judy Garland

Jane Russell

DINNER WITH GEMINI

Entertaining with Your Sun-sign

THE HOST

A Geminian dinner-party is unlikely to be an occasion for relaxing: the Geminian host will be popping up and down from his place at the table like a jack-in-the-box, checking that one dish is not boiling over, that another is not thickening too fast and that a third has not dried up. That, anyway, is the picture as far as the meal itself is concerned. But for Gemini it is the whole evening that is important – and he will hustle and bustle his guests through a varied and lively ritual of talking, eating, drinking and listening to music.

However, to return to the food, he will probably have planned a very varied menu, original and perhaps surprising, and with a range of contrasting dishes that will keep his guests happy. A tendency to fiddle too much with the dishes he is preparing may lead him to over-elaborate: so the best rule for Geminians is to stick to the recipe book, and when the recipe stops, so should they!

THE GUEST

The Geminian guest will, out of politeness, do his best to curb his nervous desire to interfere with his host's arrangements by poking around among the dishes, or by handing things around too energetically for the comfort of others at the table! But a dinner-party with a Geminian present will certainly not be dull as far as conversation is concerned; his flair for talking will keep the table lively.

THE SETTING

There is probably no need to bother much about the colour-scheme of the table decorations: Geminis like most bright colours, and the host will not go far wrong with bright yellows or oranges. Lily-of-the-valley or lavender will make pleasant additions to the table, and Gemini will find them lively and sympathetic; rather extrovert music will please him: some Vivaldi, perhaps, or light Mozart; Offenbach, or the popular music of the 1920s.

WINES

As to wines: a good light hock will be particularly enjoyed, and Gemini is likely to be rather fastidious in his tastes, so although the USA is a Geminian country, he may nevertheless decide that he prefers the richness of French and German wines to the more predictable Californian types. In fact, a bottle of Moselle will be very suitable, or a light claret.

An all-star evening for famous Geminians of past and present would very likely include the illustrious guests in our picture. For details of the various dishes on the table – every one a Geminian favourite – turn to page 82.

King Charles II

John Wayne

RECIPES FOR GEMINI

Cooking with Astrology

The Geminian, always first to sit down to table, will have devoured the entire meal with his eyes before the other guests have so much as drawn up their chairs! He may also finish first! Geminians will not like any food requiring so much concentration that they will not be able to talk at the same time! Gazpacho, besides being light, contains many elements, and is the least boring soup imaginable! Sweet-and-sour pork, with its two flavours so strongly contrasted, will delight a Geminian guest; and chicken jolanda has the same dual element, with the white meat of the chicken and the pink meat of the ham.

On the whole, elegant simplicity will commend itself to the Geminian, and although he will probably eat so quickly that his host may wonder whether his taste buds have time to react, he will appreciate good cooking, and will be the first to notice the most subtle flavours in an unusual recipe. He will enjoy wine (and all liquor) as much for its flavour as its effects, so quality rather than quantity should be the aim. In the zabaglione, for instance, the Marsala will not go unnoticed! Most certainly he will be careful to telephone you first thing next day and thank you for the evening.

'Grub first, then ethics!' Bertolt Brecht, 1898–1956.

GAZPACHO

This iced Spanish soup is a great Geminian favourite, and has many delicious ingredients. First, blend to a purée or rub through a sieve 2 or 3 peeled tomatoes and 1 peeled clove garlic. Add $\frac{1}{2}$ Bermuda onion and $\frac{1}{4}$ cored, seeded green pepper, both roughly chopped, and $\frac{1}{2}$ cucumber, peeled and diced, and blend or sieve again. Pour mixture into a pot; chill. Just before serving, add a blending of 6 tablespoons olive oil, 4 tablespoons lemon juice, salt and pepper to taste, and 2 cups tomato juice. Stir well and taste, adding more olive oil, lemon or tomato juice, salt or pepper if necessary. Serve with ice cubes. If you wish, set aside a few small pieces of the onion, pepper and cucumber, and either stir them in at the last moment, or hand round separately.

FISH SALAD

Cut into small cubes $\frac{1}{2}$ lb turbot and $\frac{1}{2}$ lb halibut. Poach them gently in a little milk until just tender. Drain fish and combine with $\frac{1}{4}$ lb cooked, shelled shrimp. Serve with a garnish of parsley, perhaps a little chopped raw onion, and an ordinary French dressing.

SWEET-AND-SOUR PORK

A dish beloved of Geminians. First, fry 1 carrot and 1 Bermuda onion, both thinly sliced, in 2 tablespoons olive oil for 10 minutes, or until lightly browned. Add an 8-oz can of pineapple chunks, drained, 3 to 4 tablespoons sweet pickle, 2 tablespoons soy sauce, 2 tablespoons sugar and 2 tablespoons vinegar, $\frac{2}{3}$ cup stock and a teaspoon of salt. Simmer for 20 minutes; then thicken with cornstarch; remove from heat and keep hot. Cut 1 lb pork (a fat cut will do) into neat cubes and deep-fry for about 5 minutes, or until cooked through. Add to sauce; reheat and serve with plain boiled rice. If you wish, the fried pork cubes can be dipped in an egg-and-flour batter and deep-fried a second time before being added to the sauce.

CHICKEN JOLANDA

Take the breasts of 2 chickens, with the wing attached, and flatten slightly. Fry in a mixture of butter and oil until cooked through and golden brown all over. Drain. Place a slice of ham on top of each breast, and cover with a slice—or slices—of cheese (classically, Gruyère; but any cheese which is not too strong will do). Place under a moderately hot broiler until cheese has melted and the ham warmed through. Serve. A very simple recipe, the only catch in it being that you can only make it with chicken breasts. These can often be bought separately, however.

ZABAGLIONE

Put 5 egg yolks, a pinch of salt, $\frac{1}{2}$ cup fine sugar and 1 cup Marsala in the top of a double boiler, or failing that, in a heatproof container perched on top of a pan of boiling water (a coin slipped between the side of the container and the pan allows steam to escape). Whip mixture over simmering water until thick and frothy and smooth. Remove from heat and continue to whip until slightly cooled. Serve warm or cold. Whisky, sherry, vodka, Madeira or brandy may be used instead of Marsala—not, however, all together! If you like, serve your creamy sweet as an addition to hot puddings, giving them an extra rich flavour and texture.

A delicious variation to this zabaglione recipe is made by substituting a white wine for the Marsala, and flavouring it with orange peel. The elegant subtlety of the combination of flavours will not be lost on the discriminating Geminian palate.

CANCER
21 JUNE–22 JULY

Cancer the Crab is the sign of motherhood: its ruling planet is the Moon, affecting the tides and women. The moon is changeable, but shines brightly, like the metal of Cancer —pure silver. Cancer belongs to the cardinal quality, which means that its subjects are 'outgoing', though they give of themselves mainly to those within their own family circle— for their lives need to evolve around a special, enclosed group of people. Cancer's element, water, is more particularly the water of the sea. The colours of Cancer are shades of smoky grey and blue, and the stone of the sign is the stone of the sea itself, the pearl, which in its turn is created by the oyster, and then protected—as the crab protects itself— in the fastness of its shell.

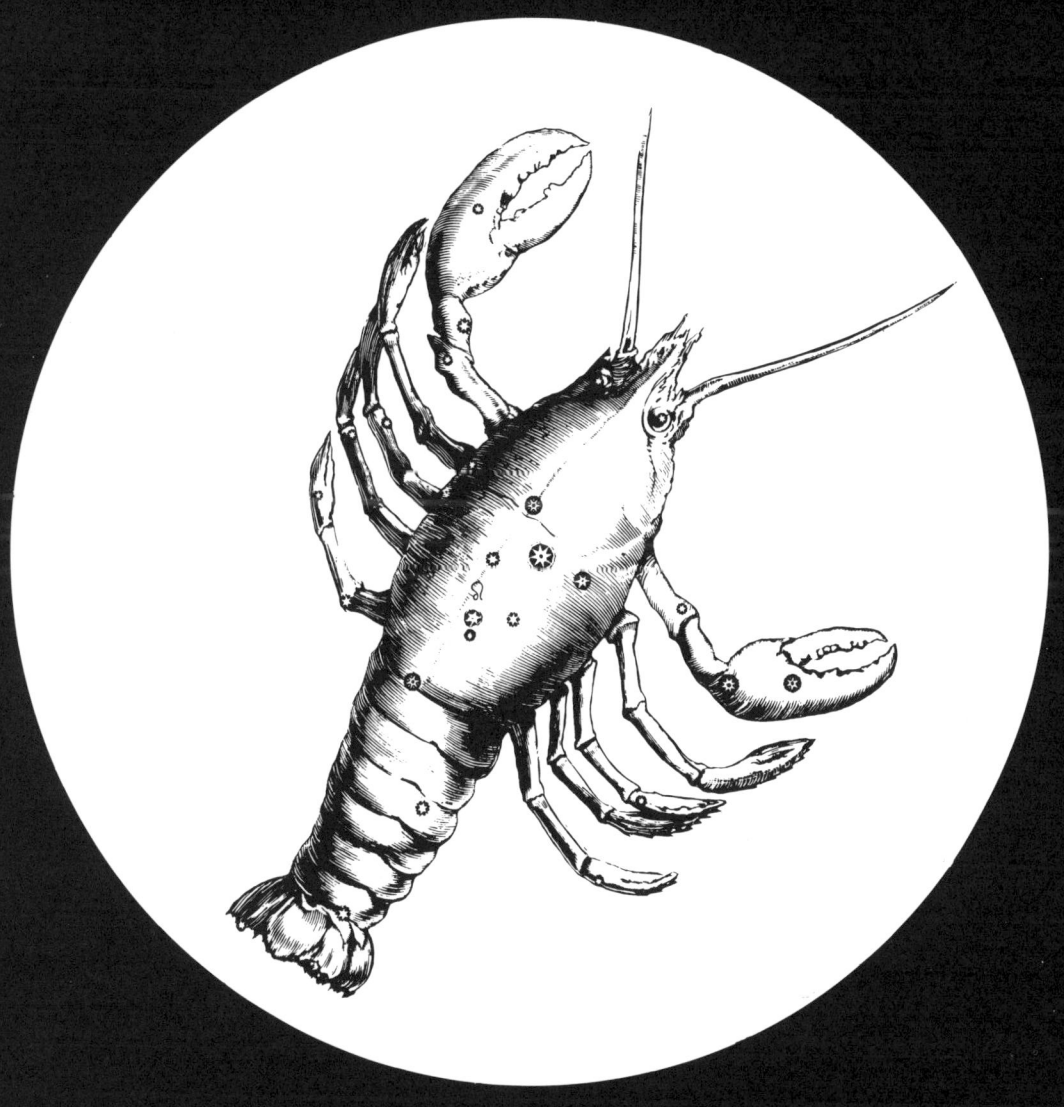

YOUR SUN-SIGN CHARACTER

The Zodiacal Self Revealed

Cancerians are kind, gentle, loving people, who have an extremely powerful urge to cherish and protect those whom they love. Generally speaking, these splendid qualities are expressed fully and whole-heartedly, but towards only a select few—those of the Cancerian's immediate circle. When he is a child, they will be his brothers and sisters, or when his father is away from home, his mother. When Cancer is adult, these qualities will be directed towards his wife and children, and when a Cancerian girl becomes a mother she is fulfilled indeed; her whole being—far more than is the case with any other sign—will be concentrated around her little ones.

EXTREMES OF HAPPINESS AND FEAR

All this is splendid, because it is so positive. But the Cancerian circle is a small one. Added to this, his protective instincts are the highly developed ones of the crab itself; he springs rapidly to defend himself—often before this is really necessary. Outsiders may feel that he is short-tempered; he will even snap at his friends. At times, too, he can seem a very frightened mortal. It is difficult for the Cancerian to take a middle-of-the-road path in this respect, and the differences between his 'family' self and his 'out-in-the-world' self are quite astonishing.

Cancer is very changeable, and this is directly related to his powerful 'swings' of emotion. One moment he will feel on top of the world, and will express himself positively and with evident happiness; and the next he will become suddenly uptight, a hard, beady look will come into his eyes, and a little frown will appear between his brows. This is the defence-mechanism coming into action; at such times, alas, Cancer's hard-hitting remarks will upset his friends more than he may realize. The situation can become more complicated if a friend retaliates. For Cancer is easily hurt and upset; that his friends should say such things! They just aren't true!

Cancerians have much natural sympathy, and will listen for hours on end to tales of woe brought to them by their friends and family. They are kind and reassuring, and will give much practical help and advice —they have the gift of identifying with other people's problems. Like the elephant, the Cancerian never forgets, and at times he may seem extremely hard. He will remember the smallest injustice done to him in the past, and will constantly bring it up in con-versation with others. Often the Cancerian is inhibited, and then his defensive shell is really useful, for it acts like the crab's shell as strong buffer against the com-plexities and difficulties of the outside world, and indeed masks his own complicated motivations from unwanted exposure.

84

CANCER IN ACTION

Mind and Body: You and Your Life Style

Cancerians are delightfully sentimental, probably far more than they realize. A bunch of flowers, an evening out ('for old time's sake') to a romantic film or a musical will touch their most vulnerable feelings. And if the moment is well chosen the outsider is almost certain to succeed, and tears of joy will pour down the Cancerian's cheeks at the kind thought, or indeed at the thought of the lovely musical, or at both! Once again, like the elephant, our Cancerian always remembers such moments of kindness.

The Cancerian has extremely powerful instincts, and will quite rightly live by his intuition. It is often said that women are the intuitive sex; but it is true that the Cancerian male is also highly intuitive. He should not try to ignore this quality, or laugh at it, or think it effeminate. It is not; and if the Cancerian—either male or female—feels that something is 'right', or that something will happen, he can afford to rely on his feelings. For 98% of the time, he will be right. His inclination always is to say 'I feel', rather than 'I think', and he must remember this, for it is a natural, powerful and positive asset.

Cancerians are enormously shrewd, and perhaps this is another aspect of their intuition. Their shrewdness often comes to the fore in their working lives, for they are good businessmen—a trait which is shared by the girls of the sign, who are unlikely to allow others to take advantage of them, either emotionally or in terms of their careers or household work.

The Cancerian is very clinging, and will hang on to anything—whether it is a pair of old socks or an outworn relationship. He is not possessive in a straightforward way, but he does find the act of parting difficult. For this reason, possessions tend to pile up and there may be clutter everywhere; this extends beyond physical objects to a mental state as well, where all may be jumble and confusion.

CHANGES OF MOOD

Perhaps the most difficult obstacle of all for the Cancerian is to find a balance between his extremes of feeling and action; he is a victim of his moods and of his changeability. All too often he becomes confused by conflicts within himself, and also by other people's reactions to him; but this may be because his attitudes towards other people can change so quickly—so much so that it is sometimes difficult to know exactly what the Cancerian's true feelings are. On one occasion his response to a friend or acquaintance will be a pleasant greeting, a positively enthusiastic 'Yes' to a suggestion; but another time the friend's proposals are—for no apparent reason—treated with a scowl or an extremely black look, whereupon the Cancerian turns sharply and walks off in the opposite direction!

If he can once find a balance between these extremes, he will emerge as a marvellous person in whom kindness and sympathy are predominant, and who will exude love, a delightfully warm air, and tenderness.

POWERFUL MEMORIES

Almost inevitably, the Cancerian mind looks to the past. It is extremely difficult for most Cancerians to look forward; all too easily, because of this, there is a strong tendency to live in the past ('We didn't do that when *I* was young!' they will say to their children). Perhaps they are prompted in this by their remarkable memories. This special ability has a splendidly positive side, of course, when for example—like the historians they often become—they will keep alive much that would otherwise be lost.

Of all the signs of the Zodiac, Cancer, it is probably true to say, is the one most prone to worry. He *needs* to have something to worry about, and if one problem clears up, he will have to find another! It is absolutely no good trying to tell a Cancerian (or anyone else, for that matter, who is prone to worry) to stop worrying; they cannot. But if they know they are the worrying type, this sometimes helps them to see problems in perspective, and also puts them on the way towards a greater understanding of themselves. Worry can often be so serious a problem for the Cancerian that it can lead to digestive upsets (to which he is extremely vulnerable); and in extreme cases we sometimes find that the Cancerian, through worry, may even develop ulcers.

MONSTERS OF THE DEEP

It is impossible to speak too highly of the Cancerian imagination. But it is up to him to make positive use of it, for it can all too easily work overtime in the wrong way—which merely has the unfortunate effect of feeding his tendency to worry. On one level, the Cancerian is excellently placed to tell lovely, imaginative stories to his children at bedtime; and there may be times in his life when he feels impelled to write poetry. He should do so: and he must not be apprehensive at any time about putting pen to paper. If he wants to write children's stories, or even a novel, he should have a go; especially if his imagination is taking him into the deep past, or into a fantasy world of sea monsters or knights in armour! Even if he feels he is not in essence a writer, or that his technique is poor, he must not be daunted; from a psychological point of view, the amount of positive good he will do himself will more than make the effort worthwhile. And when he does begin to write, the Cancerian will find his natural tenacity a great advantage, enabling him to complete his project in the face of difficulties.

EMOTIONAL RELATIONSHIPS

Couples: How You Compare in Friendship, Love and Marriage

CANCER IN LOVE

When the Cancerian falls in love, he falls with his emotions uppermost. He is essentially a lyrical lover, and possibly a hopeless romantic! Anyone who falls in love with a Cancerian will undoubtedly feel the full force of his changing moods; and while this can make for an interesting life, it can also be extremely tiresome. Evenings spent together can be marvellously romantic – ending in passionate glory – or they can be just plain miserable. In either case, the more the partner can take – whether of passion or ill temper – the more the Cancerian will give; there is no doubt about it, an affair with a Cancerian can certainly hit the high spots.

If the partner is easy-going and well-disposed to a climate of storms and sunshine (not to mention moon-light), life will be interesting indeed. More often than not, the Cancerian in love will show his romantic tendencies and will look after his loved one to the utmost. Cancerians of both sexes must, however, try to realize that they are by nature clinging, and may find it difficult to end an affair even though they may know in their hearts that it is over.

THE CANCERIAN AND HIS FRIENDS

A friendship formed with a Cancerian will usually last for a lifetime. Whatever the circumstances, even if, for instance, the friendship was formed during student days, and the friends now live miles apart, birthday cards and presents will arrive as regularly as clockwork.

Friends who live nearby should watch out for arguments: perhaps the Cancerian takes life more

Friendship

Aries: Quite good, you may be afraid of their energy, but Arian straight-forwardness is beneficial.

Taurus: This should work out well, you will feel safe with a Taurean friend and will know exactly how you stand.

Gemini: You are changeable in mood and feeling, and Gemini is always changing his mind; there may be mis-understandings at times.

Cancer: You are two of a kind and sympathize with each other when the rest of the world becomes impossible. Develop mutual interests.

Leo: Leo may seem pompous and rather grand, but if he wants to spend a fortune, why not sit back and let him? Enjoy yourself.

Virgo: You probably met at the local gardening club, so already share a common interest. Try not to be upset by critical Virgo's remarks.

Love Life

Aries: Arians like their freedom, so try to forget your tender, somewhat clinging habits.

Taurus: Excellent at its height, but don't be bogged down by this affair once it is over. You are clinging and Taurus is possessive.

Gemini: Gemini likes to feel fancy free, so do not expect ultra fidelity; this should be fun and may make you see life in a different way.

Cancer: Emotions, sentiment and a lot of love will engulf you, so enjoy every minute, but try to recognize when all is over between you.

Leo: If he wants to rule the roost, let him – he's better at organizing; meanwhile, tempt him with your favourite recipe.

Virgo: Virgo is far less emotional than yourself, so you may be surprised by a chilly response to your early advances.

Marriage

Aries: You are both hard workers, but essentially different types; they may laugh at your worries.

Taurus: Very good, you both need security and will achieve it between you. This should be an excellent basis for your marriage.

Gemini: You are far more emotional than Gemini; in place of instinct, try to develop a rational outlook.

Cancer: Very good, but try not to spoil the fun by worrying over trivialities; you both tend to inflate what may be best ignored.

Leo: Leo will not like your worrying tendencies; tell him your problems but listen to what he has to say.

Virgo: Sympathetic: Virgo can help you to channel your emotions and give you a rational outlook. You are both worriers and hard workers; remember to take time off.

seriously than they do; allowances will have to be made in any case, but especially if some joint hobby or interest is involved. Even so the Cancerian may be an ideal close friend—his may be the shoulder to cry on, the sympathetic ear which can always be relied on, no matter how many miles intervene or how many other relationships have been formed since the Cancerian friendship was first cemented.

THE FACTS OF MARRIAGE

Generally speaking, Cancerians are more forcibly motivated towards marriage than any other Zodiacal sign; it could be that the Cancerian will not be a fully integrated person until he has achieved marriage. Cancerian husbands and wives will use their tenacity to build their marriage and make it permanent.

The Cancerian is nearly always an excellent cook, and the men as well as the women are usually adept around the house. However, the Cancerian mother can become ensnared by her domestic ties. She is liable to say that she cannot go out because of the ironing when the real reason springs from a deep-seated psychological fear of leaving the security of her own four walls. Cancerians tend to moan from time to time about their troubles; those who are in close contact with them will do well on the whole to ignore this.

Below: Use this Friends and Lovers Sun-sign chart to check how Cancer is likely to make out with others in friendship, love and marriage. Relationships are listed from left to right, Cancer to Aries, Cancer to Taurus, etc., and from top to bottom in friendship, love and marriage.

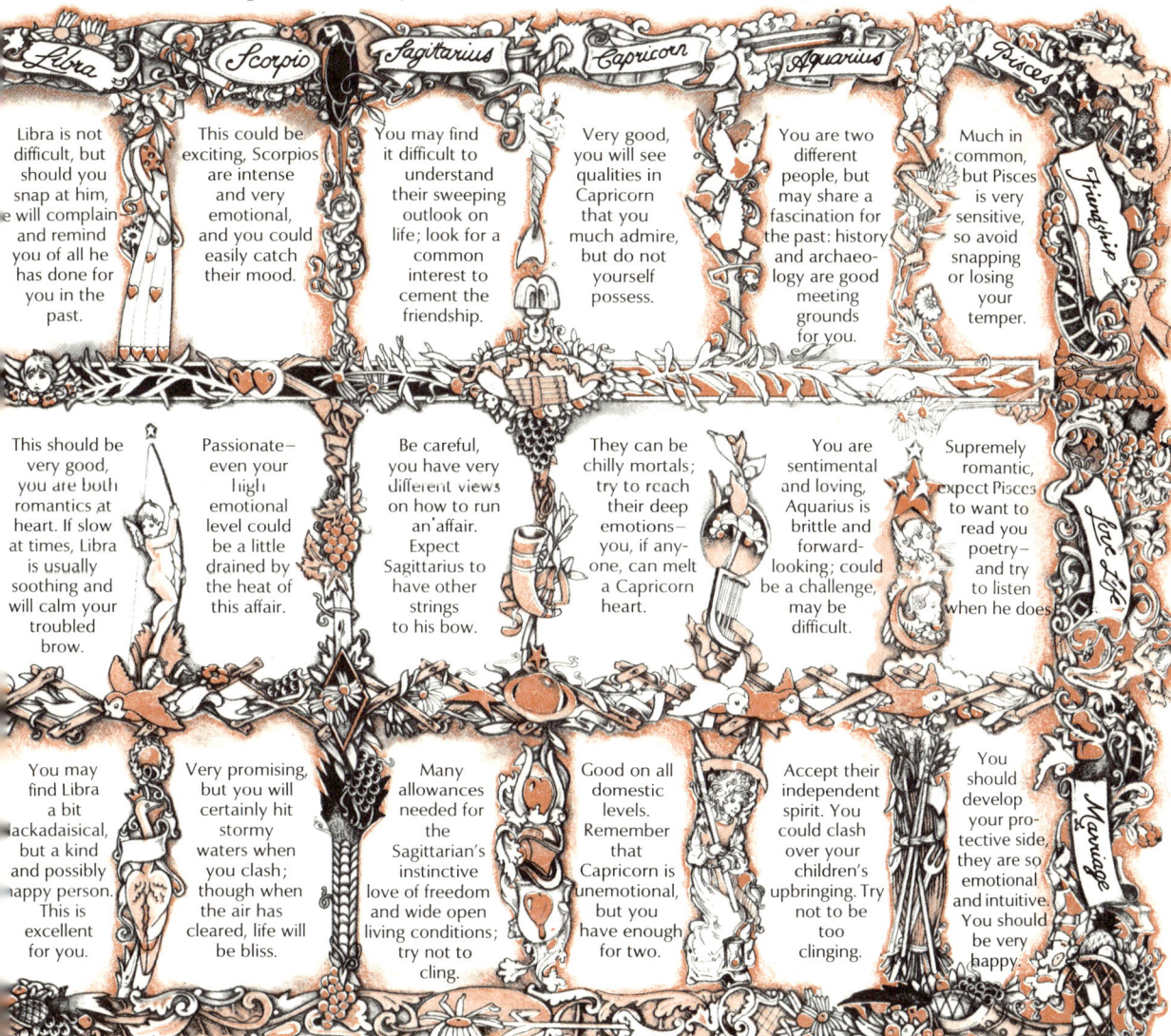

	Libra	Scorpio	Sagittarius	Capricorn	Aquarius	Pisces
Friendship	Libra is not difficult, but should you snap at him, he will complain and remind you of all he has done for you in the past.	This could be exciting, Scorpios are intense and very emotional, and you could easily catch their mood.	You may find it difficult to understand their sweeping outlook on life; look for a common interest to cement the friendship.	Very good, you will see qualities in Capricorn that you much admire, but do not yourself possess.	You are two different people, but may share a fascination for the past: history and archaeology are good meeting grounds for you.	Much in common, but Pisces is very sensitive, so avoid snapping or losing your temper.
Love Life	This should be very good, you are both romantics at heart. If slow at times, Libra is usually soothing and will calm your troubled brow.	Passionate— even your high emotional level could be a little drained by the heat of this affair.	Be careful, you have very different views on how to run an affair. Expect Sagittarius to have other strings to his bow.	They can be chilly mortals; try to reach their deep emotions— you, if anyone, can melt a Capricorn heart.	You are sentimental and loving, Aquarius is brittle and forward-looking; could be a challenge, may be difficult.	Supremely romantic, expect Pisces to want to read you poetry— and try to listen when he does.
Marriage	You may find Libra a bit lackadaisical, but a kind and possibly happy person. This is excellent for you.	Very promising, but you will certainly hit stormy waters when you clash; though when the air has cleared, life will be bliss.	Many allowances needed for the Sagittarian's instinctive love of freedom and wide open living conditions; try not to cling.	Good on all domestic levels. Remember that Capricorn is unemotional, but you have enough for two.	Accept their independent spirit. You could clash over your children's upbringing. Try not to be too clinging.	You should develop your protective side, they are so emotional and intuitive. You should be very happy.

PARENTS AND CHILDREN
The Zodiac Family Portrait

THE CANCERIAN FATHER

The Cancerian father will have many of the qualities that make an excellent parent; while he may tend to reprimand his children too sharply and suddenly for small faults, he can also be an enormously kind and understanding soul when really difficult problems arise. He will often find it difficult to understand his children, especially as they grow up, and may not make quite as much effort to do so as he could.

He is probably at his best when the children are very young, for he can be intolerant once they begin to form their own opinions. He must make a special effort to see life through their eyes, and not as he saw it when he was their age. Keeping up with the young and their ideas will call for a considerable effort on his part, but he must try and make that effort; if he fails, the generation gap will be a great source of difficulty for him.

The Cancerian father may come into his own by using his powers of imagination: the bedtime stories that he tells should be the highlight of his children's day; and it should not be difficult for him to stimulate an imaginative attitude in his children.

THE CANCERIAN MOTHER

Generally speaking, the whole essence of this sign is involvement in motherhood: Cancerians are deeply maternal. They are good cooks—the sort who make endless apple pies!—and often they are endowed with ample bosoms, made to snuggle into; for them, home is what they themselves have made it, through their own efforts and with their own dedicated, and probably overworked, hands. At their best, they love everything to do with home life; there will be a warm welcome not only for their children, but for the friends of their children whenever they appear on the doorstep.

All the same, the Cancerian mother is likely to reach true serenity only after much heart-searching and worrying about her children! Her most worrying times will be when her children are small. The Cancerian mother can be a fussy hen, not giving her chicks a moment's peace; but once she has resolved these tendencies, she may develop into the supreme ma-

ternal ruler of hearth and home, and all will be warm and secure. She will be more than repaid for her efforts when grown-up children with their own families bring her grandchildren to see her.

THE CANCERIAN CHILD

The Cancerian child has many virtues, and perhaps the highest of these is his natural protective instinct. He will not hesitate to bring this into play where his brothers and sisters are concerned; they will feel safe with him, and the way he manages to look after them efficiently and well is a thing to be admired.

It is sometimes the case that Cancerian children tend to want to stay at home rather more than their brothers and sisters; this characteristic is one that parents should look out for, because Cancerian children tend to rely too heavily on the security and psychological protection of their own four walls.

There is an above-average possibility that the Cancerian child will be shy, and parents must deal carefully with this; if the child is pushed—into singing for friends, for instance, or playing the piano—this could have a profoundly adverse effect on him, and may make him even more retiring. He is a sensitive creature, but can be very artful; it is easy enough for the young Cancerian to give way to tears if he knows he is going to get his own way by doing so!

Cancerian children should be encouraged to learn how to swim comparatively early in life, and will probably turn out to be good swimmers. Their favourite school subject will probably be history. They have colourful imaginations, and these must be stimulated. Visits to art galleries and museums will be greatly enjoyed, and stay in their memories for a long time.

The Cancerian child will not necessarily suffer from indifferent health but he may tend to look rather pale, and may not respond well to long periods in the sun: particular care is needed to protect his very sensitive skin. If he becomes mysteriously sick, it is more than likely that this has been caused by worry about a school problem, so parents must try to encourage him to talk about his problems. However, this may not be easy.

CAREERS AND PASTIMES

A Sun-sign Guide to Work and Play

CAREERS

The Cancerian should have no real difficulty in finding a career that he will enjoy, for the range open to his talents is extremely wide. It is more than likely that the Cancerian man or girl will enjoy cooking, and many professional cooks and chefs are born under this sign. Indeed, all branches of the hotel trade are good areas for Cancerians, who should be happy working in that kind of atmosphere—inspiring hotel guests with confidence and making them feel at home and well protected.

Cancerians are also excellent businessmen and women, for they have great shrewdness. Thus, if they feel they want to start their own business, they should realize that they have plenty of natural ability for this, and should succeed—provided they can also manage to keep their worries in perspective.

MIDWIVES AND CURATORS

The Cancerian usually makes a splendid teacher—especially of young children. The girl will be very happy working in a nursery school or kindergarten, and the man too will find teaching extremely rewarding, especially with young children up to the age of eight or thereabouts. Another sphere of teaching that Cancerians could find very interesting is domestic science—especially when this is taught as a specialist subject.

Nursing is in essence a career for the Cancerian; both men and women are well suited to it, and may be especially good with old people or with babies. The Cancerian girl may be attracted to training as a midwife, which she would find a sympathetic and worthwhile career.

Another important area of the Cancerian personality would be happily satisfied by museum work. This could well be ideal for the Cancerian with a flair for objects of bygone days—whether these take the form of early American silver or dinosaurs! History is a natural Cancerian subject because the past is ever present for him, and working among relics of the past will prove a most rewarding occupation.

BOAT-BUILDERS AND BIOLOGISTS

Often the Cancerian's protective urge works on a large scale, and many Army generals are born under this sign! Thus the life of a professional soldier can be an excellent choice. Boat-building, especially designing small boats, is another good area; so is the fishing industry. If the Cancerian wants an artistic career, he might do well to specialize in interior decoration, or some form of work that involves a delicate and imaginative approach—perhaps in the field of fabric design. If he inclines towards the scientific biology might attract him.

A Cancerian will also make an excellent estate agent or estate manager, and perhaps the young Cancerian thinking about a career should ask himself if, at some time in the future, he sees himself running his own business: if so, a training in the lucrative real estate business is well worth considering. He will also derive great pleasure from the more peaceful satisfactions of market gardening. He may well have a natural flair for growing vegetables, and this would suit him admirably; a smallholding—a piece of land to cherish—would be psychologically good for him, and he should feel fulfilled by that kind of life.

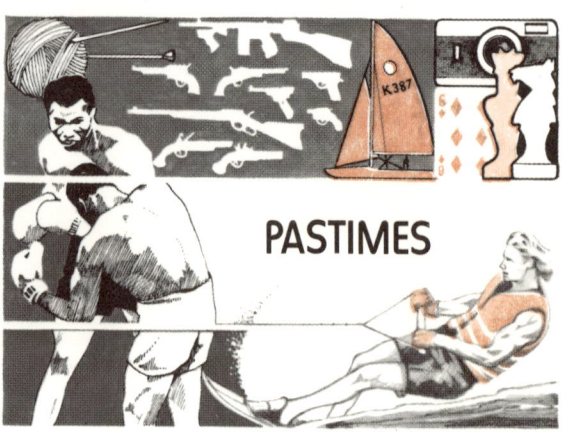

PASTIMES

The Cancerian needs his spare time to repair his frayed nerves; and the top Cancerian hobby is probably collecting. This could mean collecting anything from pins to steam engines. Messing about in boats is marvellously Cancerian, but Cancer must not forget actually to *sail* his boat—rather than spending the whole year maintaining it—which it is quite possible for him to do! Many excellent amateur photographers are born under this sign. The Cancerian may also enjoy tough sports, such as boxing, wrestling, and water sports. But he also needs peace and quiet, and may well enjoy chess or a game of patience. Cancerian girls usually excel at knitting and crochet, which they find restful and not too demanding as well as satisfying their home-loving instincts.

AT HOME

A Sun-sign Guide to Home Décor

The Cancerian will undoubtedly have soft shades of grey worked into the colour scheme of his or her home. White will also feature. The overall effect will be pleasing, and perhaps the furnishing fabrics will include shiny textures–the quiet glitter of fibreglass, for instance, with its pleasant shimmery quality.

Surfaces tend to be hard and durable, for the children of the house will be considered to the full, and sometimes elegance will be sacrificed to practicality. Alas, all too often the Cancerian home is rather a mess. Cancerians are not very tidy people; their idea of tidiness may be just to pile odd toys or magazines together–which may upset the whole balance of a room's appearance. This may be because the house is very much a *home*, and is geared to the children in it; but Cancerians should be a little careful, for looking at a pile of clutter is not particularly relaxing, and will not ease their tense nerves. Visitors should keep an eye on the floor and make sure they are not tripped up by toy cars or sent skidding off on a stray roller skate.

A Cancerian's furniture will be comfortable, but will tend to look and feel 'old'. There will probably be loose covers–perhaps in a pale colour–and these may even have additional protective pieces over the corners. Cancerians love flowers and there could well be an arrangement of large pale flowers, preferably white against dark green foliage.

The Cancerian's kitchen will be the powerhouse of the home, and very often kitchen and dining room will be merged. Cancerians like open-plan living, so that the family can be together as much as possible; that way, too, mother is not isolated in the kitchen.

IN SEARCH OF 'ANCESTORS'

The Cancerian's choice of paintings is delightful: he will favour charming pictures of children, such as those by Gainsborough. Cancerians will also try to collect some 'ancestors', and will delight in portraits of ladies and gentlemen of past ages, or reproductions of family portraits. Delicate watercolours will also enhance their walls, and the ornaments and objects around the room will inevitably include holiday souvenirs, such as pieces of coral, shells and perhaps a stuffed trout in a case on the wall, or model boats made by the children.

At its best, the Cancerian home will contain superb antique furniture, and if the owner is really wealthy each individual piece will be of the same period. Coffee will be served from a silver pot. A visit to a wealthy and well-appointed Cancerian home will be something to remember, not only for the ambience but for the food, too; which should be really spectacular!

Gina Lollobrigida

Yul Brynner   Louis Armstrong

Amy Johnson

DINNER WITH CANCER

Entertaining with Your Sun-sign

THE HOST

Ah, to be the guest of a Cancerian! With his admirable, detailed memory and natural talent for cooking, together with his deeply felt urge to look after people, Cancerians can be absolutely ideal hosts. They can remember what they gave you when you last dined with them—and whether you enjoyed it or not; they are solicitous even to the extent of remembering what wine you like, whether you like a hard chair or a soft one, coffee with or without sugar, and music or silence while you are eating. They will be great worriers, in cookery as in everything else, and it is best for your peace of mind that you should not see their faces as they hover anxiously over their pots and pans in the kitchen.

THE GUEST

A Cancerian guest can be, frankly, a little difficult; like his other half, the host, he also has a good memory, and may well recall only too clearly that he has eaten a particular dish at least three times before in your house. He may well also be an expert in wines, and while this may be pleasant if it means that he will recognize the rather special wine that you have provided, it could also be embarrassing as he makes it quite clear that he recognizes the rough stuff in the beautiful carafe, obtained from the bargain shelf in the cut-price store down the road. An evening for a Cancerian must go smoothly. Any tension may all too easily go to his stomach, so do *not* seat him next to someone with whom he is likely to disagree! (If you are in some doubt about who will or will not go well with Cancer, try referring to the Friendship panels in the Friends and Lovers chart on pages 88–9.)

THE SETTING

Cancerians like smoky greys and greens, which are rather good colours when it comes to table decorations. They also love sparkling silver cutlery, and wild flowers, which in season can be used to decorate the table. Restful, calm music will soothe the troubled Cancerian, especially, perhaps, music associated with calm seas and prosperous voyages: Elgar, for example, or the more placid works of Debussy.

WINES

Wine should be chosen with discrimination; if it has to be cheap, make sure it's good value for money. Perhaps a good Rhine wine would be ideal.

An all-star evening for famous Cancerians of past and present would very likely include the illustrious guests in our picture. For details of the dishes on the table—every one a Cancerian favourite—turn to page 96.

Ginger Rogers

Julius Caesar

RECIPES FOR CANCER
Cooking with Astrology

Sliding into the dining room, tentative and crablike, the Cancerian will wait to be shown his place, wait to be handed his food, and wouldn't trouble anyone to pass the salt or pepper. In the case of Cancer its element—water—plays an important part. Cancerians are happy with rather smooth, bland recipes: hence the vichyssoise, the pâté and the sole—nothing to worry an uneasy Cancerian stomach. You will almost certainly receive a return invitation to dinner by the next post.

VICHYSSOISE
This most delicious of cold soups is a joy both in winter and summer. In the pan in which you intend to make soup, fry the whites of 4 leeks and 2 small onions, both finely chopped, in butter until soft but not coloured. Add 3 large potatoes, peeled and sliced, and 5 cups chicken stock (stock cubes will do perfectly well). Boil for $\frac{1}{2}$ hour; then either blend to a purée or rub through a sieve, adding $2\frac{1}{2}$ cups creamy milk. Season to taste with salt, pepper and a pinch of nutmeg; bring to boiling point, stirring, remove from heat and leave until quite cold. Stir a tablespoon of heavy cream into each portion and serve garnished with chopped chives. The merest touch of curry powder adds an acceptable tang.

SALMON PATE
Can be made with canned salmon; but, as with everything else, the real thing is by far the best. Skin, bone and dice salmon, and marinate for a couple of hours in dry sherry with a bay leaf, salt and pepper. Meanwhile, place $\frac{3}{4}$ cup raw cod and $\frac{3}{4}$ cup raw haddock in a blender with any odd scraps of remaining salmon, 2 slices trimmed white bread, soaked and squeezed out of milk, 2 egg yolks and 4 tablespoons softened butter. Blend to a purée, adding sherry in which salmon was marinated. Spread base of a deep, fireproof baking pan or terrine with a layer of blended mixture, then some pieces of marinated salmon, then more puréed mixture, and so on until pan is full. Cover tightly with foil and bake in a slow oven for about 1 hour. For added protection, stand baking pan in a larger pan with water to come halfway up sides. Cool and serve cold. Without doubt, an expensive dish; but how rich and satisfying and perfect in its smooth richness for the delicate but choosy Cancerian stomach.

'What is patriotism but the love of the good things we ate in our childhood?' Lin Yutang.

SOLE BONNE FEMME
A classic way with sole. Line an earthenware casserole with chopped shallots, sliced white mushrooms and a pinch of parsley. Arrange cleaned, skinned sole on this bed and moisten with a glass of dry white wine. Cover dish with a buttered paper or foil. Bring to simmering point on top of the stove; then transfer to a 325°F oven and bake for 15 minutes, or until fish flakes easily with a fork. Drain off cooking juices into a small pan; reduce over a high heat and pour over sole. Serve immediately.

CHICKEN A LA KING
A splendid American way with an elderly fowl. Boil her for 2 hours with 2 carrots, 2 small turnips, 1 head celery, 2 leeks, a sprig of thyme, some parsley, 1 bay leaf, 2 cloves, 6 black peppercorns, some salt, and water to cover. Let chicken cool in its stock. Skin chicken; carve breast meat; bone legs and dice meat. Place white and dark meat in a fireproof baking pan. Make $2\frac{1}{2}$ cups white sauce, using chicken. stock, and stir in $\frac{2}{3}$ cup cream and 1 large glass dry sherry. Beat 3 egg yolks and gradually beat in some of the hot sauce. blend this mixture with remaining hot sauce; season with salt, pepper and the juice of $\frac{1}{2}$ lemon, or to taste. Pour sauce over chicken meat and stir over a low heat until chicken is hot and sauce has thickened, taking care not to let it boil, or egg yolks will curdle. Core, seed and shred 2 sweet red and 2 green peppers; toss in hot butter and use to garnish chicken.

CANCERIAN SOUFFLE
In a double boiler, dissolve $\frac{2}{3}$ cup sugar in 4 tablespoons water over simmering water. Cool. Add 4 beaten egg yolks and whisk over simmering water until mixture thickens. Cool again. In a heavy pan, dissolve another $\frac{2}{3}$ cup sugar in 4 tablespoons water over direct heat. Swirl pan gently until syrup turns into a deep golden brown caramel, taking care not to let it burn. Stir in 1 cup blanched almonds, chopped and quickly poured on to an oiled surface. Allow to set until quite hard. Prise off this praline and shatter with a hammer or in a mortar. Mix resulting bits and pieces into egg mixture, and fold in 6 egg whites, stiffly beaten. Pour into individual dishes and chill until set. This is a very rich mixture which will serve about 10 people.

LEO
23 JULY—22 AUGUST

During late July and August, the lion Sun majestically shines in
the heavens in Leo, the fifth sign of the Zodiac. Here the Sun
—the ruling planet of this regal sign—is supreme. Leo is the
king, the ruler, the all-powerful but magnanimous one;
he is crowned, inevitably, by a diadem of gold (this being his
metal). Leo's element is fire, that which burns purely and
fiercely; nor is Leo easily swayed, for his quality is fixed.
His colours are the colours of the Sun in the morning and
evening sky, ranging from pale orange to deepest flame;
and his stone is the rare ruby, used by Noah to light the ark
while the Sun himself occupied his own sign.

YOUR SUN-SIGN CHARACTER

The Zodiacal Self Revealed

Whatever his background, education or finances, the Leo will possess his own kingdom. It may be the size of a pinhead or as big as Texas—this does not matter. What is important is to recognize Leo as a ruler—though in more everyday terms perhaps 'organizer' is a better word. Every Leo knows he can organize better than anyone else—he has, furthermore, a special Leo way of going about it.

When Leo hits town, the only course for lesser mortals is to let him take over. If he is worth his salt he will rule and organize with great magnanimity; usually he only needs to be taken down a peg if this magnanimity turns into condescension. Leos can, alas, fall into this trap, sometimes even without realizing it, and sometimes in just a light-hearted way; but also from time to time because they are growing too big for their boots.

This can happen if, for instance, they have risen suddenly to fame and fortune. If they have not had experience of life and a sound, sensible upbringing, the glamour of money can go to their heads. But generally speaking they are not without a good measure of common sense, and once over an initial stage of wanting the biggest and best of everything, they become steadier. Then their natural generosity and zest for life, together with their ability to bring sunshine into other people's lives, really come into their own.

NOTHING BUT THE BEST

Nevertheless, the extrovert, Sun-loving Leo finds it difficult not to go too far. *She* will wear just one ring too many, and her mink will be just that bit richer and more opulent than other women's furs when she sweeps off to the opera. *He* will boast of the progress of his investments, and will dash around in an expensive car—perhaps well above what he can really afford. In both sexes, the excuse, if one is needed, will always be: 'I like the best!' And they do.

There is nothing worse than a pompous, boastful Leo. He is a crashing bore, who does little or nothing but pretends that his life is full. Not surprisingly, he has personality clashes with people from time to time. He always wants his own way; he is dogmatic and will seek to rule other people's lives in an unpleasant way—like some unscrupulous dictator. The reason why a Leo goes sour in this fashion can generally be attributed to some personal tragedy in the past or it may simply be that he lacks real strength of character and prefers to hide behind a boastful and brassy façade. Fortunately, though, this kind of extreme Leo is not found in large numbers. This is perhaps because they rarely lose all trace of their original magnanimity, usually retaining at least some sense of proportion—if on a rather sweeping scale.

LEO IN ACTION

Mind and Body: You and Your Life Style

Leos are extremely sensitive—far more so than many people realize. They do not easily show it, but they can be easily hurt; this, with them, is not simple affectation or pretence—they may be deeply upset. They do not harbour resentment over injustice; mostly, their magnanimity will come into play and prevent them from having malicious thoughts. In a way such petty, small-minded feelings are beneath them—they leave this to more insignificant people!

Perhaps the best Leonine quality is enthusiasm; they are usually very cheerful and optimistic—in extreme cases, blindly so. This is something they should watch out for. But if the Sun goes behind a cloud, they will be deeply depressed, and their mood will be all the more deeply sensed because they will be depressed about being depressed. This particular Leo mood is exactly like a sudden summer shower, when the air is rapidly chilled. But it will soon pass because before long some friend or partner will come out with an encouraging phrase, or give them some tiny present, even perhaps a cup of coffee at an opportune moment —and out will come the Sun once more!

The Leonine sense of drama is renowned, and he will put on great scenes for various reasons and at various times. Whereas an unstable Leo may decide to make himself a centre of attraction by playing to the crowd, other, better adjusted Leos will reserve such dramas for their own private amusement—and for that of their friends.

Dinner-parties will be 'staged' rather than simply arranged! All this forms a very important area of the Leo's self-expression: in essence, self-expression is more important to the Leo than to those born under any other sign. The Sun, ruling self-expression, also rules Leo. This means that, whatever the Leo's main interest, we will find that he must not, indeed cannot, hold back. If he wants to paint or dance he will do so (even if he is very bad) and to blazes with his critics!

EXCELLENT STAYING POWER

The Leo generally has extremely high standards, and if he sets his heart on learning something, he will do it thoroughly and well. Once he becomes interested, he will not switch to some other topic—or indeed to another person, whether wife, friend or whatever—for the Leo, once he has committed himself, usually has excellent staying power. The interests he forms in childhood are often carried with him to the grave; it is in fact quite usual for him to decide on a specific line of thought or action at a very early stage, and then to keep to it.

Despite his regal tendencies the Leo is extremely hardworking; surprisingly, too, he can be a very willing slave. His 'master', however, must needs be someone whom he respects to the full—and whose abilities he knows to be greater than his own. In such cases even the most regal of Leos will—with splendid ceremony and much feeling—elevate the one he admires to a symbolic pedestal (probably made of gold) and persuade others to join him in unrelenting praise and adoration!

BREADTH OF VISION

Leo can be extremely stubborn, and must try consciously to develop flexibility. If he does not, opinions formed when he is young tend to predominate for too long. In such cases, advanced opinions that were held in youth become out of date; and, if he is not careful, as he grows older he may lag behind the times. He has, however, excellent breadth of vision, and can take in new ideas at a glance. Many Leos are very good at this, but they all tend to ignore the details of a situation, which they may find boring.

Leo's thought patterns are constructive and careful, and while in arguments and discussions he will come straight to the point he will not do so bluntly or roughly, for that would be undignified. He can very often give shape and form to other people's rather amorphous feelings; creative and imaginative projects may well make steady progress when a Leo is in the team of planners. Here, too, his excellent organizational ability will come into play.

Leo is not a worrying type; his attitude is too positive and too optimistic for worry—which he generally thinks is unproductive and absurdly time-consuming. His thought patterns are generally constructive, and he will not give an answer until he is certain about it. Usually decisive, he will not be rushed into decisions— at least not more than once, for he is one of those who learns from his past mistakes and is strong enough not to make the same one twice.

He is very emotional, and will for instance be prone to floods of tears at the theatre or cinema. He will be moved in all forms of art by scenes of grandeur and by vast epic productions in general—they will appeal to his sense of drama. On a more human level his tears will be genuinely shed for suffering humanity—especially children. And his reaction will not merely be one of distant sympathy; he will be more likely to reach for his chequebook.

Perhaps the best way to sum up the Leo mind is to say that it is 'big'. The Leo generally does things in a big way: he thinks big, does not deal in half-measures, and is broadminded in his own individual way. He will at times quite unconsciously slip into using the royal 'we'; if he is married, it may take some time for friends to realize that he is not referring to his wife as well as himself—despite his claims to the contrary!

101

EMOTIONAL RELATIONSHIPS

Couples: How You Compare in Friendship, Love and Marriage

LEO IN LOVE

If you have a Leo admirer, you will not be unaware of it. He is an emotional but enthusiastic and ardent lover, able to make his loved one feel the centre of attraction. He will sing her praises with great generosity. Don't turn up on a date with a Leo in anything but the most attractive or dashing dress or suit that your wardrobe has to offer. Make a special effort; they will expect it, not for any particular reasons connected with background, finance or anything else beyond the basic Leo motto of trying for the best.

The Leo in love is very constant. He will tend to have a few grand affairs rather than flit from one love to another. Life will be a succession of large 'treats' with him, and each will hopefully be better than the last.

LEO AS A FRIEND

You will be entertained royally and well by a Leo friend: and when it is his turn to repay hospitality he will do so with great generosity. There is no need to worry, however, if you cannot afford to keep up with him. Nor must you put yourself into financial difficulty on his behalf—this would embarrass and upset him. He is happiest when giving, and seeing that his gifts are enjoyed.

If the Leo feels that his friends are not very skilled at organizing their lives, he will be tempted to take over. He can indeed be extremely useful and constructive; but, although by no means inquisitive, he can be bossy, and may have to be told that he is! He will then climb down. He is always ready to say he is sorry if he is

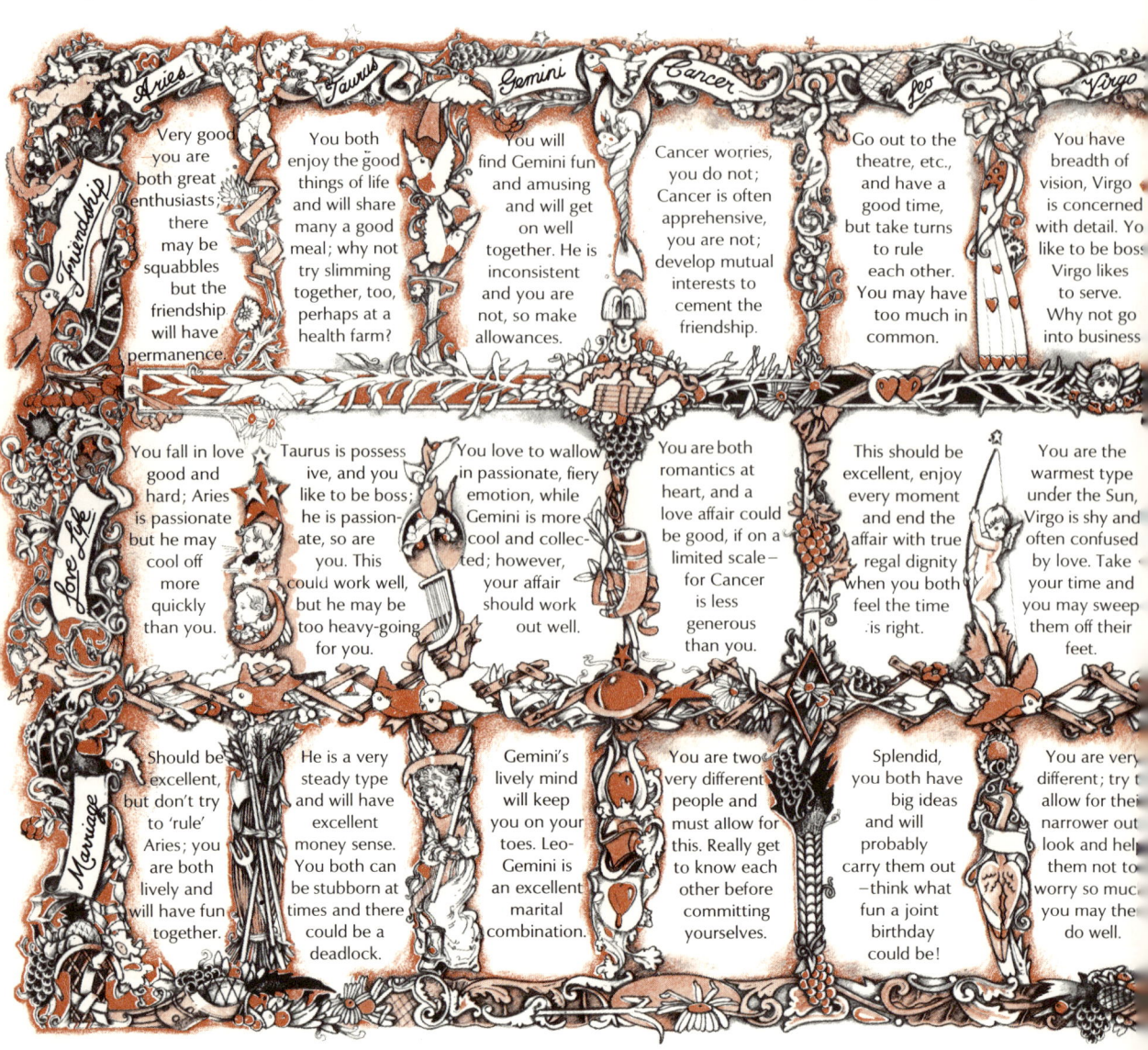

Aries — Taurus — Gemini — Cancer — Leo — Virgo

Friendship

Aries: Very good — you are both great enthusiasts; there may be squabbles but the friendship will have permanence.

Taurus: You both enjoy the good things of life and will share many a good meal; why not try slimming together, too, perhaps at a health farm?

Gemini: You will find Gemini fun and amusing and will get on well together. He is inconsistent and you are not, so make allowances.

Cancer: Cancer worries, you do not; Cancer is often apprehensive, you are not; develop mutual interests to cement the friendship.

Leo: Go out to the theatre, etc., and have a good time, but take turns to rule each other. You may have too much in common.

Virgo: You have breadth of vision, Virgo is concerned with detail. You like to be boss, Virgo likes to serve. Why not go into business

Love Life

Aries: You fall in love good and hard; Aries is passionate but he may cool off more quickly than you.

Taurus: Taurus is possessive, and you like to be boss; he is passionate, so are you. This could work well, but he may be too heavy-going for you.

Gemini: You love to wallow in passionate, fiery emotion, while Gemini is more cool and collected; however, your affair should work out well.

Cancer: You are both romantics at heart, and a love affair could be good, if on a limited scale — for Cancer is less generous than you.

Leo: This should be excellent, enjoy every moment and end the affair with true regal dignity when you both feel the time is right.

Virgo: You are the warmest type under the Sun, Virgo is shy and often confused by love. Take your time and you may sweep them off their feet.

Marriage

Aries: Should be excellent, but don't try to 'rule' Aries; you are both lively and will have fun together.

Taurus: He is a very steady type and will have excellent money sense. You both can be stubborn at times and there could be a deadlock.

Gemini: Gemini's lively mind will keep you on your toes. Leo-Gemini is an excellent marital combination.

Cancer: You are two very different people and must allow for this. Really get to know each other before committing yourselves.

Leo: Splendid, you both have big ideas and will probably carry them out — think what fun a joint birthday could be!

Virgo: You are very different; try to allow for their narrower outlook and help them not to worry so much you may then do well.

in the wrong, and he will quite often send flowers as proof of his repentance. He lives life at quite a lively pace, but does not panic easily – he is too well organized for that. He is usually very punctual; he takes the view that it is ungracious and unkind to be late – and, after all, royalty seldom are!

LEO IN MARRIAGE

Because Leos have such strong characters, they need to approach marriage with care: for one thing, they will want to be boss. This is not an easy situation for the Leo girl, who can dominate her partner all too easily if she is not careful (especially if he is weaker or has a less clear-cut personality). Leo women therefore must learn the gracious art of being a wife. Although her role

is that of the power behind the throne there is no need for her to worry about taking a subservient role – she shines too brightly for that, anyway. The Leo man can infuriate his wife by his condescension. In fun, he may misguidedly call her 'the little woman'; and any self-respecting girl will fly off in a fury, and quite rightly so. However, he does really love her, and she will have no need to worry when birthdays or anniversaries come round. He will not forget!

Below: Use this Friends and Lovers Sun-sign chart to check how Leo is likely to make out with others in friendship, love and marriage. Relationships are listed from left to right, Leo to Aries, Leo to Taurus, etc., and from top to bottom in friendship, love and marriage.

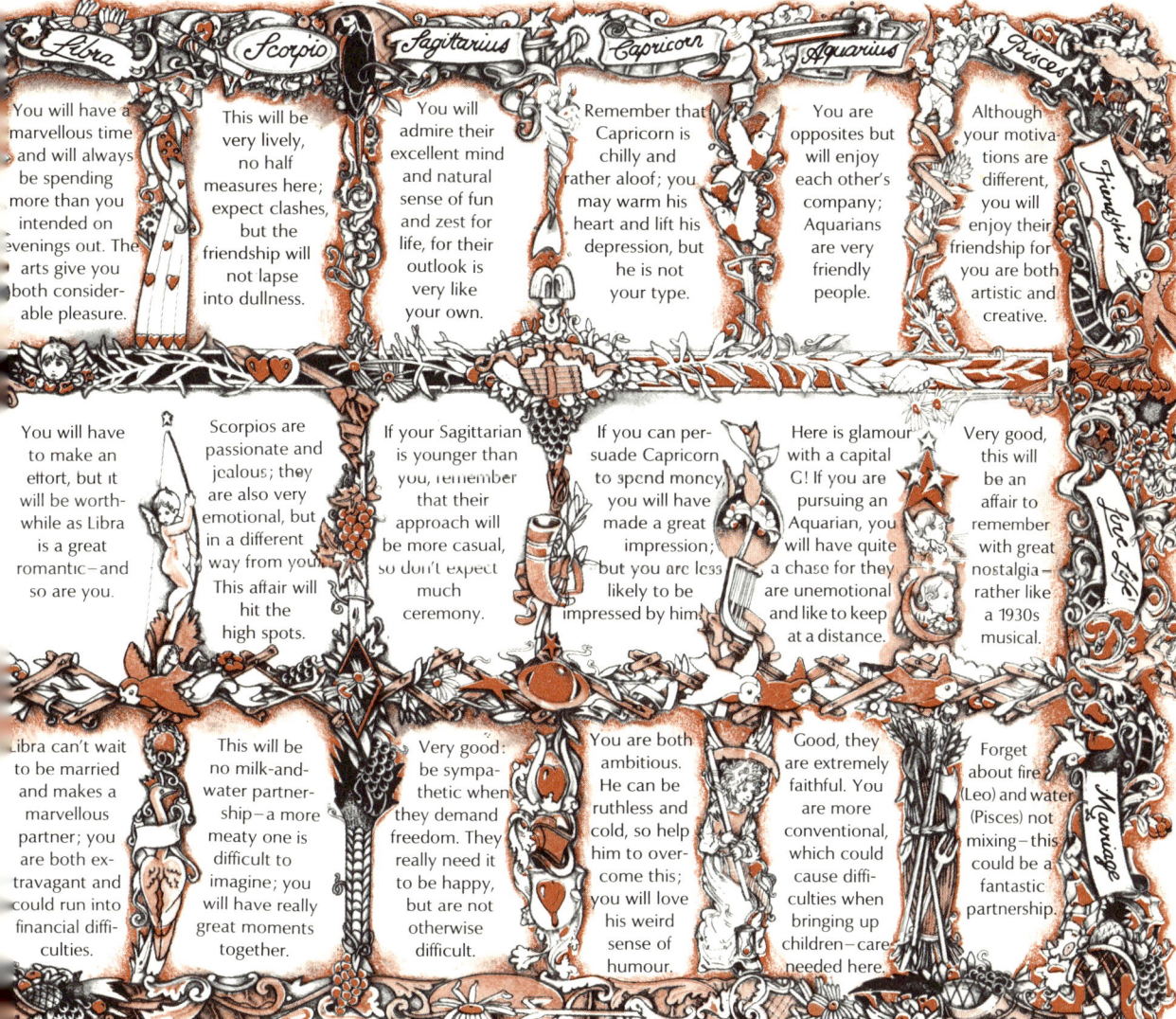

	Libra	Scorpio	Sagittarius	Capricorn	Aquarius	Pisces
Friendship	You will have a marvellous time and will always be spending more than you intended on evenings out. The arts give you both considerable pleasure.	This will be very lively, no half measures here; expect clashes, but the friendship will not lapse into dullness.	You will admire their excellent mind and natural sense of fun and zest for life, for their outlook is very like your own.	Remember that Capricorn is chilly and rather aloof; you may warm his heart and lift his depression, but he is not your type.	You are opposites but will enjoy each other's company; Aquarians are very friendly people.	Although your motivations are different, you will enjoy their friendship for you are both artistic and creative.
Love Life	You will have to make an effort, but it will be worthwhile as Libra is a great romantic – and so are you.	Scorpios are passionate and jealous; they are also very emotional, but in a different way from you. This affair will hit the high spots.	If your Sagittarian is younger than you, remember that their approach will be more casual, so don't expect much ceremony.	If you can persuade Capricorn to spend money, you will have made a great impression; but you are less likely to be impressed by him.	Here is glamour with a capital G! If you are pursuing an Aquarian, you will have quite a chase for they are unemotional and like to keep at a distance.	Very good, this will be an affair to remember with great nostalgia – rather like a 1930s musical.
Marriage	Libra can't wait to be married and makes a marvellous partner; you are both extravagant and could run into financial difficulties.	This will be no milk-and-water partnership – a more meaty one is difficult to imagine; you will have really great moments together.	Very good: be sympathetic when they demand freedom. They really need it to be happy, but are not otherwise difficult.	You are both ambitious. He can be ruthless and cold, so help him to overcome this; you will love his weird sense of humour.	Good, they are extremely faithful. You are more conventional, which could cause difficulties when bringing up children – care needed here.	Forget about fire (Leo) and water (Pisces) not mixing – this could be a fantastic partnership.

PARENTS AND CHILDREN

The Zodiac Family Portrait

THE LEO FATHER

Leo is the sign of the father, and in one sense he should be the epitome of fatherhood, doing precisely the right thing at the right time, expressing his love for his children equally and with great warmth. Generally speaking, this is indeed what happens; but Leo must not be too dogmatic towards his children when they are growing up, and he really must be careful not to rule their lives: a fault, alas, too common in the Leo father.

On the other hand he is kind, loving, loyal and a splendid father in many ways. He is enthusiastic, too, for he never loses a certain childlike quality—nor does he (or the Leo mother) really forget what it was like to *be* a child. So it is easy for Leo to tune into his children's wavelength, and he will enjoy the role of parenthood. He is demanding, and may expect high standards from his children—so high in fact that they may seem quite unattainable at times, and the Leo father should guard against taking a too-severe attitude should such goals not be reached. Nevertheless he will enjoy his children's company, and will love to take them to sporting fixtures or cultural events.

THE LEO MOTHER

The Leo mother will share some of the father's attitudes towards her children. For instance, if she is divorced, she will cope better than any other sign with bringing up her children alone. She will manage the boys well, even if they are more difficult than the girls. She will organize her children's lives to the full with out-of-school activities; and they will never be at a loss for something to do. Because she remembers her own childhood very vividly, she may tend to project her own unfulfilled dreams onto her children, so that they will excel where she has failed to make a name for herself. She needs to be extremely careful in this respect; she could very easily have her daughter slogging away in ballet class or at the ice rink when the child really wants to be on a pony, or just quietly reading.

Her enthusiasm for motherhood will grow as she becomes used to the role, and she will be affectionate towards her children. She will be particularly good at coping with them during their teens—for this is usually the age-group that fascinates her most. She herself must guard against the customary Leo tendency to 'rule' or be too bossy.

THE LEO CHILD

The Leo child is usually exuberant; if anyone earns the term 'full of himself', he does. This is fine in many ways; but he can go too far—especially if he has adoring parents who think, and probably tell him, that he is the greatest. At the other extreme, if the Leo child lives in an over-restrictive atmosphere and his high spirits are dampened, he will be very unhappy and will not be able to develop all his excellent qualities in ways that are most suitable for him. The great thing is to tell him that he is by no means the only child in the world, and that others can do things just as well as he can, and very often a great deal better. As he is basically generous he will want to help other children who are less fortunate, and he should be encouraged to do so by passing on toys and (excellent for him) organizing theatrical performances with his friends to collect money for charity.

It is essential that the Leo child should be carefully taught not to be bossy, though any activities in which his organizational abilities or aptitude for leadership are put to the test are excellent for him; just watch that he doesn't become too domineering.

The Leo child is a great 'doer', and will want to be busy, to have plenty of hobbies and interests, for he is an enthusiast and is basically very creative. With careful guidance his delightful sense of freshness should stay with him all his life.

If he is happy at school, he will have much to contribute there; he will work hard and take a pride in his lessons. But he will not like discipline, and will crumble if he has unsympathetic or unenthusiastic teachers who expect reverence from their pupils. They won't receive it from young Leo!

The Leo child needs to be given his head, and it is excellent for him to have more responsibility than may be usual for a child of his age. He will probably want to prove himself, and parents will soon see that he is made of excellent stuff. He will be especially good at looking after younger members of the family.

HEAD PREFECT

CAREERS AND PASTIMES

A Sun-sign Guide to Work and Play

CAREERS

Generally speaking, the Leo is happiest in a position that brings him in front of the public—where he can show himself off. In more ways than one, he likes putting people in their place! On one level, he will be marvellous as a head waiter, greeting rich clients and making them feel grateful to him for finding them such a marvellous table (and collecting such huge tips that he will soon have his own lush establishment!) On another level, he will be a managing director—with the emphasis on *managing*. The natural splendour of the sign leads Leo to enjoy being loved and generally held in high esteem. He is, too, a hard worker, setting himself difficult targets and knowing that he will achieve them. Leo's childhood and teenage dreams become reality more often than for any other sign. However, he is not usually ruthless: if he is, he may suffer for it. 'Pride before a fall' is a phrase that has a special significance for Leos.

LURE OF THE THEATRE

Leo is the sign of the actor, and many dancers are also born under this sign. The glamour of the theatre is a big attraction for Leos, and Leo, furthermore, rules the spine; a professional dancer of course needs a strong spine if he is going to execute pirouettes with any dexterity.

Leo will work well and hard in most spheres of activity—in offices and factories including, if need be, jobs in heavy industry. But what he will not do is suffer fools. If a superior is stupid, he will not be obeyed. This is such a powerful trait in the Leo's character that it can in many cases make him change jobs. It may not be the work itself that will bother the Leo (though of course he will always want to make progress) so much as being bossed about by someone he cannot respect.

Leos make marvellous teachers, usually with most age-groups but particularly with children over eight— and the teenage/student generation also fascinates them. By tradition Leo is the sign of the father and this may be why Leos are successful in this taxing profession. They also find it easy to win pupils' and students' hearts,

and their own natural enthusiasm will drive them to organize out-of-school activities which their particular flock will enjoy and remember. For instance, many Leo teachers will run the drama group and take their pupils on theatre visits, or perhaps in a slightly different capacity will take them on outings or on holiday trips, and generally encourage them in a great variety of ways.

Leo is the sign of many professional astrologers; we also find painters, jewellers, professional sportsmen, and more generally people who are concerned with high-quality work in 'the professions'; nothing second-rate, cheap and nasty, or done in the service of speed will appeal to them. Leos have to be careful, however, that because they are emotionally involved in their work they do not burn themselves out. They can often go on working right into old age; this may be excellent, of course, but if they are told to slow down by their doctors, they should do so. They are prone to heart trouble, and will strain their hearts quite easily. They will not like slowing down, for they really love life and will be bored by any reduction in pace. What they then do will be a matter for them; but the chances are that they will carry on enthusiastically to the end.

PASTIMES

It may be that Leo will blend his working life and spare-time interests; he will be particularly lucky, then, if he is engaged in creative work. He is not a 'hobbies man', for he will want to take most things he does to a very high standard, and may well enrol for an extra-mural study course, and so end up fully qualified in whatever fascinates him. Dolly Levi in *Hello Dolly!* says: 'Some people sew, some paint—I meddle.' Well, many Leos sew, if they cannot afford the best clothes that Harrods or Bonwits can offer; and if we substitute 'organize' for 'meddle', we have a fairly clear picture of the Leo and his or her sparetime life! Dolly goes on to say that she arranges 'poker games, daffodils, and lives.' This would make a marvellous portrait of a Leo, for it is precisely what they adore doing.

AT HOME

A Sun-sign Guide to Home Décor

A Leo's home is his castle. As he grows in prosperity so will the comfort, opulence and beauty of his home. However, he must be extremely careful; he can make mistakes, and in his love of opulence he could fall into the occasional lapse of taste. He might for instance be captivated by a fur bed-cover; this may be very well, provided he has not also chosen to put carpets on the walls and to pile on more trimmings and fittings than a bedroom can take, including perhaps a leopard-skin rug under his feet!

Usually, the Leo has excellent taste. He will want all his possessions to look right, be right and also to be of the finest quality.

The furniture he chooses will be extremely elegant. If anyone has an eye for what is 'right' for a particular setting, it is the Leo. Leo homes usually have good-quality carpets, sometimes shaggy-textured ones, with plain-coloured walls or perhaps a really exotic wall-paper (such as those designed by William Morris). The colours will be warm: plenty of orange, flame, clear golden yellows, and sometimes for contrast pale turquoise or Aquarius blue. There will be plenty of light, but it will not be glaring for although Leos hate switching off lights they equally hate garish lighting.

HOUSE OF SUNSHINE

The Leo's home will be warm. Cold makes him intro-verted, and he will feel slightly out of sorts in anything but a hothouse! Elegance and all those qualities that make life worthwhile are vital to the Leo. The Leo wife will probably have her husband well trained, so that while she is playing the role of elegant hostess in a flowing gown and her latest diamond earrings, he will be in the kitchen putting the finishing touches to the meal. 'He enjoys cooking,' she will say. There will be at least one classic dish; the evening will be well-organized and comfortable, and Leo will always devote a great deal of attention to his guests.

Leo will be enormously attracted to paintings that are exuberant, optimistic and full of sunshine. Van Gogh's *Sunflowers* is bound to be a firm favourite; Leo will also like the Lascaux cave-paintings, for these are from the dim 'Age of Leo' in roughly 10,000 BC. He prefers paintings that present an optimistic view of life; these are not necessarily without realism but they are not gloomy or sordid either. In essence he wants to see people who are happy and enjoy the sunshine. The Impressionists he will like particularly, especially the ballet and theatre paintings of Degas. Grand works from the Italian Renaissance will appeal, and Leo also loves classical art and will perhaps invest in museum reproductions of Greek or Roman heads. These will be dramatically lit and, like the pictures, they may take the visitor's breath away. In essence, Leo's taste is rich, elegant and exciting. 'A thing of beauty is a joy forever': this may well be his motto.

DINNER WITH LEO

Entertaining with Your Sun-sign

THE HOST

If money is no problem, Leo will more than likely take his guests off to the best restaurant in town. But if he entertains at home, he will want to make an equally splendid impression; here the danger is of course that he will attempt to do too much with too little, spreading very good things a little thinly.

Even so, Leos should try to curb their instinct for the very best, the very richest, and be perhaps a little more realistic about the food they serve. Most people would rather, in the end, have enough of a good reliable dish than too little of the most splendid food! The same is true of parties: Leo's instinct will always be to give a first-rate party for four hundred people, with champagne flowing like water. But it may be a better idea to hold a first-rate party for fifteen people, with a good sparkling wine rather than cheap champagne. Of course, it all depends on your Leo. If he needs persuading, perhaps it would be best to point out that organization, not size, is what really matters!

THE GUEST

The Leonine guest will probably always expect too much, and really must remember that not everyone shares his predilection for the luxurious. He may also be something of a snob. Unfortunately, there are few less pleasant or insensitive types than the food-and-wine snob (it must have been a Leo who, raising a glass of cheap Spanish wine to his ear, commented: 'I fancy I hear castanets!'). If he can cure himself of such pomposities, so much the better.

THE SETTING

Scatter your table with solid gold cutlery and serve your meal off fine Sèvres—then you won't go far wrong with your Leonine guest. Failing these, decorate the table in shades of golden yellow or orange. Rather grand music will be to the Leo's taste, which may introduce complications: the closing twenty minutes of *Götterdämmerung* tend to drown the conversation! But a rich, full sound will always be appreciated – plenty of strings and a good flowing melody!

WINES

As for wines, serve champagne – if you can afford it. But remember that it must be good champagne (you'll soon hear about it if it is not). On a less ambitious level, try a burgundy or some full-flavoured wine that will appeal to the Leo's sense of opulent well-being.

An all-star evening for famous Leos of past and present would very likely include the illustrious guests in our picture. For details of the dishes on the table—every one a Leonine favourite—turn to page 110.

Mick Jagger

Neil Armstrong

Dorothy Parker

Princess Anne
Alfred Hitchcock
Napoleon Bonaparte
Percy Bysshe Shelley
Mae West

RECIPES FOR LEO

Cooking with Astrology

Sweeping into the dining room, the Leo will make straight for the head of the table, and the hostess may have some difficulty in displacing him! He will accept food with a gracious air. In the case of Leo, oxtail soup, smoked salmon, boeuf stroganoff and duck à l'orange all have the air of a royal banquet table. The rich brown colour of oxtail soup will appeal straightaway to the Leo, as will its robust flavour. Smoked salmon, over which a sliver of lemon has been squeezed to give it a typical Leonine tang, has the proper air of luxury, and boeuf stroganoff will appeal to a sophisticated palate that nevertheless demands a satisfying fullness. Duck à l'orange, too, has the air of distinction which will remind the Leo of the dining-rooms of power (and is, moreover, a dish containing a sympathetic citrus fruit!). Pears, smelling of the sun and drenched in rich red wine, are somehow thoroughly Leonine. Given such a meal, the Leonine guest will feel sure that you have recognized his natural superiority and are anxious to pay it tribute. This works both ways of course: the Leo host will be just as delighted to offer you the same fine fare! The day after your own party you will receive a small avalanche of flowers, thanking you in style.

'I look upon it, that he who does not mind his belly will hardly mind anything else. Dr Johnson, 1709–1784.

OXTAIL SOUP

Admittedly, oxtail soup can be bought in cans. But, as with everything else, you will not really know what it should taste like until you have made it yourself. Fry 1 oxtail, jointed, in butter with 2 chopped onions, 1 sliced carrot, 2 chopped stalks celery for 5 minutes. Cover with 4 pints or so of beef stock; bring to a boil; add 2 slices chopped bacon and a bouquet garni, and simmer gently for about 4 hours. Skim off fat from time to time. Strain soup; remove meat from bones and chop finely before returning to the liquid. Thicken with a little cornstarch if necessary; add a squeeze of lemon juice; correct seasoning and serve very hot. Too much trouble? So open a can—but don't expect it to taste the same.

SMOKED SALMON

Simplicity itself: just buy your smoked salmon and serve with little slices of lemon and thinly sliced brown bread and butter. No trouble; always delicious, and as expensive as any Leo could desire.

BOEUF STROGANOFF

The favourite dish of many a Leo. You should use fillet (ends) but a cheaper broiling steak will do. Cut steaks into very thin slices about 1 inch long, or into matchstick pieces. Beat with a meat bat and season with black pepper. Fry $\frac{1}{2}$ Bermuda onion, finely chopped, in butter until transparent; then add steak strips and continue to fry lightly for a few minutes until meat is browned all over. Remove meat and onion with a slotted spoon, and keep warm. Add $2\frac{1}{2}$ cups thinly sliced white mushrooms to remaining pan juices and fry lightly. Then add $1\frac{1}{4}$ cups beef stock mixed with 2 tablespoons tomato paste. Return beef and onion to pan, and cook gently for 15 minutes until meat is thoroughly hot. Thicken sauce with cornstarch; stir in $1\frac{1}{4}$ cups sour cream and continue to stir over a low heat until mixture is hot again. Serve with plain boiled rice.

DUCK A L'ORANGE

There are many ways of preparing duck with orange: this is a relatively simple recipe, not classical, but rich and delicious. Joint duck; coat joints with flour and fry for 10 minutes until well browned all over. Transfer to a heatproof casserole. In the same fat, fry $1\frac{1}{4}$ cups sliced mushrooms for 4 minutes; add to casserole. Stir $\frac{1}{2}$ cup flour into resulting fat and juices, and brown lightly over a very low heat, stirring constantly. Remove from heat; add 2 cups chicken stock and $\frac{2}{3}$ cup orange juice gradually, stirring vigorously to prevent lumps forming. Return to heat; bring to simmering point and simmer, stirring, until thickened. Pour over duck; cover casserole and simmer very gently until duck is tender, at least 1 hour. Peel 1 orange very thinly, avoiding white pith, and cut zest (i.e. coloured part of rind) into thin strips. Divide orange into segments, removing pith and pips—the only really tedious part of this recipe. Simmer zest in water until tender; drain well. When serving, stir orange segments into sauce and garnish duck with strips of zest.

PEARS IN WINE

One large pear per guest: peel pears, leaving on stalks, and stand upright, side by side, in a casserole. Pour in almost enough red wine to cover pears. But first bring the wine almost to a boil and stir in a great deal of sugar; keep on tasting until it tastes very sweet. Then pour over pears. Put in a slow oven (325°F) and bake gently until pears are tender. Serve with plenty of chilled heavy cream.

VIRGO
23 AUGUST–22 SEPTEMBER

Virgo the Virgin is the sixth sign of the Zodiac. This is the sign of the pure, unsullied one. Virgo's metal is quicksilver, the metal of Mercury, the ruling planet of the sign. Like Mercury, Virgo is restless and always on the move. Virgoans are hard-working and their work often embodies an important, instinctive element of service to others. The Virgoan quality is mutable: this means that Virgoans are adaptable to change, and able to use their restless energy for the good of others. They will love, but with great purity. Virgo's colours are the colours of the earth, the Virgoan element—shades of brown and green. The Virgoan stone is the sardonyx, reflecting once more the colour of the earth so beloved by all subjects of this sign.

YOUR SUN-SIGN CHARACTER

The Zodiacal Self Revealed

The Virgoan is supremely neat, clean and tidy. He is also extremely careful and hardworking. The latter is, in fact, his most important feature: his ceaseless activity, the way he keeps himself 'on the go' from morning to night—this is the key to his whole motivation.

But the Virgoan's intensity is something of a mixed blessing: for in his haste to move from A to B, he may well miss a few opportunities to enjoy the quieter, more reflective moments of life. As it is, he tends to work constantly—to get up, move around, and busy himself with something at the least possible excuse. Many Virgoans would do well to interrupt their ceaseless rush from time to time; if they can manage to stop and consider for a while, they may well benefit from doing so in the long run.

ENERGY TO BURN

But what is the reason for all this compulsive activity? Basically, it is because the Virgoan has an abundance of nervous energy which must find an outlet. If he drops in to pay one of his quick social calls, he will sit restlessly on the edge of his chair and constantly waggle one foot in the air. The Virgoan girl must always have something to occupy her; many knit, sew or crochet as they watch television.

Much of this has a good side—so long as the Virgoan recognizes that he has a high energy level which must be given proper expression, and that the outlets he chooses should be of the kind to satisfy his own individual requirements. His career is usually not enough for him, and of all the twelve signs of the Zodiac, Virgo is the one most favourably inclined to leisure activities. The Virgoan will probably have several pastimes. This is excellent, for in them he will be burning to good purpose all the energy that he has left after the working day. It is therefore advisable for Virgoans to find and develop at least one spare-time activity.

SIGN OF THE CRITIC

The Virgoan's neatness and tidiness can be taken to extremes: if he is not careful, he may become obsessional over small matters such as the exact angle of the telephone on his desk; anyone interfering with that telephone once it is in position will receive a fierce reprimand from Virgo, who is also a severe critic of others.

He has high standards, and finds it difficult to understand why others are slovenly, careless, impractical, and so on. Because of this, he may seem rather harsh at times. This critical faculty can of course be used to advantage. If Virgo wants to criticize and analyze, let him do so to the full by working on research projects, examining and assessing the value of products and theories put forward by others.

VIRGO IN ACTION

Mind and Body: You and Your Life Style

The Virgoan is enormously practical and careful. He will miss nothing, and will scrutinize the tiniest details. However, his concern for detail may lead him to lose sight of the overall picture. He must remember this, for he will inevitably, from time to time, become bogged down in the minutiae of a problem. At such times, he will do well to recognize his limitations. He should try to step outside himself, as it were, and grasp the total situation, so that he can then see the whole way from A to Z, and not let himself be stuck somewhere between B and D!

A HELPING HAND

The Virgoan is always ready to lend a helping hand. He is not necessarily the one to whom people can pour out their troubles; nor is his shoulder especially well-equipped for crying on. But if you are moving apartments, or need an extra hand in organizing some special occasion, he will be so keen to help, he may want to take over the whole job. But be careful: he is not such a good organizer as he may seem. Although he will be by far the busiest member of any group, he can tend just to run round in circles.

The Virgoan does try to be practical, however, and should someone have a problem to tell him about, his reaction will at least be positive. 'Well,' he will say, 'what are you going to *do* about it? Why not . . .' And a suggestion will follow. Other signs may prefer debate or discussion but his approach to life is an active one, and he will be glad to help in a practical way when others are in difficulties.

CLINICAL ATTITUDES

As the name of the sign suggests, there is in all Virgoans a sense of purity. If they are doing a dirty job, they seem to act on dirt like a magnet in reverse, repelling it so successfully that they manage to keep even their shirt-cuffs clean.

There is, too, a hint of something in their personalities that seems to set them apart from other people: not a shrinking from contact – that would be too strong – but perhaps a subtle distancing. Virgoans tend to be rather shy or slightly inhibited, and sometimes other people wrongly interpret this as standoffishness. This is not the case: with them Virgo is just being Virgo. He is in essence rather a clinical person, and the feeling he sometimes has of being apart from others can be sensed by those around him. This can produce misunderstandings, and is something Virgoans themselves should obviously try to recognize and come to terms with for the general good.

On a more positive note, the Virgoan's natural reserve is often extremely charming; as a quality, it tends really to blossom when the Virgoan has resolved his

youthful personality problems. The young Virgoan may tend to hide this reserve or shyness in a tendency to be over-talkative. He will, however, gain in both poise and assurance when he learns to take a deep breath first and use all his splendid analytical qualities with due caution. Then, when he speaks, he will have something to say that others will really want to hear.

THE TRUTH-SEEKER

Many Virgoans are specialists. It is important for them, if possible, to devote their minds to one specific area of a subject. Virgoans may find that they are at their best in research work : they will leave no stone unturned in their search for the truth, seeking out reasons to explain why A plus B does in fact equal C. But the Virgoan can turn his excellent mind to many things; indeed, he may easily settle in some area of study that many people would find too demanding or too per-nickety—requirements that may positively *attract* a Virgoan, with his unique brand of persistence and nervous energy.

THE WORRYING KIND

In his quest for perfection down to the last detail, the Virgoan must be extremely careful that his mind does not become so thoroughly involved in a problem that he cannot escape from it. Virgoans are one of the types most vulnerable to worry; for example, they are inclined to bring their career problems home with them and then stay awake all night thinking about them.

It is extremely difficult for them to avoid this; a worrier cannot 'turn off' his career as easily as he might switch off a light. But at least if he recognizes his ten-dency to worry, this can help him from a psychological point of view. The Virgoan's partner can help a lot here, if he or she can make the Virgoan see his particular problem in perspective.

If the Virgoan persists in worrying, his health will inevitably be affected. A loss of appetite is one sign that the Virgoan has become obsessed by some deep-rooted problem, which has become so engrained in his mind that he cannot for a moment forget it. He begins to sleep badly; his digestion suffers and he may fall victim to obscure stomach upsets, and these may, in extreme cases, lead to ulcers.

In general, however, the Virgoan's strong practical streak should be adequate to preserve him from excess-ive worry and the ill effects that this can bring. The practical person knows that, in the end, nothing is achieved by worry alone; the only proper cure is through action. This knowledge should be the Virgoan's saving strength. Eventually, it is to be hoped that all Virgoans will manage to resolve their worries in a sound, sensible and *practical* way.

EMOTIONAL RELATIONSHIPS

Couples: How You Compare in Friendship, Love and Marriage

VIRGO IN LOVE

It is often sadly the case that the Virgoan, before he can fall deeply and passionately in love, needs to overcome some fairly difficult psychological barriers. He appears to be seeking perfection, and can be highly critical of his partner. This kind of behaviour may be prompted by some deep-rooted personal problem. It is not impossible, for instance, that the Virgoan may unconsciously believe that there is something unclean about physical love. Even today, when so much more information and advice on such matters is available, the Virgoan may be full of doubts. He needs not only a kind and understanding partner, but one who is firm enough at times to take command and guide doubting Virgo through his difficulties.

VIRGOAN FRIENDS

With a Virgoan friend, life will never be dull. But it may be somewhat embarrassing at times: Virgoans are so hard-working and eager to help, they forget that they are not the best organizers in the world. After a meal, for example, when it is time to wash the dishes, the Virgoan will rush to the sink and insist that you sit and relax in an armchair while he or she does it all. But, of course, rest will be impossible: the clatter of pots and pans as the Virgoan fusses and frets in the kitchen will be enough to rouse the whole street!

Virgoans are good-hearted, and although they have a restless nature, they do make excellent friends. Virgoans can be put out by luxury, which they may tend to feel is 'not for me', but if their restlessness and

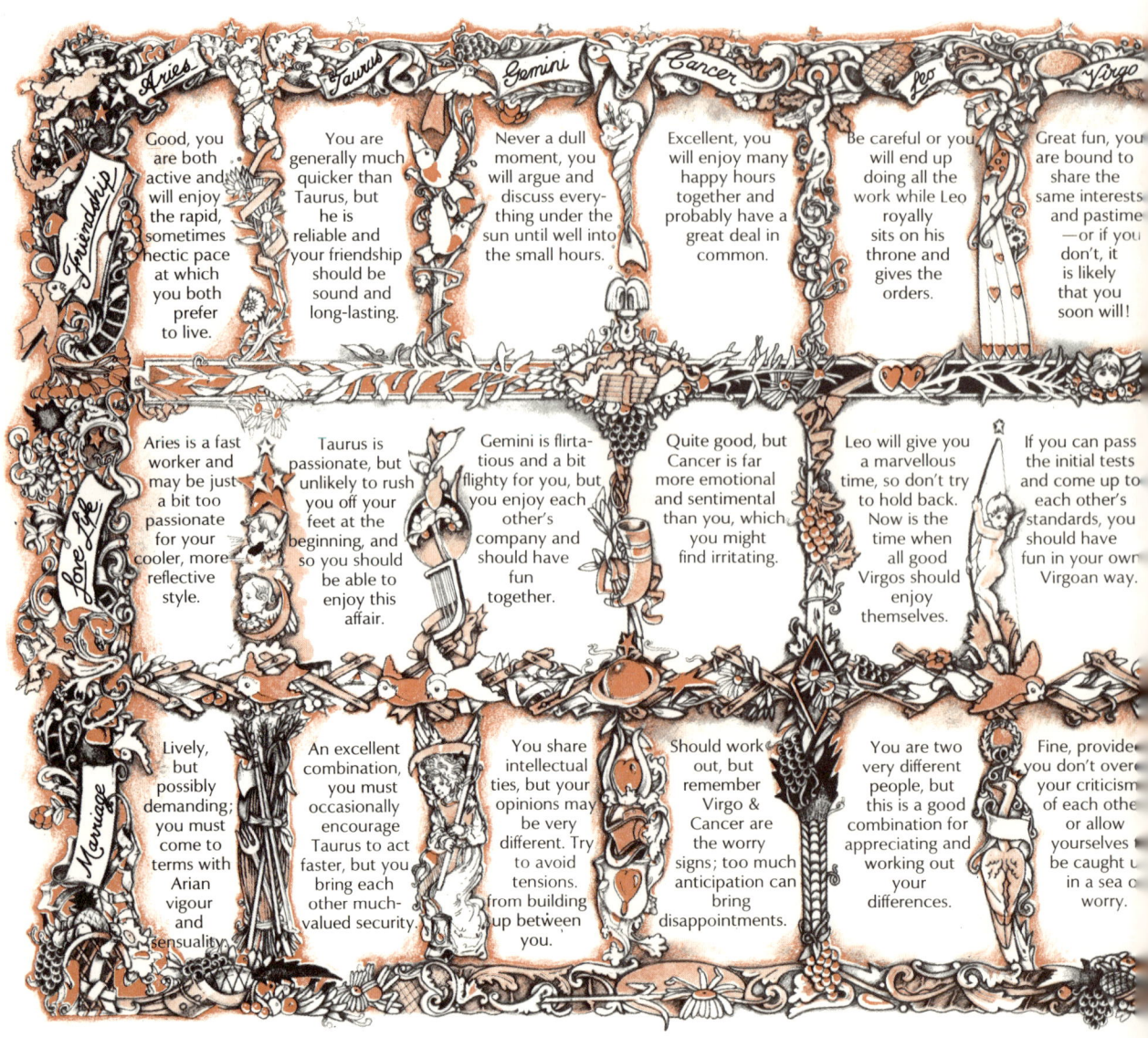

Aries

Friendship: Good, you are both active and will enjoy the rapid, sometimes hectic pace at which you both prefer to live.

Love Life: Aries is a fast worker and may be just a bit too passionate for your cooler, more reflective style.

Marriage: Lively, but possibly demanding; you must come to terms with Arian vigour and sensuality.

Taurus

Friendship: You are generally much quicker than Taurus, but he is reliable and your friendship should be sound and long-lasting.

Love Life: Taurus is passionate, but unlikely to rush you off your feet at the beginning, and so you should be able to enjoy this affair.

Marriage: An excellent combination, you must occasionally encourage Taurus to act faster, but you bring each other much-valued security.

Gemini

Friendship: Never a dull moment, you will argue and discuss everything under the sun until well into the small hours.

Love Life: Gemini is flirtatious and a bit flighty for you, but you enjoy each other's company and should have fun together.

Marriage: You share intellectual ties, but your opinions may be very different. Try to avoid tensions from building up between you.

Cancer

Friendship: Excellent, you will enjoy many happy hours together and probably have a great deal in common.

Love Life: Quite good, but Cancer is far more emotional and sentimental than you, which you might find irritating.

Marriage: Should work out, but remember Virgo & Cancer are the worry signs; too much anticipation can bring disappointments.

Leo

Friendship: Be careful or you will end up doing all the work while Leo royally sits on his throne and gives the orders.

Love Life: Leo will give you a marvellous time, so don't try to hold back. Now is the time when all good Virgos should enjoy themselves.

Marriage: You are two very different people, but this is a good combination for appreciating and working out your differences.

Virgo

Friendship: Great fun, you are bound to share the same interests and pastimes —or if you don't, it is likely that you soon will!

Love Life: If you can pass the initial tests and come up to each other's standards, you should have fun in your own Virgoan way.

Marriage: Fine, provided you don't overdo your criticism of each other or allow yourselves to be caught up in a sea of worry.

116

natural humility can be penetrated, the Virgoan will blossom as a true friend. Once that stage has been reached, the pleasure they will take from receiving presents is a delight to the beholder.

Others should try to help their Virgoan friends to relax a little and enjoy life—even though this may not be easy. They must expect to be criticized; but less careful or less sensitive friends may benefit from this, and should try to see the Virgoan's criticisms in a positive light—for this is how they are intended.

MARRIAGE AND THE VIRGOAN

The Virgoan's tendency to nag, to be hypercritical, and perhaps at times to become obsessed by detail, can make them difficult partners. The Virgoan wife may for instance become unduly upset over untidiness or dirty footprints. This kind of petty annoyance can quickly assume too much importance. The Virgoan should use his rational outlook to prevent a build-up of tensions. He needs a partner who, like himself, will work hard for the marriage; and together they will then forge a bond of great stability and permanence. But he must consciously develop those qualities of warmth and affection which all too often do not come easily to him.

Below: Use this Friends and Lovers Sun-sign chart to check how Virgo is likely to make out with others in friendship, love and marriage. Relationships are listed from left to right, Virgo to Aries, Virgo to Taurus, etc., and from top to bottom in friendship, love and marriage.

Libra — **Scorpio** — **Sagittarius** — **Capricorn** — **Aquarius** — **Pisces**

Friendship

You could enjoy the Libran's relaxed attitude to life, but you yourself cannot be so easy-going.

Very good, you both love to delve deeply into whatever captures your interest—so away you go!

You will clash at times, but in a good-natured way. Your eye for detail could fill in the gaps that Sagittarius leaves.

Very promising indeed, this friendship is one of the really sound ones and should last for years and years.

You two are the friendliest signs of the Zodiac; this should be a most agreeable friendship.

You are opposites, but will recognize your individual qualities—this should work out well.

Love Life

The Libran's tendency to be 'In love with love' will amuse you, but be careful, you might laugh at the wrong moment!

Scorpio is potent, emotional & extremely passionate. You are none of these—therefore watch it!

He is passionate but likes his freedom; his hectic pace will suit you, but in other ways he may not come up to your high standards.

Capricornians tend to be chilly and very selective; but if you both like the idea, this could be a great affair.

You are both very unemotional, so if you somehow manage to rouse each other's passions, this will do you both a lot of good.

They are very romantic, but not usually strong; you are good for each other but tolerance needed.

Marriage

The Libran likes a balanced life, and hates disturbing scenes; you must accept this and try not to criticize too much.

Good—if you can cope with Scorpio's physical demands; take care not to arouse their jealousy, they are the suspicious type.

You will look up to his splendid mind, but could be over-critical of his bright and breezy, freedom-loving manner.

Good, you will both work hard for your marriage. They are very faithful; you both need stability.

You can seem distant at times. Good for friendship within the marriage, but tensions may be hard to break down.

Could be marvellous if you control irritation at their untidy ways; much to offer each other

PARENTS AND CHILDREN

The Zodiac Family Portrait

THE VIRGOAN FATHER

The Virgoan father is good at encouraging his children to take up interests outside their school activities. As he himself is likely to have several interesting hobbies that consume his own leisure hours, he will expect his children to do the same. So he will urge them to be active and busy in their own ways, which is excellent for them.

However, from the children's point of view, he may seem slightly distant and not over-affectionate. He must think about this possible flaw in himself, and try to see himself as he appears to the children. He must, too, make a conscious effort to praise say, his children's drawings or paintings, and generally show enthusiasm for their efforts. He has a tendency to be over-critical even in the smallest matters; to say, 'It's all right, *but . . .*' when simple praise and encouragement would be much more appropriate.

On a more positive note, the Virgoan father can be a great storyteller, and he will also find it easy to communicate his ideas to his children. This they will enjoy, and will take notice of his remarks; but once he has said his piece, he must learn to sit back and let the children do it their way, if necessary biting his own tongue when he feels the need to suggest 'improvements' bubbling up from somewhere within.

THE VIRGOAN MOTHER

As far as the Virgoan mother is concerned, never will the babies have a crumb on their little cheeks; and the baby's clothes will be as bright as for a detergent commercial. Everything from playpen to prayerbook will be in its place. However, when baby grows into a grubby schoolboy order and cleanliness will not be so easily maintained; junior will play football, and will come home along the muddiest path. While her washing machine will always be loaded, sometimes even the most energetic Virgoan mother will grow a little tired of the unending housework. When she is tired, she may become 'difficult' and annoyed with her children's untidiness. So it is up to her to try to keep a broad, rational outlook on her domestic ways, and make sure that these do not dominate her life too much.

She will love to sew and make new clothes for herself and the children, and while this is fun for her, she must escape from the home atmosphere from time to time. When she does, she will be surprised how much she enjoys a real evening on the town. If necessary, outings should be made compulsory for Virgoan mothers—for the good of all the family as well as their own hard-pressed selves.

THE VIRGOAN CHILD

The Virgoan child will constantly surprise his proud parents by his adult and sensible ways—though these may from time to time be tinged with quaintness. He will be a very willing member of the family—always ready to help clean and tidy the house—and will delight in doing things for his younger brothers and sisters; and above all he will like running errands or taking messages, both to neighbours and on the telephone—which he will probably begin using at a very early age (this is of course being one of the favourite instruments of Mercury the Great Communicator, and the Virgoan's ruling planet).

The Virgoan child is a teacher's dream: he is that ideal pupil whose exercise books are always neat—no smudges or blots to be seen. His handwriting will be clear and legible and the child himself will always look tidy and not be the sort to arrive late for classes. The Virgoan at school is prepared and able to take quite a lot of responsibility, but he is not one of the best organizers in the world. He likes to know exactly what he has to do, and when it has to be done. If anything, he should be encouraged to take the initiative more than he does, even if the idea tends to make him rather apprehensive. This could be because the Virgoan's role is to serve rather than to lead; all the same, he needs a certain amount of responsibility for his own good.

The Virgoan child will ask question after question, and if the answers given are not completely satisfying, quick as a flash back will come some shrewd comment or criticism, and the answerer will feel very small because there is no point in attempting to gloss over facts or details. At the same time, the young Virgo can take criticism and indeed will thrive on it—provided that it is always practical and constructive.

opposite leaves

This may be a
with alternate in
produced singly in pa
spiral formation on
ste

CAREERS AND PASTIMES

A Sun-sign Guide to Work and Play

CAREERS

As with every other sign of the Zodiac, it is essential when choosing a group of suitable careers that the special attributes and talents emphasized by the sign be given full consideration. For the Virgoan, there are plenty of different areas which all offer scope for his kind of enthusiasm. The Virgoan is very definitely a worker, and will not like a job where there is little or no activity to keep his lively, rather restless mind occupied. His flair for detail can take him into all areas of research – chemistry and scientific research being high on the list of his preferences.

He will also be extremely happy in an outdoor occupation, and many Virgoans find what they are looking for in agriculture (all branches of farming) and horticulture. They are often naturally accomplished gardeners, and take great delight in growing things. They have very active minds, and some combine this with a natural critical faculty, and make excellent critics, often specializing in the field of the theatre or that of the cinema. As Mercury is their ruling planet, communication (the keyword for Mercury) is vital to them; thus work in newspapers, broadcasting, and the telecommunications industries in general is both stimulating and enjoyable.

THE IDEAL SECRETARY
The Virgoan girl makes an ideal secretary: orderly, rational, smart, generally a good typist, and ever-willing to do all that is necessary for her boss (though she will, it is certain, be careful to keep the relationship on purely business lines!).

Virgoans have excellent business sense, and will do well not only working in large stores (perhaps gaining experience of a specialist trade) but also in establishing their own businesses; if they feel ready and experienced enough to do this, they should do extremely well, for they are careful and not likely to rush into any business project before they feel properly equipped to do so. Many a one-man business has progressed steadily with a determined Virgoan as its founder.

FASHION, HEALTH AND HYGIENE
Because the Virgoan is neat and careful, many girls will be very happy in fashion and dressmaking; and if the Virgoan boy or girl has an artistic flair, this may be best expressed through design or pottery, which are sympathetic media for them.

There is often an interest in health, hygiene and perhaps diet; when this is related to careers, we can see Virgoans as dieticians, health food specialists, physiotherapists, masseurs, and indeed, more conventionally, as doctors or nurses. The Virgoan girl makes a splendid nurse: she has many of the qualities necessary for that profession, being fastidious and inclined towards work in clinical surroundings, as well as having a natural wish to help others.

Many Virgoans are excellent with figures, so all forms of work involving statistics are suitable. If a Virgoan wants to teach, he will be better with older children, or perhaps at an adult educational centre teaching those who want to learn out of a spirit of pure interest.

PASTIMES

Of all the signs of the Zodiac, Virgo is the one that astrologers most associate with pastimes. The Virgoan is likely to become deeply involved in his particular hobby, and will derive from it immeasurable pleasure and satisfaction. Married male Virgoans will be in their element fixing up a beautiful new kitchen, or re-papering the living-room, so much so that the Virgoan home may never be without a patch of wet paint or a cupboard in the making. The Virgoan will also be excellent at building all manner of objects, from ships in bottles to full-sized boats. Always his work will have the beautifully neat, careful appearance that he himself has; and a dress made by a Virgoan girl will look as though no human hand has ever touched it! Generally speaking, the Virgoan's hobby will cut right across his career interests rather than being just an extension of them. Favourite Virgoan sports include walking, cycling, golf, tennis, athletics and squash; mainly they thrive as solo performers.

AT HOME

A Sun-sign Guide to Home Décor

As might be expected, the Virgoan home will be as neat as a new pin. At least one room will tend to have plain white walls. However, the Virgoan boy and girl both love small patterns: a great Virgoan characteristic is to wear spots, very often in a scheme of navy blue and white; and spots and small floral patterns are likely to feature to quite a large extent in Virgoan decorations. Despite the tendency for all Virgoans to be somewhat clinical, they also like to collect lots of small ornaments, and at times their rooms will have a cluttered, fussy appearance. Lovely indoor plants will be favoured, especially when the Virgoan is a city-dweller, for these will help to compensate him for his lack of a garden.

Rush matting may cover part of the floor. The floor itself may consist of a well-polished parquet design, or perhaps of black and white vinyl tiles. The furniture is likely to be functional, and covered in a small floral chintz. It could be modern, but will more probably tend towards a colonial style, with wooden rocking-chairs and four-poster beds.

ICONS AND FLOWER PAINTINGS

The Virgoan has an interesting taste in pictures: his house may well contain reproductions of Dutch interiors or perhaps Dutch flower paintings. Alternatively, he may specialize in paintings showing people at work; and if he likes religious works he may well choose an early primitive painting or an icon. He will like the

Douanier Rousseau's paintings of exotic plants in landscape settings, and on another level the simple lines of Modigliani's portraits are certain to appeal to his somewhat clinical appreciation of clean lines and orderly use of colour—though he may not entirely sympathize with that painter's more voluptuous effects!

The Virgoan's hobbies are bound to intrude into the home: at least a corner of the living-room (or a whole room if possible) will be devoted to his interests. For instance, a dressmaking dummy may be attractively placed as part of the whole scheme, or there will be a work-table at which models, perhaps of ships, are made. There may even be a pottery wheel in the garden shed, or perhaps the Virgoan will find pleasure in making flies for fishing. The visitor to the Virgoan's house may find a microscope and various specimens awaiting scrutiny by his host's keen eye. The Virgoan is an interesting person, and his rooms will reflect this; there will not be a dull section, any more than there is in his life.

A visitor's first impression will probably be that the Virgoan possesses a well-kept house or apartment; and a closer inspection usually proves fascinating, for their rooms are filled with pretty objects. Guests may be left to their own resources, for Virgo will spend too much time in the kitchen fussing over his various preparations. But, to make up for this, there will be plenty to look at and enjoy.

Greta Garbo

Sean Connery   Rocky Marciano   Queen Elizabeth I

DINNER WITH VIRGO

Entertaining with Your Sun-sign

Jesse James

Maurice Chevalier

THE VIRGOAN HOST

You will tend to receive a rather precise kind of meal from a Virgoan host. Everything will be neat and in its place: a succession of classical dishes that have been carefully and properly cooked. What may well be missing is that dash of individual inspiration that some other sign of the Zodiac may give to a dish. Of course, sudden dashes of inspiration have as often ruined dishes as they have made them! All the same, the Virgoan should see to it that his meals are not too plain, too simple or too modest. Perfectly cooked toast and beautifully clear, sparkling water are all very well, but . . .

THE VIRGOAN GUEST

The Virgoan guest will like everything just so: an ill-laid table, an ill-presented dish will be agony, and will completely spoil the occasion for him. He is a severe critic even when he is out and meant to be enjoying himself in someone else's home. The Virgoan's desire for everything to be perfect tends to override any concern he may have for his host's feelings. A good try is not enough, for him; he expects 100 per cent results.

So the Virgoan is *not* the person before whom to set a rather sloppy curry, or a dish of spaghetti: someone else will dig in uninhibitedly, but a Virgoan would as soon face a firing squad as try to eat spaghetti in company! It will be worth asking your guest whether he is vegetarian before fixing the menu: many Virgoans are –and there are some extremely good vegetarian dishes, too; so don't despair if the answer is 'yes'.

THE SETTING

A neatly-laid table will mean a lot to a Virgoan. He will choose a spotlessly white cloth and beautifully folded white napkins–or perhaps navy-blue napkins against a white cloth. Very small, brightly coloured flowers make good table decorations and will be especially appreciated by Virgoans. As for background music, they may well prefer to eat in silence; and those who favour a few sounds at table will anyway want nothing more intrusive than a little piano music.

WINES

Wines should be gentle: perhaps a little Graves? Nothing too dashing–that would not be in keeping. One Virgoan country is Greece; some Greek wines are soft and would be suitable–though Retsina is probably too fierce for Virgo.

An all-star evening for famous Virgoans of past and present would very likely include the illustrious guests in our picture. For details of the dishes on the table–every one a Virgoan favourite–turn to page 124.

RECIPES FOR VIRGO

Cooking with Astrology

Carefully straightening his knife and fork, the Virgoan will be tempted to wipe them with his napkin, but may politely refrain. He will arrange the food on his plate like an artist's still-life! Virgoans are often vegetarians, so minestrone and aubergine salad will be safe enough; and the large number of ingredients in the paella recipe should interest them.

Virgoans can be picky, and will be delighted with any complicated dish which calls for meticulous study! A very correct, probably printed, card of acknowledgement will thank you.

MINESTRONE

This is the king of winter soups: freshly made, it is a meal in itself, bearing no resemblance to its distant canned cousin. Basically, the idea is to have a good beef stock and throw into it any vegetables that come to hand. So: in the pan in which you intend to make soup, melt butter, and in it fry ½ leek, shredded, 1 Bermuda onion, finely chopped, and 1 clove garlic, crushed, for 10 minutes, stirring. Add 5 cups beef stock, bring to a boil and toss in 1 turnip, peeled and chopped, 1 stalk celery, chopped, and 2 to 3 tablespoons macaroni or rice. Simmer for 30 minutes. Then add ¼ cabbage, cored and shredded, 3 snap beans, trimmed and thinly sliced, and 2 to 3 tablespoons green peas. Simmer for a further 20 minutes. Stir in 2 tomatoes, peeled and seeded (or some tomato paste) and 2 slices bacon, chopped and crisp-fried. Serve with grated cheese.

'A host is like a general: it takes a mishap to reveal his genius.' Horace, 65–8 B.C.

EGGPLANT SALAD

A simple appetizer: peel 4 medium-sized eggplants and slice thinly; sprinkle with salt and put aside for ½ hour to draw out bitter juices. Then rinse with cold water and pat dry. Slice 3 large ripe tomatoes and 2 Bermuda onions. In a baking pan or ovenproof casserole, arrange a layer of onion slices. Cover with a layer of eggplant, followed by one of tomato. Season with salt and pepper; then repeat layers until everything is used up. Pour in olive oil until ingredients are almost covered. Bake in a slow oven (say 300°F) for 3 hours. Cool; chill and serve.

PAELLA

No classic recipe for this Spanish dish, but good for a party. For 8 people, shell 6 to 8 mussels and peel about ¼ lb large shrimp (though bottled or frozen ones will do). Remove meat from a small cooked lobster, and dice it. Bone and shred or dice meat from a small cooked chicken. In a large, heavy pan, fry 1 clove garlic, crushed, 1 Bermuda onion, chopped, and 1 sweet green pepper, cored, seeded and chopped, in olive oil for about 5 minutes. Add tomatoes and the chicken meat, and continue to fry lightly. Stir in 2 cups long-grain rice, 4 cups chicken stock, a little powdered saffron for colouring, and salt and pepper, to taste. Bring to a boil and simmer for 25 minutes. Then stir in mussels, shrimp, lobster meat and about ½ cup green peas; moisten with a further 4 cups stock (add this earlier if there are any signs of the rice drying out) and simmer for a further 10 minutes, or until rice is cooked through but still very moist.

ROAST STUFFED BREAST OF LAMB

A good economy dish: have a breast of lamb boned for you. Lay it flat, skin side down; stuff with a forcemeat, roll tightly and tie with fine string. Roast in a slow oven (325°F), allowing 30 minutes per lb, plus 30 minutes over. Serve with a plain salad: how Virgoans love salad!

APPLE PIE

Peel, core and quarter 1½ lb tart green apples. Simmer in 4 tablespoons water, tightly covered, until soft. Stir in a mixture of ⅔ cup brown sugar, and 1 teaspoon each cornstarch, salt and cinnamon. Then stir in 2 to 3 tablespoons lemon juice and cook gently, stirring, until mixture is fairly thick. The mixture may either be placed in a pie pan and covered with pastry, or you can first line the pan with pastry as well. The latter perhaps gives a little too much starchy pastry for most guests' digestions. Bake pie for 10 minutes on the top shelf of a hot oven (425°F); then reduce heat to 375°F and bake for about 30 minutes longer. Brushing the crust with a little milk will result in an extra shiny, brown surface.

LIBRA
23 SEPTEMBER—22 OCTOBER

Libra, the seventh sign, begins exactly halfway through the
Zodiacal year, when the Sun leaves the northern hemisphere
and passes south. The symbol of Libra, the scales, echoes the
basic need of all Librans for a balanced life. Their ruling planet
is Venus, and love is expressed to the fullest in this sign.
The Libran element is air, which must be freely inhaled.
Their quality is cardinal, which means that Librans are 'outgoing',
perhaps more so than any other sign. Their metal is
glowing copper; their stone is the rich sapphire, and their
colours are pale, delightful shades of blue and pink.

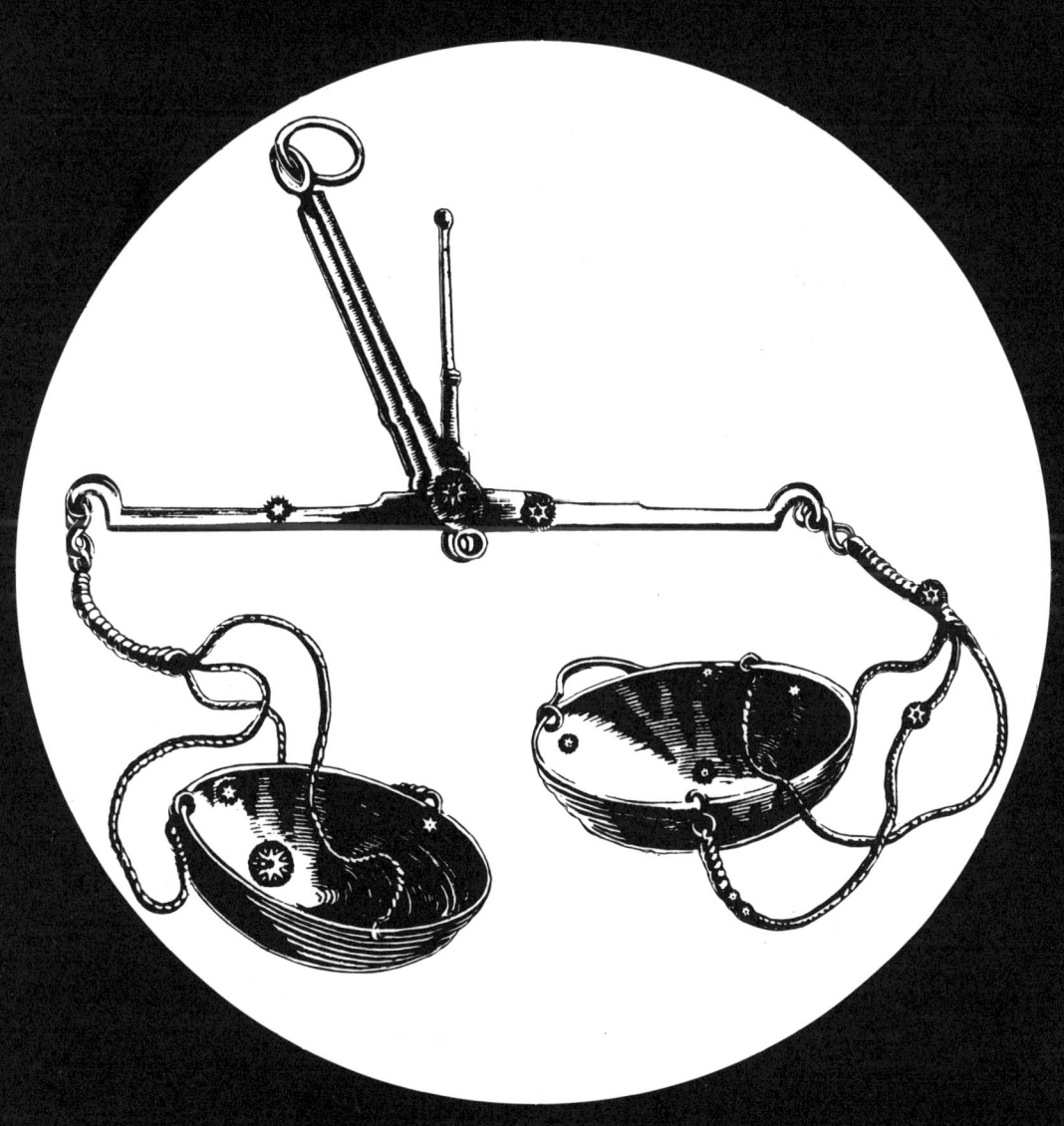

YOUR SUN-SIGN CHARACTER

The Zodiacal Self Revealed

The Libran is an uncomplicated, easy-going type. He tries to respond positively when suggestions are put to him, and manages to appear unworried even at difficult periods in his life. Not surprisingly, the Libran's life is not always as simple or straightforward as it may seem. There are in fact many reasons why he prefers to conceal his problems and present a calm and collected face to the world.

Many Librans put on a relaxed appearance in order to cover up the great difficulty that they have in making decisions. Often they can never bring themselves to reach a decision at all, choosing rather to live through such moments, perhaps until the opportunity or the need has passed. To their friends (and to themselves) they will say: 'I must wait and see what happens.' And, with each successive delay, deciding *when* to decide becomes almost as difficult as choosing a course of action and may be beyond some Librans altogether.

FAIRNESS TO OTHERS

Some of the Libran's problems arise because he tends always to relate to others and automatically sees life through their eyes—even when they are opponents rather than friends; and in the process of relating to others his own opinions and reasons for action may become completely clouded. He is usually driven by a strong inner need to be fair to others—and in return he expects them to be equally fair to him. The Libran is enormously kind-hearted and will do many good deeds in his life; but he also likes recognition for any good that he does. Indeed Libra—more than any other sign of the Zodiac—positively enjoys being showered with thanks, kind remarks and affection. So, when friends or members of his family are less warm or responsive to him than he expects, he will feel that the 'scales' are tipped against him and he will become upset. He must try to realize that not everyone is as gushing as he, and that a curt 'Thanks very much' is about as much as many people are capable of giving; and, what is more, that those few words can mean a very great deal when they come from a more 'uptight' person than himself.

Perhaps the worst Libran fault is resentfulness. In extreme cases this can even lead to a persecution complex, which by its nature will obviously erode the qualities of natural charm, gaiety, love of life and genuine happiness that are so characteristic of the Libran.

The Libran cannot bear quarrels, and will try to break up even a comparatively mild argument between two of his friends. Quarrels upset the necessary 'balance' and 'harmony' of life, and can make the Libran ill. He needs to be extremely careful in this respect, for sometimes he can be his own worst enemy, worrying when there is no real need to do so. His sensitivity will also at times make him surprisingly aggressive.

LIBRA IN ACTION

Mind and Body: You and Your Life Style

For many years the Libran has had a reputation among astrologers for being lazy. Certainly he likes to take life easily. He will, nevertheless, do all kinds of unpleasant jobs about the house and garden. However, this is not because he is particularly attuned either to horticulture or hygiene, but because he cannot bear the sight of disorder about him. It will offend and upset the housewives of the sign, for instance, to see a dusty shelf or a pile of objects in the wrong place. This is the basic motivation for much of the hard but run-of-the-mill work that many Librans undertake.

In a more general way, they like to carry out tasks and complete them. Librans are often at their best while surrounding themselves with a well-balanced flow of activity, doing jobs well and in good time. There must be no last-minute rushes or dramas—these could lead to upsets, and the Libran worth his salt will avoid them by careful advance planning.

BLOSSOMS IN PARTNERSHIP

Most Librans do not really blossom or become psychologically rounded people until they are settled in a permanent relationship. They must have another person to relate to—another pair of eyes through which to see life; and finding a partner is crucial to their well-being. It is very difficult at the best of times for Librans to step outside themselves and take an objective view of their situation. And in his youth the Libran is likely to live through stormy times, for in his need to find the right person he will rush into relationships which he thinks will be fulfilling, but which may then fall a long way short of his expectations.

When the Libran is a child this psychological urge will be expressed towards his parents and other members of his family; but as he grows older he will find this less and less satisfying, and he will tend eventually to break away from his family and set himself up in his own apartment. Soon, he will realize that he is lonely; this may be upsetting and will anyway remind him of his need to relate to someone. And so the search for a partner will begin.

The Libran, such are his needs, will feel compelled to keep trying until he finds someone. He will probably suffer a number of heart-breaking experiences in his quest for the perfect relationship—one which will satisfy his own high standards and also his demanding and deep-seated psychological needs.

MASTER OF THE MELTING LOOK

The Libran's greatest asset is his charm. The Libran man will use this to great advantage both in his career and in his approaches to women, who will probably wilt at the knees as soon as he casts them a first melting look. The girls are perhaps even more fortunate, and at their best may epitomize the spirit of womanhood. But they must let their natural charm develop with dignity as they grow older, otherwise there may be a tendency, for instance, to wear dresses that are too young for them—when they should be displaying themselves in romantic, flowing gowns.

Basically, the Libran mind is cheerful and optimistic and not in the least gloomy or apprehensive. The Libran will always look on the bright side. His sense of judgment is renowned and he will always do his best to see that there is fair play. And if he does feel that something or other is going awry he will be one of the first to point this out—and he will go on worrying until peace and contentment are restored.

The Libran should always try to form his own opinions: while he may think that he does so, this may not always be the case, for he can be easily swayed. A favourite phrase is, 'Well, yes, I *do* see what you mean . . .' And he does—to the point of suppressing his own feelings in the matter. He tends also to borrow his intellectual notions from minds that are more forceful and direct. He is not without resources, however, when the occasion demands; although on the surface he is gentle, kind and perhaps rather soft, there are times when he will assert himself and stand up for his rights.

STRONG BASIC INSTINCTS

He is surprisingly intuitive and has some fairly strong basic instincts. If he follows them he will usually be right. This in itself is perhaps a splendid antidote to his indecisiveness, and if he can bring this facet of his mind into play when confronted with the bugbear of decision-making, he really could give a considerable boost to his self-confidence.

Diplomatic and tactful to a fault, the Libran may give way to other people's ideas more often than he should. But usually he will have sufficient foresight to be able to gauge the longer-term effects of his decisions; and by weighing the future with the present he should manage to make allowances for his own easygoing tendencies. Sometimes, however, the Libran mind reveals an uncharacteristically critical streak, and while this can be of help to him in assessing his problems, it does seem to cut across the Libran personality as a whole. It may for example confuse and even mildly horrify the kindly Libran, who would not normally favour this trait in others.

The Libran's powers of concentration may be very good, but at the same time he cannot cope with interference when, for instance, he is studying. He will *like* the distraction of a friend's arrival, or a long telephone conversation; yet he also knows that it is difficult for him to pick up the threads after the visitor has left or after he has finished his call.

EMOTIONAL RELATIONSHIPS

Couples: How You Compare in Friendship, Love and Marriage

LIBRA IN LOVE

The Libran easily falls in love; and not only that, he or she is very often 'in love with love'. He is essentially romantic, and will be marvellously generous towards loved ones, giving them expensive presents and thoroughly charming their hearts. He will pursue his choice gently but firmly, and any girl considering a relationship with a Libran will not be rushed off her feet by sudden displays of passion. The Libran girl may tend to play up the romantic element in her life. However, although she will be anxious to have a boyfriend, she may take a long time before fully committing herself. This is partly because she is such an easy-going type.

Despite their lazy side, Librans can also be over-critical towards their loved ones, and they should take care that this does not mar relationships. They must use all their other virtues of kindness and diplomacy to restore a proper balance.

THE LIBRAN FRIEND

It is always pleasant to have a Libran friend: a congenial atmosphere seems to surround them, and they often have a happy knack of helping others to forget the worries of the day, intuitively sensing their mood and suggesting some pleasant diversion. But Librans do not like to be rushed! Both sexes will want to look their best and may take a long time to get ready for an evening out. However, this does not concern them at all. 'Not to worry,' they will say, 'the show won't begin without us.' And, infuriatingly, they are very often right!

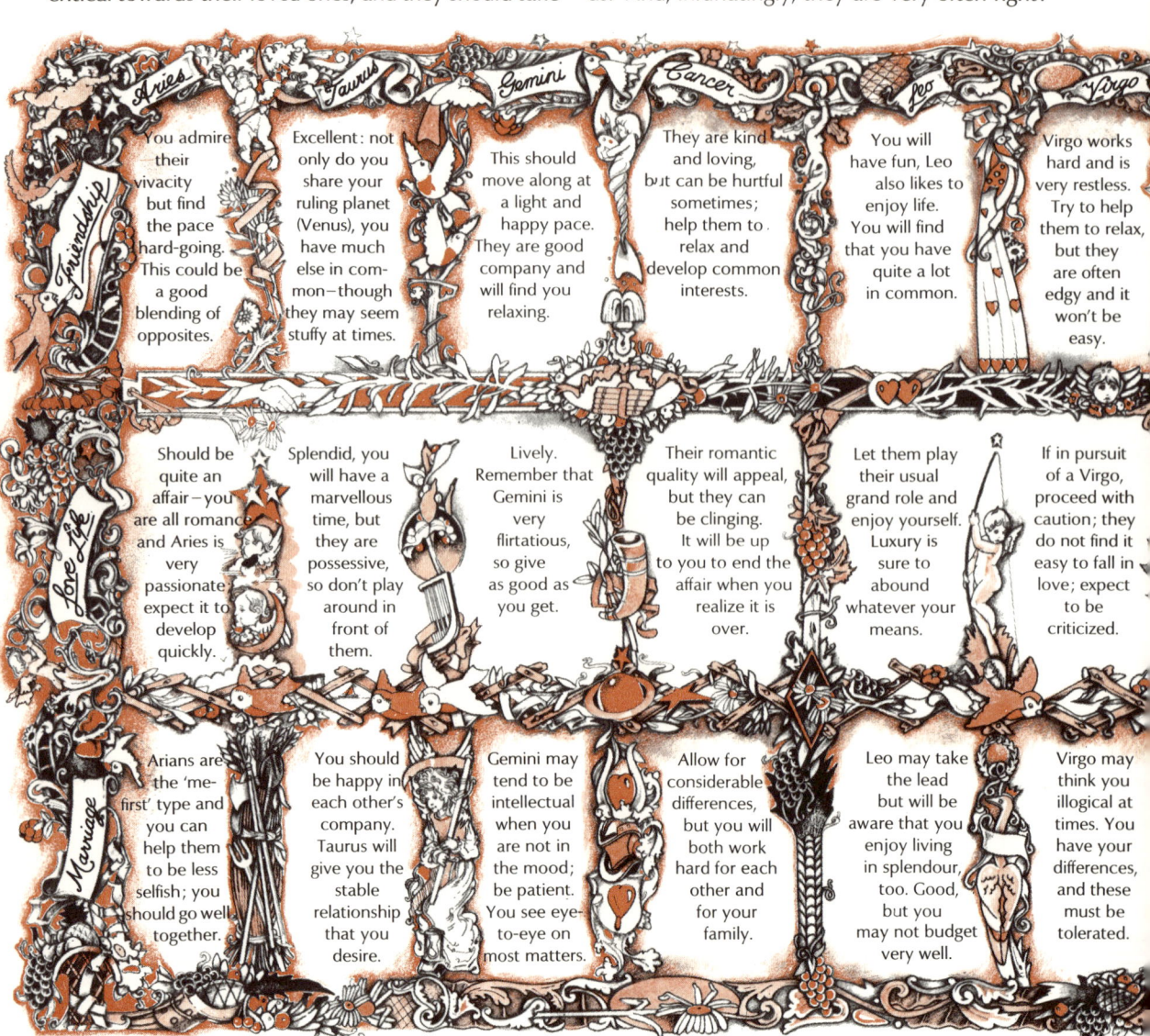

Aries · Taurus · Gemini · Cancer · Leo · Virgo

Friendship

Aries: You admire their vivacity but find the pace hard-going. This could be a good blending of opposites.

Taurus: Excellent: not only do you share your ruling planet (Venus), you have much else in common—though they may seem stuffy at times.

Gemini: This should move along at a light and happy pace. They are good company and will find you relaxing.

Cancer: They are kind and loving, but can be hurtful sometimes; help them to relax and develop common interests.

Leo: You will have fun, Leo also likes to enjoy life. You will find that you have quite a lot in common.

Virgo: Virgo works hard and is very restless. Try to help them to relax, but they are often edgy and it won't be easy.

Love Life

Aries: Should be quite an affair—you are all romance and Aries is very passionate; expect it to develop quickly.

Taurus: Splendid, you will have a marvellous time, but they are possessive, so don't play around in front of them.

Gemini: Lively. Remember that Gemini is very flirtatious, so give as good as you get.

Cancer: Their romantic quality will appeal, but they can be clinging. It will be up to you to end the affair when you realize it is over.

Leo: Let them play their usual grand role and enjoy yourself. Luxury is sure to abound whatever your means.

Virgo: If in pursuit of a Virgo, proceed with caution; they do not find it easy to fall in love; expect to be criticized.

Marriage

Aries: Arians are the 'me-first' type and you can help them to be less selfish; you should go well together.

Taurus: You should be happy in each other's company. Taurus will give you the stable relationship that you desire.

Gemini: Gemini may tend to be intellectual when you are not in the mood; be patient. You see eye-to-eye on most matters.

Cancer: Allow for considerable differences, but you will both work hard for each other and for your family.

Leo: Leo may take the lead but will be aware that you enjoy living in splendour, too. Good, but you may not budget very well.

Virgo: Virgo may think you illogical at times. You have your differences, and these must be tolerated.

MARRIAGE—THE FACTS

The Libran's wedding day will be a great occasion. To them it represents almost a rebirth, and from that moment on many of them become properly integrated people for the first time. They make marvellous partners: they are so good at relating to others, they almost seem able to acquire aspects of their partner's personality and in return they seem to transfer something of themselves to their wife or husband.

The Libran husband is usually very kind and considerate towards his wife, and generally speaking is not over-demanding (the wife of a Libran may find it easy to wind him round her little finger). The Libran wife, on the other hand, will entertain well and lavishly, and will do much to help her husband make progress in his career. She likes to impress others, and uses her natural charm to good effect.

The most serious Libran fault, resentfulness, can from time to time rear its head in marriage. It is sometimes difficult for Librans to realize that they can be too demanding in their need for praise in response to their good deeds. This may well be the root cause of any difficulties that may arise in a Libran marriage.

Below: Use this Friends and Lovers Sun-sign chart to check how Libra is likely to make out with others in friendship, love and marriage. Relationships are listed from left to right, Libra to Aries, Libra to Taurus, etc., and from top to bottom in friendship, love and marriage.

Libra	Scorpio	Sagittarius	Capricorn	Aquarius	Pisces	
You will enjoy life together enormously. As well as the company you can help each other to unwind.	They will keep you deeply involved in joint interests; they like to enjoy life so you should have fun.	Could work out well, but if they are the studious type you will have to keep up with all the latest philosophy, literature and so on.	Your dry and crusty Capricorn friend will amuse you, and you will bring fresh air and optimism into his life.	This should work out very well indeed; you are easy-going and Aquarius is the most friendly person in the world— have fun!	You will be interested in their emotional approach even though it is not yours; should work out well.	Friendship
You both may be wearing rose-coloured spectacles, so try to take them off sometimes. Romance will engulf you.	Scorpio is highly passionate and may not be as purely romantic as you would wish. Go forward with care.	Sagittarius is free and easy and hates to feel tied in love relationships. Give them the freedom they need as well as your abundant affection.	Feel honoured that Capricorn has set his heart on you, he's very choosy. But if he says he wants to be alone, he really means it.	Aquarius can be romantic, but prefers ties of friendship to more emotional bonds—so love may be a long time coming.	You will take off into a romantic wonderland. Fly with Pisces and enjoy yourself.	Love Life
This should be excellent—you both need someone to relate to permanently; but don't rush into it—as you could easily do.	Scorpio is a jealous type— allow for this. Their emotional level is very high and you may find this rather wearing.	Good, life should be fairly free and easy. You are both extravagant, so money could be a source of tension.	Can be marvellous; once committed, they are enormously loyal and faithful, though they are also rather stingy.	Very good. Although unconventional, they are loyal and faithful; you should be mentally in tune.	Pisces is not a good organizer. Use your flair for partnership and your diplomatic approach.	Marriage

131

PARENTS AND CHILDREN

The Zodiac Family Portrait

THE LIBRAN FATHER

The Libran father is kind, generous and can usually be won over. The consequences of his easy-going ways can be wide-ranging. On one level the shrewd child will soon find that when he wants more pocket money, perhaps to take up some new and expensive hobby, he only has to ask. Under such circumstances it may be hard at times for the child's mother not to blame the Libran father for spoiling him.

The Libran father will be rather soft, and may tend to be weak in his other relationships with his child. He needs to watch this tendency: if his usual solution in a sticky situation is to look for the easy way out, he could weaken his child's character. Not surprisingly, the child, finding that things come easily to him, will almost inevitably develop idle ways.

However, the Libran father has his own brand of fighting spirit, too. In particular, he will want to ensure fair play for his children. He will go to see the head teacher soon enough if he thinks that some injustice has been done to his child, and he is persistent enough to fight hard both for his rights as a parent and for those of his child.

THE LIBRAN MOTHER

The Libran mother will work extremely hard if necessary to make sure that her children are always smartly dressed; to do this she may either take on work outside the home or go to dressmaking classes (dressmaking is one of the Libran's special skills) and make the children's clothes herself.

She will emphasize the virtues of politeness in bringing up her children, and one can expect pleasant thank-you letters, for instance, from the child who has a Libran mother. Interestingly enough, to encourage her children to write such letters of thanks, she may well decide gently to warn them that if they do not write their letters, no more presents will come. Soon the children will be scurrying for pen and paper!

She will not find it easy to discipline her child, and her bark will usually be worse than her bite. Threats will abound, but alas the child will become aware that they are *only* threats. Occasionally, though, she will bring herself to carry out one such threat: there will be

an uncharacteristic flare-up and the child will be punished, perhaps quite heavily and in a way that he or she will not forget in a hurry!

THE LIBRAN CHILD

The Libran child is not especially active: he will not bother to stir himself for anything he finds boring, perhaps a subject at school. During dull lessons he will all too often be accused of day-dreaming, but in the great majority of cases this will be because his mind is focused on some other activity that he enjoys. He will tend to benefit from art lessons, and will appreciate music; if he wants to play an instrument, he should be encouraged. The Libran child will be aware of his abundant charm, and will use it to the best advantage. Both boys and girls have a strong tendency to lay on the charm to an extent that some may find oppressive. If parents give in too often to their winning ways, there may be difficulties later on; and although strict discipline should not in general be really necessary, some guidance is needed to give them a certain basic strength of character. The Libran child will soon express his need to relate to others, and this can be positively directed if he is allowed and encouraged to help others, perhaps running small errands. If he does wrong, it is easy to appeal to his instinct for fair play.

The sub-teen Libran girl will soon be drawn to the romantic idols of her generation; indeed, she may hit this particular period of her life rather earlier than most of her friends. If she becomes too dreamy, romantic, forgetful and 'out of this world' parents must realize that her Libran need for romance and love is beginning to express itself.

Above all, the Libran child must be taught to make his own decisions. Perhaps his first lesson in decision-making could involve choosing a toy or game, or perhaps clothes (within reason!). Instinctively, he will appeal to his elders; but they should limit themselves to pointing out the various pros and cons, and they must insist that the final decision is his. In later life he will be grateful for such firmness when he was young.

CAREERS AND PASTIMES

A Sun-sign Guide to Work and Play

There is a wide range of careers which are enormously suitable and rewarding both to Libran men and girls. Working in the somewhat rarified atmosphere of the diplomatic corps at once springs to mind as being eminently suitable for both sexes. This is because most Librans would enjoy utilizing their tactful, diplomatic qualities to the full, and at such a high level. The social life, too, would certainly appeal. So would the challenge of using their charm to win over people whose way of life and cultural and religious backgrounds may be different from their own.

Many artistic Librans of both sexes become dress designers, and the girls are often attracted to dressmaking, millinery and all branches of fashion.

On a more serious level, the community-spirited Libran would also do very well as a welfare or social worker. But he needs to be a little careful; he will have to accept, for example, that the job involves constant contact with the less savoury elements of life; this in many ways could be upsetting for him. However, he is an excellent listener to other people's problems; this will help him, as will the knowledge that he is in a position to bring a little more comfort and stability into other, less fortunate lives.

CHARMING RECEPTIONISTS
Many of the most charming receptionists are often Librans: this kind of rather graceful work suits them well—they will sit happily at their desk in the entrance hall, with a beautiful bowl of flowers arranged each morning by their own dainty hands, and will love to help strangers coming into the office block to find their way to the right floor, or cheerfully show them to their hotel rooms.

If the Libran is considering starting his own business, he should first think very carefully about whether he really does want to go it alone. In the long run, taking the responsibility for all policy decisions himself could be quite a psychological burden, and from the outset he should very seriously consider the possibility of partnership. If it is possible for his wife also to be his business partner, so much the better.

Work in an art gallery would be an extremely pleasant occupation for a Libran; he is enormously appreciative of art, and will be happy finding the right picture for the right customer. His artistic interests could extend to musical instruments, which he would also enjoy selling.

ARMY OFFICERS AND HAIRDRESSERS
A large number of Librans become splendid hairdressers: if they are not set on collecting academic honours, this is a marvellous choice of career for them. For girls, beauty culture in general is attractive and they will do well in this and perhaps in stage, film or TV make-up. Responding to different urges, a great many Librans join the armed forces; thus the armies of the world are by no means lacking in Libran officers, nor is the technical world without its Libran engineers and construction specialists.

Unless he is very young and naturally attracted to sport, the Libran is not inclined towards physically active hobbies or sparetime interests. He needs to guard against inertia, indeed, and although he may not like energetic hobbies, he should have one that makes him move around a bit. Perhaps golf would be best; and if Librans can be persuaded to play tennis, this will be marvellous.

BIG ROMANTIC NOVELS
The Libran will almost inevitably have a large collection of records, and will spend many happy hours listening to them. Many Librans read quite a lot, too, and tend to like big romantic novels such as *Rebecca* or *Gone with the Wind*. The Libran girl will take to making and perhaps designing her own clothes. Entertaining, giving small dinner parties and large cocktail parties, is a great delight to the Libran, as is simply having a quiet conversation with friends.

AT HOME

A Sun-sign Guide to Home Décor

The Libran living-room will be pleasant to look at and very comfortable. There will be cushions in plenty, soft and covered in a good furnishing satin or taffeta. Couches and armchairs will be large and commodious.

The carpet will run from wall to wall and many Librans will choose a pretty floral design rather than a plain colour. Sometimes the room will look fussy, with perhaps one pattern or several ornaments too many; and although the individual pieces may be extremely attractive, they may not be shown to the best advantage.

CHAIRS TO SNUGGLE INTO

The furniture itself will be conventional, but its design will merit attention: there will be wing chairs to snuggle into, for instance, and well-proportioned tables. If there is a piano, it will be a baby grand, perhaps swathed, 1920s style, in an old Spanish shawl and bearing a large flower arrangement and family photographs. There will be plenty of sheet music in evidence, and on the music rest perhaps a tattered copy of Beethoven's *Moonlight Sonata* or a book of Chopin nocturnes. The stool will, of course, be of the 'duet' type!

How the Libran likes curtains and drapes! These will be made with masses of extra fullness, and will sometimes be caught up at the sides. Fabrics will be of the heavy sort, such as thick velvet, and the nets will certainly be of the very best lightweight nylon, often with wide frills on the edges.

It is easy to recognize a Libran room from the choice of colours alone: warm pinks and shades of pale blue will predominate and for contrast there will perhaps be an occasional splash of rich red.

CLASSICAL RUINS

The Libran has, of course, very decided tastes in paintings, and high on the list of his favourites is Gainsborough—the portrait of Mrs Siddons and the *Morning Walk* are so to the Libran taste that it makes one smile! Impressionist flower-paintings, the Guardi views of Venice, and more generally pictures that make the viewer take a deep breath, then relax and enter a peaceful and idyllic world of allegorical scenes and classical ruins—all of which are highly Libran in their suggestive power.

The visitor to a Libran home will be enormously well entertained: after a huge, rich dinner the company will move to the living-room where further comforts (as well as brandy and liqueurs) will be offered. The choice of music will of course be romantic—Chopin, Tchaikovsky, Rachmaninov (especially the piano concertos) and nostalgic musicals will all appeal, as will the songs of sophisticated entertainers such as Juliette Greco, Marlene Dietrich and Maurice Chevalier.

DINNER WITH LIBRA

Entertaining with Your Sun-sign

Dwight D. Eisenhower   Julie Andrews

THE HOST

Librans are likely to have comfortable, pleasant homes. As host, the Libran will like his efforts to be appreciated, so plenty of compliments will be in order. Whatever the food and wine are like, guests will have a pleasant, relaxing evening, be welcomed enthusiastically and made to feel thoroughly at home. Librans have a great dislike of draughts—unlike some of the more chilly signs!—and will take care that room temperatures are maintained at a steady, pleasant level.

The Libran's guests will find themselves in good company, for the Libran hates being alone and usually has plenty of friends; he is tactful, so will probably have taken the touble to find out what his guests like to eat.

THE GUEST

As a guest, a Libran will enjoy a friendly welcome, a warm room, good conversation and comfort. He will make a particular effort to fit in with whoever else may be present, and if for some reason the host feels that two of his guests may not get on too well, a Libran is the ideal person to seat between them. He will accept what he is given, and will eat it with every appearance of enjoyment—even if he hates it!

THE SETTING

Librans have a very good eye for decoration, and the Libran host will tend to provide a well-decorated table in a rather romantic setting, with low lights and sweet music. The Libran guest will be very mildly distressed by an untidy table (though he will do his best not to show it because he will not want to cause offence); on the other hand, he will particularly appreciate the effort taken with an attractive table, perhaps featuring Libran pink or pale blue, or with a course served in a dish of Libran copper. Perhaps because he is usually very fond of music, he may not want to have it used as a background for eating; if he does—then rather discreet, again fairly romantic music will probably be best received by him.

WINES

The Libran's taste in wines may be for sweeter wines than many other signs would choose: perhaps a Sauterne, with fish or sweet, would be an appropriate choice. But he is comparatively easy to please and will in most cases be content to leave the choice to his host or partner (decisions, decisions!).

An all-star evening for famous Librans of past and present would very likely include the illustrious guests in our picture. For details of the dishes on the table—every one a Libran favourite—turn to page 138.

Oscar Wilde   Horatio Nelson   Pope Paul   Graham Greene

Shirley Temple

RECIPES FOR LIBRA
Cooking with Astrology

The dinner party will start, for the Libran, with a careful look at the guest sitting opposite him; and he may go on toying with his food, and spending much time in talk. Astrology sometimes has its effect by opposites ('polarities'), and Aries—the opposite sign to Libra—will commend to the Libran the dull red colour of tomato soup, while as a Libran he will appreciate its smooth texture and full flavour. Librans generally appreciate white meat, and the pork chop recipe will appeal to them for that reason as well as for its slightly sharp flavour.

Turkey will go straight to their hearts as well as their stomachs: every turkey day is a special day to the Libran, who by his nature will give a festive air to any meal. The Libran will be famed among his friends for his sweet tooth, and the strawberries in brandy and sugar will appeal to this, while bolstering the spirit of goodwill already laid down by the fowl! The one thing not to expect at the Libran table, or to require a Libran guest to put up with, is undue economy: only the best available will be good enough. A letter of thanks from your Libran friend will arrive next day; they will expect a card from you thanking them for theirs!

TOMATO SOUP
Still probably the most popular of all soups, but one infinitely improved by being actually made, rather than poured from a can. And simplicity itself to make: prepare $2\frac{1}{2}$ cups stock and rub 3 or 4 peeled, seeded tomatoes into it through a sieve (you can even use canned tomatoes if you must). Add salt, pepper, a bouquet garni and $1\frac{1}{4}$ cups milk. Simmer gently for 20 minutes or so, and serve. A little cream at the last moment enriches the soup.

AVOCADO AND SHRIMP
A very simple dish: halve avocados lengthwise, removing stones. If not to be served immediately, brush cut surfaces with lemon juice. Place a few shrimp in each half and serve accompanied by an ordinary French dressing and black pepper. Easy, elegant.

PORK CHOPS IN LEMON
An easy dish which is always delicious and really tastes as though it had been very difficult to prepare. Trim and bone pork chops. Lay them in a dish; season lightly with salt and pepper, and pour over the juice of 2 or 3 lemons. Let them soak in this for 3 hours, turning from time to time. Then drain chops, dip them in beaten egg and coat with breadcrumbs, pressing them on firmly. If there is time, chill for an hour or two to 'set' coating. Fry chops in very hot fat for 5 minutes, browning them (but not burning them) on both sides. Arrange in a fireproof dish. Mix $\frac{3}{4}$ cup grated cheese with $\frac{1}{4}$ cup chopped mushrooms. Sprinkle over chops. Add remains of lemon juice and bake in a moderate oven for $\frac{1}{2}$ hour, basting occasionally. This dish has a fairly strong flavour, so it is best served with rather bland vegetables.

'Give me neither poverty nor riches; feed me with food convenient for me.' Book of Proverbs.

ROAST TURKEY
Librans can overeat; and if anything prompts overeating it's a large, succulent, roast turkey. Clean and truss a turkey. Wash $1\frac{1}{4}$ cups long-grain rice and boil in plenty of water for 7 minutes. Drain and combine with a dozen cooked and peeled, crumbled chestnuts. Add $\frac{2}{3}$ cup currants and season the mixture with salt, pepper and perhaps a touch of cinnamon. In a large pan, melt $\frac{1}{2}$ cup butter. Add rice mixture and stir over a low heat until all the butter has been absorbed. Cool mixture before stuffing turkey with it. Sew up turkey; put it in a roasting pan and cover breast with foil. Roast in a moderate oven, turning bird from time to time and basting with more melted butter. Judge roasting time by piercing a leg with a fork: if the juices run pink, it's not done. In a moderate oven, it will take roughly 25 minutes per pound, but perhaps longer. Remove foil from breast for the last 20 minutes to give it a chance to brown.

STRAWBERRY OOFF
Ease itself: wash, hull and thinly slice your strawberries, and put them in a bowl with sugar, to taste. Pour over them as much brandy as you feel justified in spending on them. Chill for an hour or so. Meanwhile, stiffly beat 1 egg white. Whip $1\frac{1}{4}$ cups heavy cream and fold in egg white. When ready to serve, fold strawberries into cream mixture and either serve directly, or pile into a hollowed-out sponge cake. You can have this with meringues, but that is really a little too sickly sweet!

SCORPIO
23 OCTOBER–21 NOVEMBER

Scorpio is intense, passionate and reforming. Until recent years
Scorpio was ruled by Mars, the warrior planet, and even today
astrological thought recognizes its enduring influence.
However, distant Pluto, the planet of reform, revolution and
irrevocable change, is now more closely linked with this,
the most penetrating and forceful of all the signs. Dark red and
maroon have long been the Scorpionic colours. Scorpio's
element is water–the deep, still water of a bottomless lake.
Through it he directs powerful emotional forces, moving his
fellow humans from stillness to action. The quality of Scorpio is
fixed, which echoes the sign's intensity, as does its associated
gem, the opal. Scorpio's metal is iron–the fighting
metal of Mars.

YOUR SUN-SIGN CHARACTER

The Zodiacal Self Revealed

The most overwhelming characteristics of Scorpio are his intensity and sense of purpose. To delve deeply— this is the aim by which he is driven in every situation. He cannot skim the surface, whether he is preparing for a university degree or simply reading the Sunday newspapers; the pitch of intensity at which he must live simply will not allow it.

In every description of Scorpio there is an emphasis on passion. This is not only the passion of love: Scorpio has powerful feelings, and will express himself passionately in whatever he is doing. He must live his life at a high emotional level. If he does not, he all too easily becomes resentful and brooding, and his highly charged feelings will remain imprisoned within him rather than be positively expressed.

At such times Scorpio can run into trouble. He may feel that he is unfulfilled or dissatisfied with life. He must then be made aware that such moods may occur, but that they can be prevented so long as he does not repress his *true* feelings. Psychological upsets can be especially damaging to Scorpios.

From a practical point of view, how he directs his emotions is of course a matter for him to decide; but he may well, for instance, feel very strongly about social injustice, bad housing conditions or financial exploitation; it is in areas of this kind that the Scorpio will show up evil, indeed root it out from the dingiest corners.

SIGN OF THE DETECTIVE

It is good for Scorpios to have some 'cause', something in which they can fully immerse themselves, channelling all their powerful feelings positively; and, if they want to, stirring others into action. The Scorpio is a natural detective, and is in his element bringing things into the open. This is a valuable outlet for his energies.

The Scorpio works hard and plays hard. He is no middle-of-the-road man—or girl, for that matter! Over-indulgence is something that needs conscious control, but this will be a never-ending battle with him, as he finds restraint difficult. If, on the other hand, he swings too near to excess, the only practical answer is to take drastic remedial action. For instance, if Scorpio discovers he is overweight—this is quite likely from time to time—he must go off to a health farm and live on lemon juice for two weeks. On his first night out afterwards, he may want to celebrate his freedom; but this, to those who know him, is only a first step to new heights of excess, leading him back to the health farm. That's how the Scorpio pendulum swings!

Scorpio's worst fault is his jealousy. Conquering it will not be easy, but he must learn to put up a fight whenever he feels its pangs boiling up inside him. As with all negative traits, recognition is a vital step towards victory.

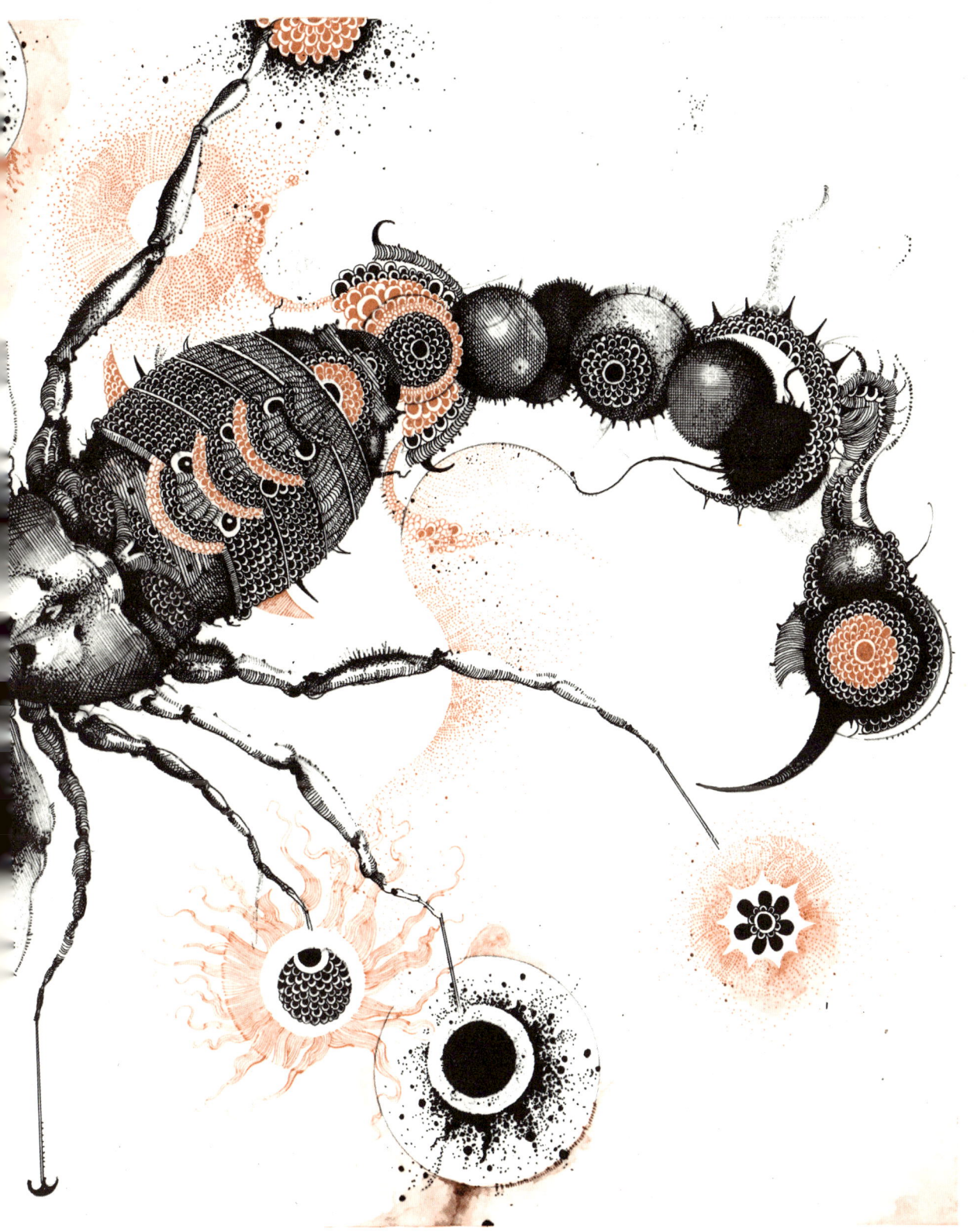

SCORPIO IN ACTION

Mind and Body: You and Your Life Style

Scorpio has magnetic charm: others cannot help but be attracted. This is one of the good-looking signs of the Zodiac, in a dark, intense way. The Scorpio girl may well have a passionate, gypsy air about her, while the man's look is hypnotic and piercing. Both seem to have a special and very individual power, which will come to their aid in any situation, and be used either for good or evil.

The Scorpio seeks to give his life a definite pattern. He will work extremely hard to achieve his ambitions—then quite suddenly will abandon everything and start again from nothing. He will more than likely do this several times during his life. It seems that this pattern of drastic change is necessary to his psychological well-being, and it is expressed not only in his career, but often in his personal life too. There is perhaps a connection here with his intensity: like a volcano he has to erupt from time to time—and will feel all the better for it!

The Scorpio has an enormously high energy level. He is rather like a powerful engine which will deteriorate if left idle. If Scorpio's energy is not burned up it may turn sour on him and he may then fall into a poor physical state; it is possible, too, that he may become a victim of mental distress. The Scorpio cannot be bothered with trivialities, and if he finds that he is involved in work which seems to him to be unimportant, or if he thinks that he is simply a small, rather unnecessary cog in a large wheel, he simply won't function properly. He will feel that the energy he is using is being wasted. Then the rot will set in—and will continue until he decides to make an important change of direction, and sweeps all aside to start anew.

STING IN THE TAIL

Much is written about Scorpionic cruelty—the sting in the tail! Certainly this cannot be ignored, for when Scorpio hurts, he really hurts; and if someone hurts him in return he will not forget it in a hurry. But, strange though it may seem, he may then respond by goading the other person to repeat his action. This is because the Scorpio can, in certain circumstances, be something of a masochist: the worse he is treated the more he will take. But the next time he erupts, he will do so with an explosion that will really shake those who have watched him suffer.

Scorpio rules the genitals, so this area of the body is most susceptible to influence, therefore vulnerable. Scorpio is the most potent of all the signs, and such energy, which can be highly intense, may lead to extreme behaviour; so much so that Scorpios may be roused to act with violence, cruelty, even with sadism. They should recognize this lurking power in themselves, the better to control it.

THE MIND—INTENSE AND CREATIVE

The Scorpio mind, like the whole Scorpio personality, is steeped in intensity. 'Still waters run deep' is perhaps a good way to describe his mental attitude. Scorpios are imaginative but cannot easily make their imaginations work for them. Because the mind is so intense, it is not always easy to prompt it to flow positively. When it does, however, there is a wealth of creative artistic ability to be expressed. If the Scorpio can find a proper outlet, he may contribute a great deal to the world, and in so doing improve his own life. The Scorpio might, for example, do worse than try his hand at crime or detective fiction, for this is one area in which he could excel.

All too often the Scorpio's imagination works overtime—but to frustrate its owner rather than to benefit him. Some strange idea may enter his head—put there, perhaps, by a friend's casual remark. The friend may say he saw Scorpio's wife waiting in a restaurant. Scorpio didn't know she was going out that day. She must be meeting . . . and within minutes he has mentally lined up the whole divorce proceedings—and started to look hard at the girl in the outer office! Unfortunately, too, he will not clear the air immediately he arrives home, but will wait, brooding for a long while before mentioning his fears. And when he does, he will really let fly!

NO STONE UNTURNED

Scorpio is often known as 'the investigator', and can turn his mind to working on the smallest, most complicated area of a big problem. His ability to leave no stone unturned gives him obsessional tendencies, and he can easily become bogged down by his problems. He needs to make sure that this trait does not get the better of him. He has excellent reasoning powers, and these should in most cases see him through his difficulties. His sense of perception is excellent, and provided he can keep a clear perspective he will come to terms with the deeper, darker areas of his mind.

Even so, a measure of conflict may be unavoidable. This is because the Scorpio is inclined to attack all his tasks with an intensity that more easy-going signs may find ferocious and rather frightening.

When Scorpio has a problem, he is inclined to involve himself in analyzing his reactions to it rather than concentrating on the problem itself. This can be a fruitless occupation in some respects: he may gain in self-knowledge, but it will not solve his immediate difficulties. Scorpios are enormously intuitive, and it is to their advantage to use this gift. If they feel that something is wrong, or that some unexpected event is going to take place, they will invariably be on the right track—like the shrewd detectives they are!

EMOTIONAL RELATIONSHIPS

Couples: How You Compare in Friendship, Love and Marriage

SCORPIO IN LOVE

The Scorpio in love is extremely passionate. He will experience many deeply emotional relationships, each more meaningful than the last; and he will not forget past loves in a hurry. They will linger in his mind long after the farewells have been said.

The most common reason for farewells in the Scorpio's love-life is his sometimes violent jealousy. Some partners cannot cope with this; and unless they have a great deal of inner strength they may not put up with it for long. It will be the cause, too, of some hard-hitting quarrels. Unfortunately it is hard for the Scorpio to realize how potent and completely negative his jealous attitude really is.

Scorpio is an attentive escort: only the best restaurants, the best hotels will be good enough; he will certainly see to it that the setting is exactly right for his big seduction scene! Obviously, he is an expert, and the girl of his affections will be fascinated, slightly scared and completely magnetized by his approach! If Scorpio can manage to keep his jealousy at bay, then the affair could hit the high spots.

SCORPIO AND HIS FRIENDS

The Scorpio friend will be demanding, and those with a less powerful energy-level may struggle to keep up with his searching questions, his constant demands for their opinions, and his strong feelings on everything from the latest big fight to the next election results. He will always want to pursue a subject in great depth;

	Aries	Taurus	Gemini	Cancer	Leo	Virgo
Friendship	Good, but stormy: if you want a relaxing evening, don't telephone your Arian friend.	Good. They have qualities you admire; you can both get angry but the friendship should be stable and long-lived.	Not easy but you might steady Gemini's jumpy ways and make him more consistent.	Quite good, but Cancerians may be just a little too sentimental for you.	If you can really let Leo be king of the castle all will be well – but can you?	Excellent, how you will love going over the tiny details together. Your plans should never go astray, you are both too careful.
Love Life	Scorpion meets Ram. Passionate, you may never go out, but spiky too.	Taurus, although passionate, may be slow to respond to you. Take your time – it will be worthwhile!	Gemini may well have another relationship going; if you are jealous this will only make them look for a third!	Emotions will run high; they are very sensitive and you can be cruel at times. Take care.	A good time all round – here's someone who appreciates your taste for living it up; this one could be expensive, if anyone's counting.	Virgoans are extremely choosy and clinical, you are extra sensual – which could cause a lot of trouble.
Marriage	You will both fight for your highly potent marriage: control your jealous instinct.	Excellent if you remember that your worst fault is jealousy and theirs is being possessive.	Gemini is a mental lightweight, and you are a 'heavy', a prober; this needs understanding.	A sympathetic pairing if you do not trample on their sensitivity – and get your head bitten off in return.	Colourful and rarely dull, but remember you are both emotional in different ways. You brood then explode, Leo just explodes.	You both work hard, but may get on each other's nerves. If in difficulty look to your love life for explanations.

obviously, from a friend's point of view, it is advisable to confine such discussions to common ground. Scorpio is usually a big spender, and will not worry if his friend is less well-off. He is generous to a fault, and loves to spread his money around: he does this not to buy popularity, but simply because he likes life, and wants others to do so. Even in friendship, however, jealousy can occur, and tact is sometimes needed to prevent Scorpio's emotions from boiling over.

MARRIAGE – THE FACTS

In marriage, Scorpio's potency needs to find a satisfactory outlet. This is essential, because he is so highly powered. Otherwise he will become restless, and will soon look for relationships outside marriage. Anyone

contemplating marriage with a Scorpio should realize that it will be no wishy-washy affair, grey or colourless; this partnership will be bold and bright, filled with striking contrasts of happiness and moments of near-despair, or worse. The husband or wife of a Scorpio will have to work at the part, for it is a double one of husband-lover or wife-mistress. That is the challenge. The reward – though there will be great dramas, and plates may fly – is a colourful, passionate partnership.

Below: Use this Friends and Lovers Sun-sign chart to check how Scorpio is likely to make out with others in friendship, love and marriage. Relationships are listed from left to right, Scorpio to Aries, Scorpio to Taurus, etc., and from top to bottom in friendship, love and marriage.

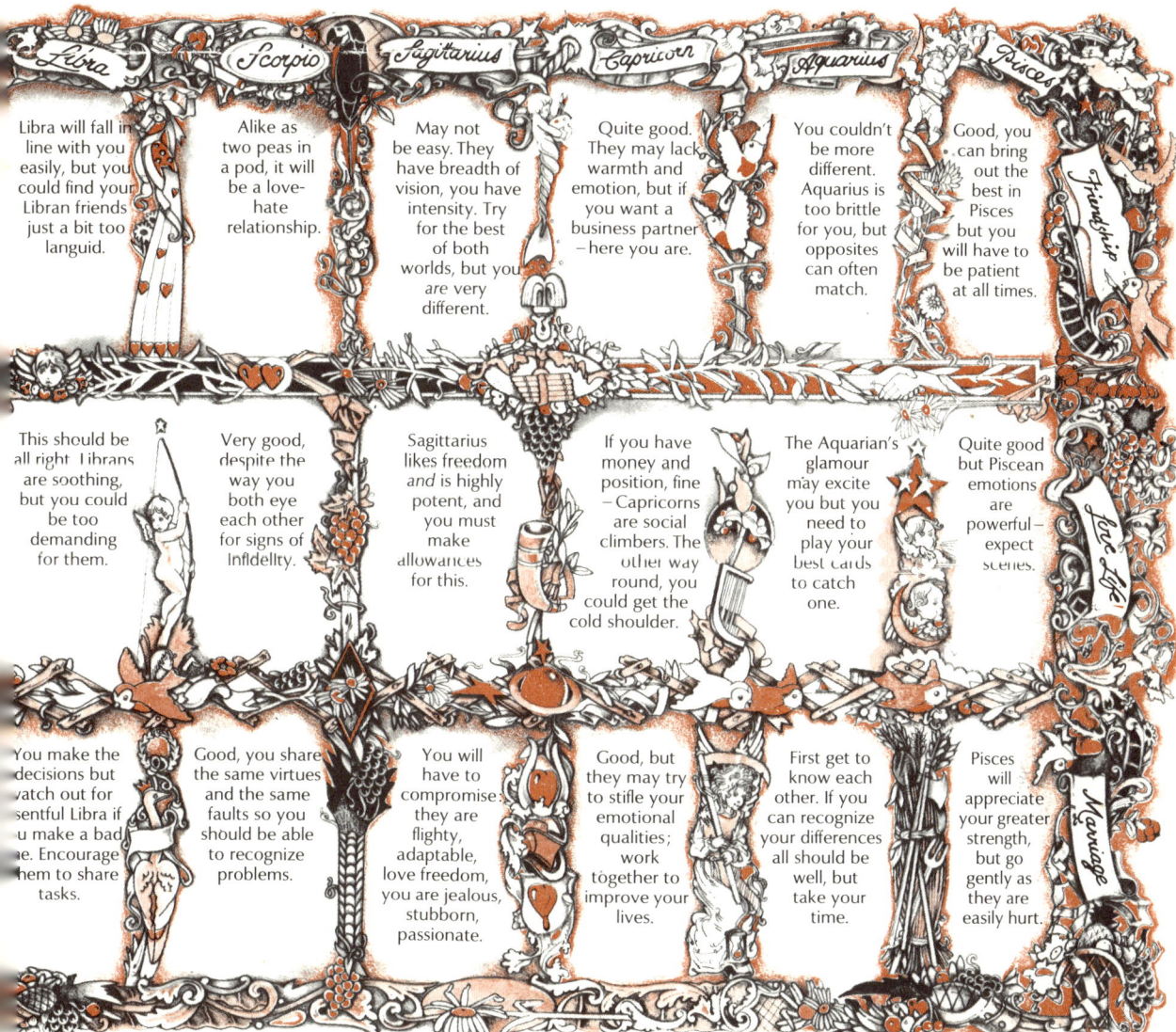

	Libra	Scorpio	Sagittarius	Capricorn	Aquarius	Pisces
Friendship	Libra will fall in line with you easily, but you could find your Libran friends just a bit too languid.	Alike as two peas in a pod, it will be a love-hate relationship.	May not be easy. They have breadth of vision, you have intensity. Try for the best of both worlds, but you are very different.	Quite good. They may lack warmth and emotion, but if you want a business partner – here you are.	You couldn't be more different. Aquarius is too brittle for you, but opposites can often match.	Good, you can bring out the best in Pisces but you will have to be patient at all times.
Love Life	This should be all right. Librans are soothing, but you could be too demanding for them.	Very good, despite the way you both eye each other for signs of infidelity.	Sagittarius likes freedom *and* is highly potent, and you must make allowances for this.	If you have money and position, fine – Capricorns are social climbers. The other way round, you could get the cold shoulder.	The Aquarian's glamour may excite you but you need to play your best cards to catch one.	Quite good but Piscean emotions are powerful – expect scenes.
Marriage	You make the decisions but watch out for resentful Libra if you make a bad one. Encourage them to share tasks.	Good, you share the same virtues and the same faults so you should be able to recognize problems.	You will have to compromise; they are flighty, adaptable, love freedom, you are jealous, stubborn, passionate.	Good, but they may try to stifle your emotional qualities; work together to improve your lives.	First get to know each other. If you can recognize your differences all should be well, but take your time.	Pisces will appreciate your greater strength, but go gently as they are easily hurt.

145

PARENTS AND CHILDREN

The Zodiac Family Portrait

THE SCORPIO FATHER

When a Scorpio becomes a father, he will feel a burst of pride and will throw himself ardently into his new role. Later on he should take care that he is not too strict; he has this tendency, and a sensitive child, perhaps a girl, could become rather afraid of him. He may find this difficult to believe, for he probably feels that his bark is worse than his bite; in reality, though, this may not be strictly true. However, the feminine charm of his little girl will go straight to his heart, and she, if she inherits her father's subtlety, should find it easy enough to win him round to her way of thinking!

The Scorpio father will be equally strict with his sons; but they will probably be quite tough in their own ways, and could well thrive on a direct, straightforward approach. The Scorpio father will plan marvellous outings from time to time, and these will help to make him popular with his children. But tolerance is one important lesson all Scorpios have to learn, *especially* when they become fathers.

THE SCORPIO MOTHER

The Scorpio mother will probably throw herself as passionately into the idea of motherhood as she entered her husband's arms on their wedding night! She will in most cases be a very good mother. Strictness may be a problem

with her, as with the Scorpio father, but her maternal pride may help her to keep a balance.

She could at times become rather too demanding. On the other hand Scorpio's great energy and flair for enjoying life will give the children plenty of splendid memories as they grow older; whether the family is rich or poor, time must be made for fun. Scorpios tend to be fixed in their opinions, and as the children grow up the parents may forget to keep abreast of the younger generation's opinions. Scorpio parents must resolve really to *do* something about the generation gap – or it could cause more difficulties than usual.

THE SCORPIO CHILD

The Scorpio child needs a great deal of careful upbringing and guidance, and strict discipline. He will have a strong personality and be determined, even quite stubborn at times. All his searching questions must be answered in detail, and parents will do well not to gloss over facts. Scorpio children need to get the facts straight, and if their parents do not supply them, they will try to find out in their own way – which could produce strange, perhaps unhappy results.

The Scorpio child loves mystery, and once he has reached the reading age will devour quantities of mystery stories – the creepier the better! He will tend to be secretive, and this trait must be watched with considerable care. It can, however, be developed positively if, for instance, the young Scorpio is entrusted with planning birthday surprises and 'secrets' for other members of the family.

Unfortunately, the great Scorpio green-eyed monster – jealousy – is certain to show its head, especially when a younger brother or sister is born into the family and begins to make his or her presence felt. But if the Scorpio child can be made to feel really wanted, and is made responsible for looking after the baby in some way, this will help. But he *must* afterwards be rewarded with great praise and affection. He will probably be an energetic child, and should be encouraged to take part in all the heavier sports. He should also learn to swim very early in life (water is his element); later he could take to underwater swimming and perhaps to skiing, either on water or snow. He will be one of the world's workers, and with encouragement will work hard at school. At the same time he may mislead teachers into thinking that he knows less than he actually does. A slightly cruel streak in him will enjoy watching the poor teacher trying to explain something to him in many different ways, when all the time he knows exactly what she means!

If the question of a boarding school arises for the Scorpio child, generally speaking he should respond well to the life. He can take the additional discipline and will soon find his own individual ways of enjoying life. His midnight feasts will not be discovered (he will, already, be a skilled secret agent) and the food he organizes will be excellent! However, all Scorpio children need care in their upbringing. They have enormously strong characters, and any negative tendencies should be checked at once or they may persist in adult life, perhaps with unfortunate consequences.

CAREERS AND PASTIMES

A Sun-sign Guide to Work and Play

CAREERS

Scorpios are hard workers, and their sense of purpose in life makes them serious in their approach to a career. They have the ability to study hard during training, whether at university or college, or in some form of apprenticeship or articles. Their determination, whatever their level of intelligence or type of job, should help them to make good progress. However, they must feel that their work is important. They hate trivialities. Scorpios have excellent business sense, and will be happy in insurance, the Stock Exchange, or working for any large business concern.

They are great researchers, and have the ability to bring out into the open that which is concealed: and many Scorpios are compulsively drawn to criminal investigation and the police force. Very often they find themselves fighting their own kind, for some Scorpio traits can be expressed, negatively, through crime.

We can of course take this theme further, for the spying profession seems to hold everything that a Scorpio needs for a satisfactory life! In addition to the attractions already mentioned, there is danger—extreme danger—which is just what Scorpio will thrive on. Although he is not reckless or foolhardy, he will be immensely stimulated by the idea of living on a razor's edge.

The Scorpio would also make an excellent psychiatrist or analyst. He is able to reveal and disentangle the complexities of the human mind. He can also turn his attention profitably to surgery, which he will perform with infinite, delicate skill. It is perhaps in this profession that the Scorpio is really at his best, using all his powerful qualities to the utmost.

The Scorpio not only likes administering discipline, but responds to it himself: it is, however, the discipline of action, of additional work and of energy expended, not the discipline of restriction, confinement or repression. He makes an ideal soldier, for he is so tough and such a strong personality that even if he advances in the ranks, which is very likely, he will inflict a strict discipline on himself to 'lead by example', as he would

say. Nevertheless, his motivations are not always so straightforward: he may inflict discipline because of his own masochistic liking for it! Both the Army and the Navy are excellent for Scorpio.

In choosing a career, Scorpio must at all times remember his need to stretch himself to the limits if he is to find satisfaction in his work. He must not only work hard, he must be able to exercise his inquiring mind, and above all else he must feel strongly that what he is doing is important to the community as a whole, and to himself in particular.

PASTIMES

As the Scorpio seeks to stretch himself in his career so he needs to in his spare-time, and his interests should act as a dynamic contrast to his working life. For instance, if he has an intellectually demanding job, he should have a physically demanding pastime; or, if the demands at work on his physical energy are heavy, he should exercise his mind to the fullest out of working hours.

Much of the Scorpio's spare time will undoubtedly be taken up with making love, and with improving his techniques. However, he has many other talents which could also be a great source of pleasure to him! As he has a high energy level, some form of sporting activity will please him. He may well go in for team games—either to play or watch. Boxing could attract him from an early age, and he will also be excellent at karate. It might be extremely good for him from a psychological point of view to have an outlet of this kind. He is aggressive, and a semi-violent hobby will help him to work it out of his system.

Scorpio is often attracted to swimming, and to some of the more challenging water sports, such as water-skiing, or perhaps under-water exploration. Indeed, any activity which entails a certain amount of risk will fascinate Scorpios—both men and girls. They will very likely be attracted to sailing, for example—but the exciting, dangerous sport of large racing craft, rather than peaceful river cruising.

AT HOME

A Sun-sign Guide to Home Décor

Exotic shades of red will dominate the Scorpio's taste in decoration. The carpets will be thick, luxurious and probably maroon; quite often black will also be used. The atmosphere might, to others, seem rather claustrophobic: and the general impression will certainly be seductive! There will be low, relaxing couches with plenty of soft, comfortable cushions. These are likely to be patterned with large tropical blossoms, or some sort of mystical Eastern design; again, the effect is mainly sensual and some may find the lack of ambiguity somewhat disconcerting.

The Scorpio may even burn incense, for he is often inclined to the occult, and adores an air of mystery. The lighting will be kept low, and directed to specific areas of the room. Light fittings will tend to be modern and sleek.

Scorpio likes good food, and the dining-area will be emphasized. The dining-table will be in highly polished dark wood, and the chairs will be comfortably upholstered. There is likely to be a special table prominently placed for drinks, for the Scorpio knows his wines and spirits well, and visitors can expect the best available, and plenty of it, too.

PEACOCK FEATHERS OR A CRYSTAL BALL

Some bizarre ornament or item of decoration may add an element of shock, surprise anyway, to the scene, such as an arrangement of peacock feathers, or unusual artificial flowers. A stuffed alligator or a case of butterflies or insects may slightly startle the visitor – or even a crystal ball!

The Scorpio's taste in pictures is as definite as his whole clear-cut, strong personality. He will love the exotic paintings of Gauguin (especially the Tahitian nudes). He will like Dali's surrealism, and perhaps the weird canvasses of Hieronymus Bosch. Dürer's marvellous knights in armour could well attract him, and if he is a student he will tend to go for posters of exotic nudes, photographs of Indian temple sculpture, or reproductions of equally sensual works by Aubrey Beardsley.

The financially well-established Scorpio will have a slick kind of taste, and may buy pictures for investment; but nevertheless he is unlikely to buy anything he dislikes. Fortunately for him, love and the human body are here to stay, and he can find both investment value and sensual pleasure in many fields of art.

If Scorpio likes pop music, it will probably be the heavier, slower numbers that will appeal to him; generally, on entering the Scorpio home, one can expect lush sounds to strike one's ears. If his taste is classical, it may be the strains of a pulsating rhythm, such as Ravel's *Bolero*, that waft out to greet the visitor in the entrance hall.

DINNER WITH SCORPIO

Entertaining with Your Sun-sign

THE HOST

If a Scorpio invites you to dinner, accept quickly before he changes his mind, because it is likely to be a splendid evening. Scorpios do nothing by halves, and playing the host is an activity they enjoy. They do find trivialities irritating, however, preferring to feel that every occasion in which they involve themselves is important. In some this sense of occasion, coupled perhaps with a wish to influence people, may mean that the visitor will find himself sitting between a senior politician and a bishop. The talk will be spirited, but an argument could quite possibly blow up over the brandy.

THE GUEST

Scorpio guests are always interesting, and have a generally dynamic air. They may, however, be a little suspicious of any new dish they have not tasted before. The best way to comfort Scorpio guests is to appeal to their imagination; this usually induces contentment.

On the other hand, if a dish is *too* successful—especially if it is a dish that your Scorpio guest is in the habit of cooking from time to time—then you may find that paeans of praise from your other guests will awaken his ready sense of jealousy, after which sparks will fly! Scorpio is the legendary lover's sign: and indeed, if you have not planned the splendid meal as a means of seducing him, he might take advantage of it to seduce you!

THE SETTING

Dark red and maroon are the Scorpio colours, perhaps with a small admixture of dark green, together producing an effect that by many standards is rather sombre. As to music, the smoother, more romantic versions of the classic pop songs form the kind of background that Scorpios find sympathetic—Sinatra, Ella Fitzgerald and others—but refer also to page 149 for a general assessment of the Scorpio's musical tastes.

WINES

Scorpio wines present a slight problem: the countries with which Scorpios are particularly associated are Norway and Syria. Syrian wine is on the whole rather rough, and a less seductive drink than *arrack* it would be hard to find! If one were to compromise slightly on the country of origin, then perhaps a Beaune would be ideal. There will also be a yen for the rather pompous kind of drinks—a good old brandy, a sound port, or any bottle with an impressive label on it.

Right: An all-star evening for famous Scorpios of past and present would very likely include all the illustrious guests in our picture. For details of the various dishes on the table—every one a Scorpio favourite—turn to page 152.

Princess Grace of Monaco

Mrs Indira Ghandi

Viscount Montgomery

Billy Graham

Katharine Hepburn

lamein

Pablo Picasso

Field Marshal Erwin Rommel

RECIPES FOR SCORPIO

Cooking with Astrology

To a Scorpio, the dining table may become a chemistry bench: he will analyse every taste, every smell, and work out the recipes in his head. And he will also analyse the guests around him.

When we use astrology to choose a menu for Scorpio we have to take into account the fact that it is a water sign, and that it is more than likely that clam chowder will intrigue and delight the Scorpio guest. Lobster Newburg has a richness that will satisfy the Scorpio diner—and the difference between a scorpion and a lobster is sufficiently slight to make an interesting comparison. Scorpio colours, dark red and maroon, can be observed in their deepest, most virile tones in the blackcurrant pie.

As for prunes in sherry, well, Scorpios do tend to eat more than is good for them, and the effect of the prune on the digestion is legendary. Scorpios will 'thank you' in advance by bringing with them a bottle of wine as a contribution to the evening; they will also help you drink it!

'Soup and fish explain half the emotions of life.'
Sydney Smith, 1771–1845.

CLAM CHOWDER
You either like shellfish, or you don't; but clam chowder is an excellently 'impressive' dish, and not difficult. Peel and chop 1 large potato; cover with cold water; bring to a boil and drain immediately. Repeat this blanching process with 5 to 6 slices unsmoked bacon, chopped. In a large pan, sauté bacon in butter for a few minutes. Add $\frac{1}{2}$ Bermuda onion, finely chopped, and continue to simmer for a few minutes until lightly golden. Add potato, a bay leaf and the juice from a can of clams. While this is simmering for 20 minutes, mince the clams. Add them to the liquid and continue to simmer for a further 15 minutes. Thicken with a little cornstarch and season generously with salt and pepper.

PRUNES IN SHERRY
Boil prunes for 15 minutes (in water, not sherry!); then soak them overnight in sweet sherry. Drain and dry prunes; remove stones and stuff prunes with a hot chutney. Wrap each prune in a strip of unsmoked bacon and secure with a wooden (not plastic) cocktail stick. Just before serving, broil until prunes are hot through and bacon lightly crisped.

BOEUF EN CROÛTE
Buy as much beef fillet as you can afford or get away with. Brush it with brandy, first removing all fat, and cover with a mixture of finely chopped and sautéed mushrooms and onion. Place in a 500°F oven; immediately lower heat to 350°F and roast for not more than 15 minutes. Cool slightly; then place a thin slice of pâté (classically, de foie) on top and wrap the lot in puff pastry. Glaze with beaten egg and bake in a fairly hot oven (425°F) for 15 minutes, or until pastry is puffed and crisp. Let no one tell you this is not an expensive dish: try it instead with pork tenderloin smothered with a mixture of chopped mushrooms, onion and parsley—no pâté. Wrap in pastry and bake. Of course, this hasn't the snobbish appeal of the beef, but if anything it's even more delicious.

LOBSTER NEWBURG
Of the many ways of cooking lobster, perhaps this is the most delicious. Boil the beast for 15 minutes; split it in half and remove meat, not forgetting claws. In a pan, heat diced lobster meat gently in 4 tablespoons butter. Stir in $\frac{1}{2}$ teaspoon paprika; add 1 to 2 tablespoons warmed brandy and set alight (a touch of the spectacular if you switch off the lights first). Pour in 1 glass dry sherry—and don't embark on Lobster Newburg unless you have both sherry and brandy! Beat 2 tablespoons heavy cream lightly with 1 egg yolk. Remove pan from heat and stir in egg mixture gradually. Season with salt and pepper. Return to heat and cook gently, stirring constantly, until sauce and lobster are thoroughly hot again and sauce has thickened. Take great care not to let it boil, or egg yolk will curdle. Serve at once with plain boiled rice. And if your guests don't finish every scrap, don't ask them again.

BLACKCURRANT PIE
Wash about $1\frac{1}{2}$ lb. blackcurrants and put them in a pie plate. Cover with $\frac{1}{2}$ cup brown sugar (more if your tooth is particularly sweet) and moisten with about $\frac{2}{3}$ cup water. Cover pie with shortcrust pastry; brush with cold water and sprinkle top with a little sugar. Bake at 390°F for 25 minutes. Serve either hot or cold, but certainly with plenty of cream.

SAGITTARIUS
22 NOVEMBER–21 DECEMBER

Sagittarius is the sign of the Centaur—a strange creature,
half-man, half-horse, both teacher and hunter. In youth,
Sagittarius is untamed and coltish, but he learns his lessons well,
inwardly knowing that fulfilment will come in middle age,
when his wilder characteristics have been calmed. Jupiter, the
ruling planet of Sagittarius, although king of the gods,
sowed many wild oats, and duality was ever-present in his nature.
We see the regality of Jupiter in the Sagittarian colour,
purple; but alas, tinkling tin is the metal of this noble sign!
The quality of Sagittarius is mutable, which means that he likes
change. The element of the sign is fire—the fire of genuine
enthusiasm, which burns long and clearly.
The Sagittarian gem is the glowing topaz.

YOUR SUN-SIGN CHARACTER

The Zodiacal Self Revealed

Sagittarians are naturally frank and optimistic. They are lively, have a good sense of humour, and are very likeable. The Sagittarian's life is, generally speaking, an open book—he would find it far too tedious as well as time-consuming to be secretive, or to dress up facts about himself or his way of life in confusing or fussy half-truths. He prefers, every time, to put his cards on the table.

There are two types of Sagittarius: the first can be over-powering, boisterous and somewhat devil-may-care, while the other likes to retire quietly to his study with his books, and is the eternal student completely caught up in an unending search for greater knowledge. But what usually happens with the former type, the racy Sagittarian, is that he takes on the more intellectual attributes of his studious brother. This in fact produces the best of both worlds—a person who has had plenty of experience of life, but who has the sense not to neglect his intellect. It is often the case, too, that the change sets in during the latter stages of further education. For if a Sagittarian fails an examination, although on the surface he may well try to laugh it off with his friends, the failure will hit him hard and he will do all he can to prevent a recurrence. The Sagittarian learns well from his mistakes, and really does mend his ways when he sets his mind to it.

OPEN-AIR OPTIMIST

The first lesson the young Sagittarian has to learn is to control his optimism. Very often he overdoes it and may therefore take unnecessary risks. When driving a sports-car, for instance, he will be the one to overtake when he really should not. He may, equally, be blindly optimistic about his finances; these are just two of the more common instances. There are many others.

Sagittarius is one of the freedom-loving signs. He cannot under any circumstances cope with claustrophobic conditions, especially living conditions: a small room with no view is his idea of hell. He likes the wide-open countryside—and even there he may find areas that are unsuitable, where he is shut in by hills, for example. But he is enormously adaptable, and does not find it difficult completely to change his way of life—if he has to. A wealthy Sagittarian enjoys all that wealth has to offer, and will certainly live it up; but, should his circumstances change, he can also cope with a move down, for that in itself would become a challenge to him; and in all spheres of his life he must have challenge. He needs, for instance, the sort of job where he can work his way through projects with reasonable speed, and where he can be thinking about the next while still working on the one in hand. Life for the Sagittarian must progress in steady strides forward, with little time for rest in between strides.

SAGITTARIUS IN ACTION

Mind and Body: You and Your Life Style

The Sagittarian seeks constantly to broaden his horizons. A quiet, limited existence is not for him. If necessary, though, he has his own individual way of making the best of his surroundings. For instance, a Sagittarian finding himself forced into working in a dreary factory job, when he was more used to travelling around, would take the view, 'Well, it's an experience!' And he would adapt himself to the new job and try to do it well – but at the same time would look round for something more suitable, for he would not want to feel himself trapped.

The Sagittarian is a splendid sportsman and also has a strong gambling streak, which he must learn to control. He loves his days out at the races, and is usually an excellent horseman. He has a natural love of horses, and indeed of all animals; dogs are probably his second favourite.

ETERNAL STUDENT

The Sagittarian often has to fight restlessness; and partly because he has considerable duality, he likes to do more than one thing at a time. He will, for instance, like to have more than one source of income, more than one job or hobby; but because he is for ever looking for new experiences, and must widen his horizons, restlessness may be a source of some difficulty. Often, older Sagittarians admit that they were victims of restlessness when they were younger, but that once having found a group of interests which really fascinated and involved them, they managed to come to terms with themselves. Perhaps the vital phrase is 'group of interests', for this is what can really provide a positive outlet for the Sagittarian brand of duality.

Perhaps more than any other sign the Sagittarian feels at his best in casual clothes. Very often he finds it irksome to dress formally or in accordance with fashion. Sagittarians are the classic example of the 'eternal student' type and will tend to cling on to their student image long after they have left university – which can seem somewhat unfortunate at times.

ENERGETIC AND VERSATILE

The Sagittarian is extremely versatile, and his interests can range from greyhound racing to a study of the use of the comma in medieval literature! He has a high energy level, and needs a lot of exercise, both mental and physical. If his work is sedentary and requires him to use his mind a great deal, he will be tired at the end of the day but will be very soon restored by some sporting activity – tennis or squash, perhaps – in the evening. But if Sagittarius is on his feet all day, or doing physical work, then he will be restored by going to evening classes, learning a language, perhaps, or

studying some difficult subject. Contrasts of this kind are essential if the Sagittarian is going to fulfil himself. This sort of pattern will also, of course, help to keep his restlessness well under control.

When the Sagittarian has come to terms with his personality and calmed his more boisterous, devil-may-care tendencies, he will contribute much to society. Even young Sagittarius, once he has begun to calm down, assumes an air of wisdom, while the really mature Sagittarius is a sage indeed. Others will come to him for advice, and because of his excellent judgment and ability to see further ahead than most people, the advice he gives will be well spiced with good sense and may also have a touch of inspiration. Above all he is able to encourage his less confident friends to make the best of themselves and their potentialities—as he himself has done.

Sagittarians love good food and wine, but are inclined to put on weight. This is another reason why they should keep up some form of physical exercise. This sign rules the liver, and after a night out the Sagittarian is likely to feel 'liverish'. The sign also rules the hips and thighs, and the Sagittarian girl is liable to put on weight around her hips.

BREADTH OF VISION

The Sagittarian mind is broad and far-sighted. Sagittarians grasp a situation quickly, and give it shape with equal speed. If they are presented with an idea they will rapidly assess its possibilities and will be busy visualizing the consequences before others have even left the starting-point! What is difficult, however, for the Sagittarian, is the business of coping with small details. Because he has such breadth of vision, he tends to ignore the ifs and buts of a situation, and he can then become very irritated when someone puts minor obstacles in his way. However, he has what is commonly known as 'a good mind', and can cross such bridges as he comes to them; or he may leave it to lesser minds to sort out the minor tangles—probably while he himself is miles away coping with the big, interesting, early stages of his *next* project.

The Sagittarian enjoys studying. He may not be much concerned with, say, dates—if he is an historian—but he has the mind of the philosopher *and* professor. He is not particularly inventive, and his results will not shatter the world by their originality.

Where the Sagittarian mind is at its best is in developing and exploring existing theories, and *challenging* them; for challenge, pure and simple, is bread and water to the Sagittarian. He cannot thrive without it in any sphere of his life, and life without some kind of intellectual challenge is no life at all, whatever his background and general education.

EMOTIONAL RELATIONSHIPS

Couples: How You Compare in Friendship, Love and Marriage

SAGITTARIUS IN LOVE

The young Sagittarian in love cannot be summed up better than by quoting Friar Lawrence, from Shakespeare's *Romeo and Juliet*:

'Young men's love then lies
Not truly in their hearts, but in their eyes'

If ever a sign appreciated a pretty face, it is the Sagittarian. This is equally true of the Sagittarian girl, who will swiftly melt when she comes into contact with a really handsome man.

But, alas, disillusion may then set in, for the Sagittarian is demanding in love, and all too soon will realize that he needs much more than a pretty face. He will not be able to put up for long with a partner who cannot match him intellectually, or who will be bored by his bookishness. Only the raciest, most undeveloped kind of Sagittarian—in the intellectual sense—will suffer a pretty girl with no mind of her own.

The Sagittarian's duality can insinuate itself into his love-life, for he will very often have more than one girl-friend, and will love them all for different reasons! He is an enthusiastic lover, but looks for something deeper than mere physical relationships.

FRIENDS

The Sagittarian friend will keep you busy: you will either be off visiting some museum or other, or else out in the open country; or if you are not rushing about, you will be in his favourite café or bar putting the world to rights. The Sagittarian sense of humour

Aries

Friendship: Lively and fairly boisterous at times—this should be a lot of fun.

Love Life: Good, you are highly potent and a very good match for the Arian's passion.

Marriage: You both love your freedom but don't forget each other. Organize your lives with care.

Taurus

Friendship: Taureans are more static, which you could find annoying, but they may help curb your restlessness.

Love Life: If you wait for a response, their passion—when it breaks—may sweep you off your feet.

Marriage: Taurus lives at a slower rate than you; also remember that they are possessive, and you love your freedom.

Gemini

Friendship: Perfect! You will broaden and deepen the Gemini mind, and they will lighten your outlook when you are too studious.

Love Life: Good, Gemini will give you a run around (you need the exercise) and you both like talking about your old conquests.

Marriage: Very good for companionship as well as love; you admire each other's mental qualities.

Cancer

Friendship: Not easy, you must develop mutual interests—perhaps in some historical subject or water sport.

Love Life: Cancerians cling: if you are asked home for dinner, you may find yourself staying longer than you had planned.

Marriage: Look out for personality clashes: they won't like your urge for freedom, or your bright and carefree manner.

Leo

Friendship: Very good, very lively, but don't let yourself be pushed around—you can beat them, for you have a better mind.

Love Life: The accent very much on fun and games; this matching should hit the high spots.

Marriage: Very good, but they may want to smarten your image; if so, let them pay the bills!

Virgo

Friendship: Your minds can complement each other: you do the general planning and leave the details to Virgo.

Love Life: Proceed with care and more slowly than usual, love can be difficult for cautious, critical Virgo.

Marriage: Your minds work in different ways, but you are both outdoor types and will enjoy journeys to the country together.

is pure fun: as a student he is the one who plans the really elaborate practical jokes. He will see to it that his sense of humour and enjoyment of life is spread around so that everyone within his circle is made just that bit happier.

LIFE AFTER MARRIAGE

The Sagittarian in marriage is demanding. He finds it difficult to settle into a permanent relationship, and will have to come to terms with his need for freedom, as will his wife or husband. Anyone marrying a Sagittarian must realize this, and give his partner room to breathe, and not be annoyed or jealous if he or she is, for instance, flirtatious at a party.

If the Sagittarian is confronted with accusations of infidelity, he will tend to react in a negative way whatever the truth of the matter; if he was innocent at first, he may then deliberately set out to be unfaithful as a kind of reprisal. But if his partner has plenty to offer from the intellectual point of view, and there is a good rapport between them, the Sagittarian is splendid in marriage. Possessiveness and jealousy are traits that he cannot, indeed will not, bear under any circumstances.

Below: Use this Friends and Lovers Sun-sign chart to check how Sagittarius is likely to make out with others in friendship, love and marriage. Relationships are listed from left to right, Sagittarius to Aries, Sagittarius to Taurus, etc., and from top to bottom in friendship, love and marriage.

	Libra	Scorpio	Sagittarius	Capricorn	Aquarius	Pisces
Friendship	Very good, Libra will take the lead from you and will find you stimulating.	There will be arguments but your breadth of vision plus Scorpio's intensity makes an interesting mixture.	Make sure you are both either sporty or intellectual – very often one type of Sagittarian loathes the other.	Not easy, Capricorn is worldly, ambitious and chilly, you are warm, affectionate and like to enjoy life.	Can be excellent, you are both far-sighted. Aquarius is a more experimental type and could surprise you.	Very good, much sympathy between you, but their emotionalism can get you down at times.
Love Life	Relax, take your time and let Libra soothe you into an enjoyable affair.	This will be passionate but remember, freedom-lover, that Scorpios are a jealous breed.	You will lead each other a dance (or a chase) which you both will think you have won Should be stimulating – and fun.	Even if you are deeply attracted, this may not be quite such a splendid affair as you had hoped.	Excellent, you will both feel free to enjoy each other's company, without being tied down too much.	Pisces will fall in line with you but proceed with caution, they are sensitive.
Marriage	You will find Libra easy to get on with, but they are full of intellectual cobwebs which you will want to sweep away.	They will resent your need for freedom: suspicion and jealousy may cloud your happiness unless you can come to terms.	Best if you are equally matched intellectually, and prepared to take an interest in each other's pet subjects.	Recognize that you are different. They are practical, so perhaps can help your schemes to come true.	Very good, while you tend more towards the traditional, their outlook will be stimulating. Children are brought up in an advanced way.	You can both be impractical (beware financial problems) but you are easy-going and happy.

PARENTS AND CHILDREN

The Zodiac Family Portrait

THE SAGITTARIAN FATHER

The Sagittarian father will enjoy his children's company. All the same, he can be somewhat intolerant when they are small; in his anxiety to put their minds to work he may expect too much of them. If the Sagittarian father is an open-air type, he may in his enthusiasm push his small son too far when teaching him, say, to ride a horse.

The relationship between the Sagittarian father and child only really blossoms when the child nears his teens; Sagittarius identifies more with youth than with young children. He is forward-looking enough to be able to understand the younger generation – what it is trying to do and how it is expressing itself – because he is the sort of person who takes the trouble to find out. The generation gap should present him with little difficulty.

THE SAGITTARIAN MOTHER

The Sagittarian mother may be faced with several quite serious problems. For her mental well-being she must first decide that she really *wants* a child. Once tied to a baby, the Sagittarian mother can become bored with the role – more so than any other sign. She needs more than marriage and motherhood to keep her happy. If she had a college education, for instance, and holds a good degree and an interesting job, she must be quite certain before she sacrifices her career. Although in true Sagittarian spirit she may exercise her natural duality and try to keep some kind of career going while the children are very young, this could make her even more restless, for the precious hours that she does manage to spend working may just not be enough for her.

But once she has reached the vital decision to be a mother, she will take up the challenge and will approach the role with much genuine enthusiasm. She will also bring her excellent intellectual qualities into play: she, if anyone, can do much to give her children a marvellous intellectual background.

THE SAGITTARIAN CHILD

Young Sagittarians are alert and extremely active. The child of the sign is great fun to be with; he tends to show off, but has a splendidly adventurous spirit. It will not be easy for his parents to let him express his natural adventurousness. He will terrify them when, for instance, he urges his pony to gallop still faster. But if he is told not to do something, the thrill of doing it will, not surprisingly, be increased. Despite his reckless tendencies, he is open and truthful, and in most cases it would not occur to him to be underhand; if he is, his parents can appeal to his sense of reason. This should be enough; it is unlikely that the fault will have to be corrected more than once.

The Sagittarian child could easily run into difficulties at school, for he will not like strict discipline. He will think many of the school rules silly; but if they are carefully explained to him, he can learn to accept them. He should be encouraged to learn languages, for which he has a special flair. He should always have plenty of challenging hobbies and interests, and will want to be kept busy – both in school and during his spare time. He may have some talent for writing, and will appreciate a good supply of pencils and notebooks in his room. He could become bored with school routine, finding some of it dull; again, he can be asked to see reason – so long as there *is* a reason. But the root cause of a bad period at school may be an unhappy relationship with his class teacher. This can be more disastrous for a Sagittarian than for a child of any other sign.

Parents will find that as the Sagittarian child grows older, so his attitude towards education will become more serious. At first he may well resent the discipline of school, and during the kindergarten years he may not want to go to school at all – he would much rather be out running free in the open fields or riding his pony (real or imaginary!). But the more involved he is with school, the more he will settle and become interested in his work; and he, of all the signs, will benefit from further education – whatever the subject. If financial sacrifices have to be made to see him through college, these should be well worthwhile in the long run, for although on the surface he may seem rather casual in his attitude towards his work, this is probably misleading and he should finish with an excellent degree.

CAREERS AND PASTIMES

A Sun-sign Guide to Work and Play

CAREERS

The Sagittarian needs a sense of freedom, even if he has to submit to the daily round of a routine job. He will be much happier if, for instance, he is given a free hand within the confines of his work, and allowed to set about his tasks as he pleases. Someone employing a Sagittarian, or asking him to become involved in a project, should bear this in mind. Consideration at the outset should bring a two-way benefit when the Sagittarian has had a chance to settle down. The Sagittarian is enormously versatile, and may well find that he will have more than one job, or source of income. In point of fact this will be excellent for him: the variety and change will help him to do well in both jobs!

If he can find an occupation which will take him out and about, so much the better. He will make a splendid travel agent, for instance. Nevertheless, despite his love of freedom, his need to use his brain is even greater, and many Sagittarians are to be found in top 'intellectual' professions, such as the law. Many are professors or teachers, although they are generally better at teaching students rather than small children, for Sagittarians can be very demanding and may expect too much from young children.

Book publishing, library work and writing are all very Sagittarian; they seem to thrive in an atmosphere that is essentially bookish. *One* type of Sagittarian thrives in this atmosphere, anyway; the other, a more outdoor type, will perhaps become a jockey (if he is small), or will train horses, or (if he is rich) own them. He will love all animals, and many Sagittarians will be extremely successful as veterinary surgeons or dog breeders.

Many Sagittarians have strong religious feelings. They are very spiritual, and can inspire others towards a less materialistic way of life. Orthodox religion is a calling for many, and a high proportion of Sagittarians throughout history have lived very devout lives as priests or rabbis.

Sagittarius is one of the sporting signs, and many Sagittarians become professional sportsmen. Horsemanship apart, there are professional drivers, athletes and skaters in plenty born under this sign. The Sagittarian ability to write can take several forms: he often has the ability to cope with the sweep of a large-scale novel; and if, as they say, there is a book in everyone, there is certainly one in the Sagittarian. He also learns languages quickly, and could well make the grade as a translator (a profession which could give him much satisfaction, and indeed the travel he adores).

Sagittarians are willing to work extremely hard in their chosen profession. Generally speaking, they love to enjoy life, and get as much out of it as possible (in and out of working hours), so it is essential for them to be in the right profession. It does happen from time to time, because of parental pressure or for other reasons, that a Sagittarian (like a lot of other people) is 'pushed' into a job. This is a particularly unhappy state of affairs, and it is advisable for him, if he possibly can, to try to change matters. He usually has far too good a mind to waste it in areas where he cannot give of his best, or where he is not much interested. While some can bear the burden of a dull, uninteresting working life this is a living death for the Sagittarian.

PASTIMES

The Sagittarian will not find it difficult to fill in his spare time: indeed, he usually has such a string of occupations that the days are often just not long enough for him. He will love to drive out into the country in his car, and if possible to visit other countries. He has a gambling spirit, and can succumb to the casino; so he needs to watch this, as it could become a serious failing. He likes archery and dancing, and sometimes hunting and shooting, the latter despite his love of animals.

He is not a great man for collecting, but could be attracted to philately. In short, the Sagittarian likes being stimulated; if he sits still watching television, it is only because, for the time being, he is mentally and physically spent.

AT HOME

A Sun-sign Guide to Home Décor

The Sagittarian home will give an illusion of space, even if it is small. Ideally, it will have a view, and an expansive view at that, for the Sagittarian would not be happy merely spying on his neighbours. If he is a city dweller, and cannot live in the wide open spaces so dear to him, he will perhaps arrange a mirror to give an impression of space within a room; or if he is in a sufficiently strong financial position to rent the penthouse which towers above all the other buildings, then he will do so. To compensate for a lack of view, he may hang several extensive landscape paintings on the walls.

Usually, Sagittarians love purple and shades of dark blue; a dark blue carpet or purple drapes will be firm favourites. The furniture will be comfortable, but the Sagittarian may not be concerned with appearances, and often what starts out as a good scheme of decoration either is never completed, or he finds that he has too many books! So the overall elegance of the room may be spoiled ('just for the time being', he says) by piles of books, papers and magazines. All too often, no matter how many bookshelves he has, he never has quite enough.

As many Sagittarians love sport, there may be model cars here and there, or prints of them on the walls. Perhaps the general effect of many Sagittarian rooms is that of a typical student 'pad'; the Sagittarian is an eternal student, and may well unconsciously cling to that image. He will hold on to an ancient armchair which his grandmother gave him when he moved into his first apartment. He might manage to re-cover it, or have new loose covers made, but comfort will dominate over style in the Sagittarian home, and the overall effect will be that the person owning it is 'interesting', and that the rooms have 'character'.

The Sagittarian choice in pictures could include eighteenth-century sporting prints or paintings of famous racehorses by George Stubbs; landscapes by Constable; and very often great master-works with religious themes, such as Rembrandt's *Belshazzar's Feast*. Many Sagittarians are interested in Elizabethan England, and will like the art of that period.

There is often a Spanish influence in the Sagittarian home; he likes colourful Spanish rugs and bedcovers, and may own several. There could well be a Spanish guitar in evidence—and not merely as decoration, for many Sagittarians appreciate guitar music and, what is more, like to play it.

DINNER WITH SAGITTARIUS

Entertaining with Your Sun-sign

THE HOST

The Sagittarian host may well decide to show his versatility by trying something new, 'just for you'. If he does, there is no need to be discouraging, only don't expect too much, because Sagittarians are given to over-optimism. Details, too, are not their strong point. In due course, on the night, things may somehow refuse to go entirely according to plan—or what, with the Sagittarian, passes for planning. Fortunately his optimism does not entirely desert him. Instead of going under in the face of crisis, he slaps the lid quickly back on the pot, glares at it and says determinedly, 'That'll be all right.' And is it? Well, not always.

The message, then, for Sagittarian cooks is: read every word of the recipe and follow the instructions carefully. This, in any kind of cookery, is half the battle. In addition, there are just two things you should watch: your Sagittarian tendency to tactlessness may lead you astray—no use planning crab salad and roast pork for Jewish guests. Secondly, refuse to allow your usual restlessness to push you into fidgeting about over-much. Relax: if the soup is dreadful, pour it away and open a tin. If the main course is burnt, make for the nearest hamburger-stall.

THE GUEST

Sagittarian guests are good eaters, have keen appetites and a liking for variety. A Sagittarian is always a good 'reserve' for a dinner-party: interested in other people, he will settle down happily to talk to whomever he finds beside him. He will enjoy most foods.

THE SETTING

As for table decorations, the Sagittarian likes rather strong colours, and this makes the choice a little difficult; nothing looks more alarming than a steak on a purple plate! Compromise with some blue flowers. For background music, something reminiscent of the open air—country and western perhaps, or Aaron Copland, or Vaughan Williams.

Oh, and put the dog in the attic: Sagittarians love animals, and if your dog cares to sit by their side with its mouth open, it will collect most of the main course.

WINES

Sagittarians are associated with Spain and Hungary. Spanish reds make suitable if run-of-the-mill clarets; and of course there are the sherries. Hungarian Tokay will bring the party to a happy end.

Right: An all-star evening for famous Sagittarians of past and present would very likely include the illustrious guests in our picture. For details of the dishes on the table—every one a Sagittarian favourite—turn to page 166.

Walt Disney

Maria Callas

Noel Coward

Sir Winston Churchill

Frank Sinatra

Jane Fonda

Ludwig van Beethoven

Boris Karloff

165

RECIPES FOR SAGITTARIUS

Cooking with Astrology

The adventurous Sagittarius, who will probably be hungry, will be eager to take in the scene—and the food—and always willing to try even something that seems distasteful! The rather gamey flavour of trout will appeal to Sagittarius the hunter; he will prefer it to the blandness of other fish; rabbit and hare, both game, should also tickle his palate—he may indeed himself have hunted, killed and presented the animal. A Sagittarian friend who is a writer will undoubtedly bring you a copy of his latest book as a gift; if he doesn't write, then a copy of someone else's.

CHILLED CUCUMBER SOUP

Simmer 1 small, sliced onion in 2 pints chicken stock for 15 minutes. Add 1 large, peeled, chopped cucumber and a pinch of fresh mint. Simmer until cucumber is cooked; then either purée in a blender or rub through a sieve. Reheat and thicken with a little cornstarch; simmer for 2 or 3 minutes longer, stirring; stir in 3 tablespoons fresh cream; cool and chill.

BAKED TROUT AND BACON

Remove backbone from trout and lay fish, cut side down, on slices of bacon in a fireproof dish. Sprinkle with salt, pepper and a little chopped parsley; splash with melted butter (more rather than less), and bake in a moderate oven (375°F) for 30 minutes, or until flesh flakes off when eased away with a fork. Serve immediately from the same dish.

> 'No animal ever invented anything so bad as drunkenness
> —or so good as drink.'
> G. K. Chesterton, 1874–1936.

RABBIT IN MUSTARD

Rabbit should appeal to Sagittarius the hunter, even if he hasn't caught it himself. Cut the animal into pieces; roll in seasoned flour, and gently fry in olive oil and butter until golden brown on all sides. Add a little diced bacon; transfer to a thick pan with a few finely chopped shallots, a bouquet garni, and just enough chicken stock (or stock and white wine) to half-cover. Cook gently until tender; drain; skim pan juices of fat and add 1¼ cups heavy cream beaten lightly with 1 teaspoon each dry mustard and Dijon mustard. Replace rabbit pieces in sauce and warm through gently. Correct seasoning with more salt, pepper or mustard, and serve.

ROAST HARE

Not really like rabbit at all in taste: gamier and not necessarily more difficult to cook (jugged hare is over-rated and messy!). Rub your hare with a damp cloth; season with salt, pepper, rosemary and thyme both inside and out. Roast or spit-roast at 450°F, lowering heat to 350°F after the first 15 minutes, and basting from time to time with a little olive oil. Catch all the juices to serve with the hare. Don't overcook him: he should be cooked through but still very moist when he comes to table. Just before hare is cooked, simmer chopped shallots in pan juices until soft; add a little wine vinegar, 1¼ cups sour cream and 2 crushed juniper berries. Stir over a low heat until sauce has reduced slightly. Serve with hare.

STEAMED SUET PUDDING WITH FIGS

To warm frozen Sagittarians after hunting. Grease a 2-pint pudding mould. In a bowl, combine 1½ cups sifted self-rising flour with a pinch of salt, ⅞ cup loose-packed shredded suet and ⅓ cup sugar, and mix well. Add 10 large dried figs, chopped, ¼ cup coarsely shredded blanched almonds, ¼ cup large white raisins (optional) and the finely grated rind of 1 lemon. Beat 2 eggs; when frothy, beat in 2 to 3 tablespoons sherry and 3 to 4 tablespoons milk. Add to dry mix and blend thoroughly. Spoon mixture into prepared mould and hollow out centre slightly with the back of your spoon. Cover top of mould tightly with foil and steam over fast-boiling water for 2 hours. Splendid with cream, custard sauce, hot jam, syrup—or what you will.

RHUBARB CRUMBLE

Lovely, fresh, glowing pink rhubarb. Clean and trim 1 lb (no stringy pieces), and cut into 1-inch lengths. Smother a pie pan with butter; put in a layer of rhubarb, sprinkle with sugar, cover with a layer of cake crumbs flavoured with a little cinnamon and a clove or two. Repeat layers until pan is full. Moisten with ⅔ cup white wine or sherry; dot with a few pieces of butter and bake in a moderate oven for 30 minutes. Serve with cream. Even those almost insatiable Sagittarians among your guests should feel well cared for after contact with a good dish of rhubarb.

CAPRICORN
22 DECEMBER–19 JANUARY

Capricorn the Goat (or Sea-goat) is the tenth sign of the Zodiac.
Here is ambition and a pillar of society, the one who rises above
his original station in life and may then appear a lonely,
remote figure, separated from the rest of society. The element
of Capricorn is earth–solid and realistic; and his metal is heavy,
base lead, the metal of Saturn, his ruling planet. His quality
is cardinal, which means that the Capricornian is 'outgoing':
this may be expressed through his ability to take the lead and
draw ahead of less assertive mortals. The colours of
Capricorn are sombre: black, greys, dark brown and greens;
and his stone is the turquoise–the brightest of the
properties of this serious sign.

YOUR SUN-SIGN CHARACTER

The Zodiacal Self Revealed

Modern astrologers recognize two distinct types of Capricorn. While these share many common characteristics, their differences are clearly marked and offer a fascinating field of study for observers of human nature as well as astrology buffs.

The two types of Capricorn were graphically described by the English astrologer Margaret Hone as 'the giddy mountain goat', making his way up the dizzy mountain heights, nimbly stepping from crag to crag—and 'the poor domestic goat', tethered to his post and only able to see one small area of the valley; for him life was a matter of plodding round in circles and getting nowhere—the post and chain being his burden in life, limiting his whole self-expression.

It is easy enough from these descriptions to conjure up a picture of the two basic types of Capricornian, but not so easy to see exactly where they converge. However, one glorious Capricornian characteristic which seems to be shared by both types is their dry sense of humour; this is usually expressed—especially by the men of the sign—in an off-beat way, and nearly always at unexpected moments! The Capricornian making an after-dinner speech, for instance, will soon break through the formalities of the occasion and give his fellow-guests a memorable few minutes that they probably had not anticipated.

However, many Capricornians have personal problems, their tendency to remoteness being one of the most serious. Many subjects of this sign are extremely ambitious, and this tends to make them cold and difficult. They are inclined to isolate themselves and make huge sacrifices to their careers and their general progress in life—all of which can make them seem daunting figures to a non Capricornian.

Their remoteness may increase as they grow older: having worked hard—often by day and night—to attain their objectives, they will then find themselves behind the top executive desk of a large company where they alone will have the power to make policy decisions; in this way their remoteness will be emphasized. This is what it means to occupy a high place on the 'mountain path'—though many Capricornians, of course, thrive under such circumstances.

Family life, marriage, relationships with children and much that really makes life worth living may have been sacrificed in the course of the Capricornian's rise to the top. It may be a power complex that motivates him, or more likely a strong urge to do better than his fellows. The Capricornian can be ruthless, but not in a scheming or underhand way. He attains his objectives through the calculating skill of his brain, by sheer hard work and persistence and because he is psychologically prepared to step out ahead of others in a goat-like series of leaps and bounds.

CAPRICORN IN ACTION

Mind and Body: You and Your Life Style

Capricorn will not take risks or behave in an unconventional manner. Of all the signs, he is the conventional one: and generally speaking he will not behave in a way that is not absolutely right and proper in the eyes of his particular circle. There are many old heads on young Capricornian shoulders: and while some elderly members of the sign will raise their eyebrows at their younger brothers, the latter will also have a strict code of conduct within their own generation.

The domestic goat sometimes needs a lot of help from more enthusiastic, positive and less repressed members of society. He is sometimes, unfortunately, inclined to spurn such help when it is offered; in extreme cases his self-pity and gloom will be so great that he will be unable to do more than moan at how badly he is treated by the rest of the world. 'If only . . .', he will say; and this may become his constant grumble. But he will plod on nevertheless, maintaining that he is making the best of his situation, when really he could be much happier if he just looked a little further than the end of his nose. He may think that he is the most hard-done-by man in the world—lonely, neglected and unloved. But if he cared to think about the general suffering in the world, he would soon agree that he had much to be thankful for.

HAPPY GOATS IN-BETWEEN

Perhaps we are painting an extreme picture of the domestic goat—perhaps, indeed, we exaggerated the characteristics of the giddy mountain species. Of course, between these two extremes there are millions of very pleasant Capricornians, who have a lot of fun and yet have big ambitions (though they are not obsessional about them); and many, too, who utilize their strong personalities and emotions to become successful powers *behind* the throne. These people are the salt of the earth. If they can keep to the middle of the path, perhaps straying from time to time towards the mountain tops, they will do enormously well and should be neither too lonely nor too remote. Nor, on the other hand, will they drift into becoming complainers and miseries to themselves and their friends.

Very often Capricorn has a reputation for being 'hard'. This is sometimes true, but he is hard on himself as well as on others, keeping to a strenuous discipline. He will expect others to do so too, and will be surprised and even shocked if they do not live up to his own high standards. He is immensely dependable and very practical; once his loyalty is given (to his wife, his club or his firm) he can be utterly relied on. He should, however, try to look at some of the warmer and perhaps less well organized people he knows, just to see if they do have something to offer. His somewhat chilly personality needs melting: when this happens, he can

become extremely amusing and very human—if in a craggy sort of way.

The area of the body ruled by Capricorn is the knees; but the skin and bones are also susceptible—and very often the Capricornian will answer to the description 'all skin and bones'. The illnesses they tend to suffer echo these rulerships, and many a Capricornian is vulnerable to knee trouble, skin eruptions (or, conversely, has an especially fine, clear complexion); they may also have dental problems, and many are prone to illnesses that 'limit' them in some way—rheumatism, for instance. Capricornians are not always very good in the sun: they can be rather pale (whatever their racial origins) and usually prefer winter to summer, finding that the heat exhausts them.

PRECISE PATTERNS OF THOUGHT

The Capricornian mind is cool, clear and calculating. Muddled thinking and woolliness have no place here; he functions only according to precise and perhaps clinical patterns of thought. Because the Capricornian's mind is made the way it is, we find him inclined towards scientific or mathematical subjects; and because he is an unemotional creature he will be less inclined to, say, poetry or the arts in general, which in essence appeal more to the emotions.

Capricorn should have no trouble in making decisions. He will carefully weigh up the situation, setting A against B and not forgetting to consider X. Then, when his thoughts have arrived at a conclusion, he will know exactly how he must make his decision—and will try to implement a solution that will be effective not only for the time being but also in the long term. This may sound almost too clear-cut and ideal; but perhaps we others could all learn a lesson from the Capricornian approach. In any event, this approach is absolutely right for him; and once he has made a few important decisions and found himself to be right, he will gain in confidence as well as in knowledge of his mental powers. This in turn will help him to obtain a remarkably shrewd view of his own character.

All in all, it is fair to say that the Capricornian's mind is constructive: he can plan ahead in great detail. He does not, generally speaking, become bogged down in detail; even so, he misses very little. His mind, although constantly directed towards the next step, is versatile enough to keep him informed of other areas. There, too, he takes in every detail, storing them up to be used at some future date.

Capricornians are prone to worry and, in a number of cases, to depression. But if they can remember to assess the positive side of their lives—what they have already achieved as opposed to their apprehensions about the future—then all should be well.

EMOTIONAL RELATIONSHIPS

Couples: How You Compare in Friendship, Love and Marriage

CAPRICORN IN LOVE

Capricorn will not easily fall in love—or do so very quickly. He will carefully watch the object of his affections from a distance and get to know them on a quiet, friendly basis before he allows himself to become emotional. Of all the twelve signs, Capricorn is the least inclined to love at first sight. Anyone attracted to a Capricornian must proceed with care if they want to win his heart; he will soon cut himself off if he feels he is being pursued. Perhaps *he* would rather choose when to begin an affair; but the *real* reason may be more deep-rooted. Despite the numerous contacts he may make in the course of his career, he may otherwise need to live a solitary life. But once he does begin a love affair, he is very faithful indeed.

CAPRICORN AS A FRIEND

A friendship cemented with a Capricornian will have two excellent qualities: it will last a very long time and it will have some extremely amusing moments. The lively, surprise element of Capricorn is his already-mentioned sense of humour, which can give his personality an immense uplift. There will be times when the prospect of an evening with a Capricornian may not seem very exciting—he is almost certain to be depressed about something. However, once he has told the story of his current troubles, the Capricornian will put them aside and let his dry humour blossom in its usual delightful way.

Capricorn is normally rather shy, and not entirely happy about meeting strangers. His friends should

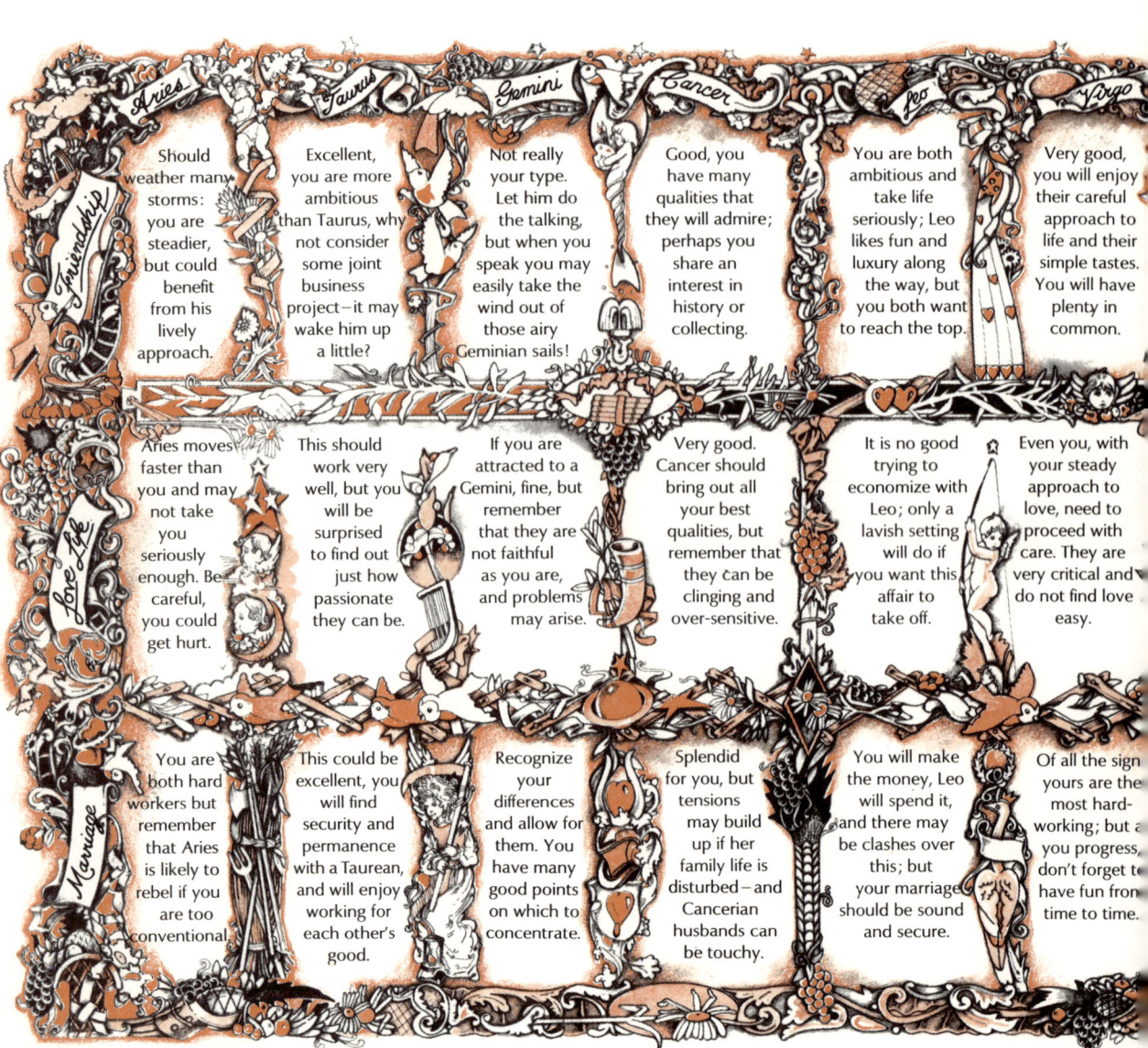

Aries

Friendship: Should weather many storms: you are steadier, but could benefit from his lively approach.

Love Life: Aries moves faster than you and may not take you seriously enough. Be careful, you could get hurt.

Marriage: You are both hard workers but remember that Aries is likely to rebel if you are too conventional.

Taurus

Friendship: Excellent, you are more ambitious than Taurus, why not consider some joint business project—it may wake him up a little?

Love Life: This should work very well, but you will be surprised to find out just how passionate they can be.

Marriage: This could be excellent, you will find security and permanence with a Taurean, and will enjoy working for each other's good.

Gemini

Friendship: Not really your type. Let him do the talking, but when you speak you may easily take the wind out of those airy Geminian sails!

Love Life: If you are attracted to a Gemini, fine, but remember that they are not faithful as you are, and problems may arise.

Marriage: Recognize your differences and allow for them. You have many good points on which to concentrate.

Cancer

Friendship: Good, you have many qualities that they will admire; perhaps you share an interest in history or collecting.

Love Life: Very good. Cancer should bring out all your best qualities, but remember that they can be clinging and over-sensitive.

Marriage: Splendid for you, but tensions may build up if her family life is disturbed—and Cancerian husbands can be touchy.

Leo

Friendship: You are both ambitious and take life seriously; Leo likes fun and luxury along the way, but you both want to reach the top.

Love Life: It is no good trying to economize with Leo; only a lavish setting will do if you want this affair to take off.

Marriage: You will make the money, Leo will spend it, and there may be clashes over this; but your marriage should be sound and secure.

Virgo

Friendship: Very good, you will enjoy their careful approach to life and their simple tastes. You will have plenty in common.

Love Life: Even you, with your steady approach to love, need to proceed with care. They are very critical and do not find love easy.

Marriage: Of all the sign[s] yours are the most hard-working; but a[s] you progress, don't forget t[o] have fun fro[m] time to time.

172

recognize this, and if they are inviting him to dinner it would be kind of them to invite some mutual acquaintance along with the other guests and so help Capricorn to feel more at ease. He is generally rather quiet and while other people—Geminians, for instance—are talking their heads off, his noble presence will contribute a strong element to the company; and when he *does* speak, everyone will stop dead in their tracks to listen!

MARRIAGE—THE FACTS

The Capricornian all too often has marital problems. He needs to realize that because his career means so much to him, it can engulf him completely; as a result his wife and children are neglected. If this occurs, he and his wife will drift apart. This is something he will

regret far more than may be apparent on the surface, for his aims in marriage are to be loyal, faithful and lastingly happy.

There is a tendency for all married Capricornians not just to keep up with the Joneses, but to *be* the Joneses; and financial sacrifices will be made to this end. They also like to climb the social scale, and although they may think that entertaining rich 'friends' is money well spent, a simple outing with the children or a romantic evening together would probably be better for them.

Below: Use this Friends and Lovers Sun-sign chart to check how Capricorn is likely to make out with others in friendship, love and marriage. Relationships are listed from left to right, Capricorn to Aries, Capricorn to Taurus, etc., and from top to bottom in friendship, love and marriage.

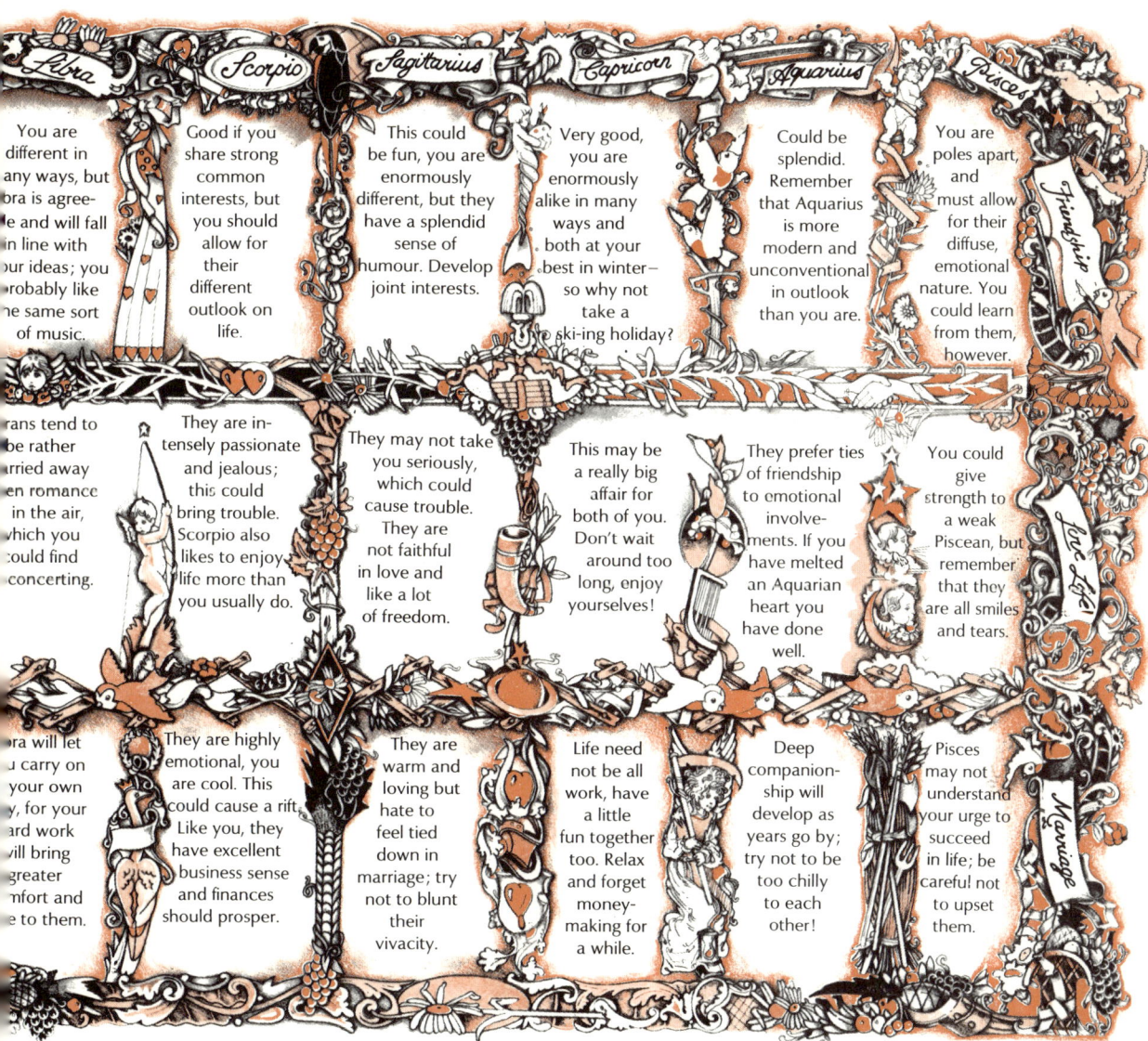

	Libra	Scorpio	Sagittarius	Capricorn	Aquarius	Pisces	
Friendship	You are different in many ways, but Libra is agreeable and will fall in line with your ideas; you probably like the same sort of music.	Good if you share strong common interests, but you should allow for their different outlook on life.	This could be fun, you are enormously different, but they have a splendid sense of humour. Develop joint interests.	Very good, you are enormously alike in many ways and both at your best in winter—so why not take a ski-ing holiday?	Could be splendid. Remember that Aquarius is more modern and unconventional in outlook than you are.	You are poles apart, and must allow for their diffuse, emotional nature. You could learn from them, however.	
Love Life	rians tend to be rather carried away when romance is in the air, which you could find disconcerting.	They are intensely passionate and jealous; this could bring trouble. Scorpio also likes to enjoy life more than you usually do.	They may not take you seriously, which could cause trouble. They are not faithful in love and like a lot of freedom.	This may be a really big affair for both of you. Don't wait around too long, enjoy yourselves!	They prefer ties of friendship to emotional involvements. If you have melted an Aquarian heart you have done well.	You could give strength to a weak Piscean, but remember that they are all smiles and tears.	
Marriage	bra will let u carry on your own y, for your rd work will bring greater mfort and e to them.	They are highly emotional, you are cool. This could cause a rift. Like you, they have excellent business sense and finances should prosper.	They are warm and loving but hate to feel tied down in marriage; try not to blunt their vivacity.	Life need not be all work, have a little fun together too. Relax and forget money-making for a while.	Deep companionship will develop as years go by; try not to be too chilly to each other!	Pisces may not understand your urge to succeed in life; be careful not to upset them.	

PARENTS AND CHILDREN

The Zodiac Family Portrait

THE CAPRICORNIAN FATHER

The Capricornian is ambitious not only for his own progress in life, but equally so for his children. He will make superhuman efforts to ensure that they are better treated than he was as a child, and will put plenty of opportunities in their way. He can, however, be very demanding, and too strict. If, for example, the child receives a bad school report, he will tend to become intolerant, forgetting to consider that perhaps the child is suffering from an unsympathetic teacher—or may even be a little afraid of his father—and is prevented through various inhibitions from making real progress.

To keep tensions from building up, a Capricornian father must try to have fun with his children; and above all else he must encourage them warmly—or at least *drily* after his own fashion (with a characteristic down-turned grin and a twinkle in his eye). He will then come to appreciate that his off-spring are made of the same excellent stuff as he is and, what is more, are worthy of their forbears (this is very important to the Capricornian). He must also listen to his children's point of view, and try to understand their new and strange ideas, even if he cannot agree with them.

THE CAPRICORNIAN MOTHER

The Capricornian mother is very keen for her children to make good progress and live a full and secure life, eventually enjoying a satisfying career. She should, however, try to give her children more pure affection. She will of course love them; but she may not show this clearly enough, perhaps for fear that it would spoil them—which she will never consciously allow to happen. She is generally a rather undemonstrative person, but she may nevertheless have an emotional child who positively needs a show of affection. Failure to appreciate this kind of need may set up tensions that could undermine the relationship. She will be skilled at stretching the housekeeping money (if she is not too well off) to ensure that her children do not go short; and in return, like the Capricornian father, she will expect her children to work hard. This is excellent—provided that the children pull their weight and recognize that sacrifices are being made for them. But the Capricornian mother must also make quite certain that her children are suited to the interests in which she involves them; she must be sure, for example, that she is not economizing in order that they should have piano lessons just because *she* once wanted to play.

THE CAPRICORNIAN CHILD

The Capricornian child is essentially a plodder. But once he becomes aware that effort brings results, parents will find that his ambitious side will begin to exert itself. He will probably have rather a serious attitude to life: to younger brothers and sisters he will seem grave, and will look after them well—though perhaps showing a rather condescending attitude at times.

If parents find that the Capricornian child is rather slow at school, there is a way of encouraging him to speed up a little. The line to take is a constructive one. For instance, he is likely to respond extremely well to such comments as, 'You *are* doing well (even if he isn't) but I'm sure you could do *even better.*' This approach should appeal to his natural desire to improve his position—and steady progress should soon result. The Capricornian child will probably do well at school in scientific subjects and mathematics; he may also develop an interest in geology and archaeology, and in athletics. Parents may discover that he is something of a loner, and they must not worry if he does not belong to a 'gang', for he is just not made that way. This is the reason why athletics is more likely to appeal to him than team games, because he is happier relying on his own efforts rather than co-operating with others. He will like peace and quiet, with good books (these are essential for him, and should be encouraged). He will enjoy listening to music, and playing any instrument that takes his fancy (even if this drives his parents crazy).

He will feel secure if he has a regular pattern to his life and if he is fairly strictly disciplined. In general, initiative is not really his strong point: he is better at being told what to do and when to do it. He likes to know exactly what is expected of him. He has a pronounced dislike of failure and will not like to think that anyone has been let down (or feels let down) through an omission on his part.

CAREERS AND PASTIMES

A Sun-sign Guide to Work and Play

CAREERS

Although the Capricornian has a strong need to feel financially secure, and ideally likes to live in the knowledge that a cheque is being paid regularly into the bank each month, he is also well placed to start his own business. From a small, cautious beginning he will then very likely build a sizeable empire. Because he is so careful and competent at coping with long-term planning, he should easily weather the difficult early stages; he will be particularly cautious about investing his capital.

If any sign excels in business, it is Capricorn. He will be happy, for instance, in a firm's contracts department working out the details of 'big deals'. The building industry may well appeal to him: architecture, town planning, building, construction and engineering are all admirable choices of career. The stock exchange, banking and insurance are also satisfactory. As an employee he will remain loyal until he retires. He is at all times careful and shrewd, and of all types the least likely to make silly mistakes.

THE ROUTE TO THE PENTHOUSE SUITE

If the Capricornian is the domestic goat he can plod happily in a secure atmosphere; if he is more ambitious (mountain goat) he will gradually climb the path that, in his case, leads to the penthouse suite. Large organizations suit him: there he can soon find his feet, and indeed in doing so will learn a lot about himself and his motivations.

In the arts many Capricornians become professional musicians. It is a little difficult to know why this is so, but perhaps it is because in essence music is a mathematical art, and the techniques of counterpart and harmony—and the extremely complex scores of the moderns—are of particular interest and fascination to them.

Without doubt the Capricornian is attracted to the idea of fame and is ambitious enough to want to rise to the top. Many Capricornians turn to politics at varying levels, and perhaps in all politically motivated Capri-

cornians there is a president or prime minister *manqué*. Some of course do become presidents and prime ministers!

SPECIALISTS TEETH AND BONE

If he is attracted to the medical profession, the Capricornian would do well to consider becoming a skin specialist or involving himself in the treatment of bone diseases and disorders. All forms of dentistry could be satisfying, and Capricornian girls attracted to some branch of medical work might consider training as osteopaths or masseuses. If the Capricornian decides to become a general practitioner he is very likely to be a man of few words—even apparently unsympathetic to patients; it may in fact be quite difficult for him to develop a comforting bedside manner.

PASTIMES

The Capricornian will like quiet hobbies which are in essence relaxing and not too much of a strain on his rather low-keyed emotions. First and foremost, he will love to read and to listen to music. He will probably find that history books interest him most of all, but he will also want to further his knowledge of business, the stock exchange, insurance, etc., in his reading. His tastes in fiction will be for large and sweeping novels such as Galsworthy's *Forsyte Saga* (which covers a family's history over several generations, and focuses on the quintessential Capricornian, Soames Forsyte); flippant, insubstantial or experimental novels are certainly not for him.

The Capricornian may well enjoy collecting—anything from impressive antiques to quite simple objects such as sea shells or rock specimens. He will enjoy going on archaeological digs and also taking part in athletic events.

Whatever type of 'goat' he may be, it is amusing to discover that a great many Capricornians are excellent mountaineers and rock climbers! They are extremely nimble and even on long walks over moorland or hills will stride out well ahead of their friends.

AT HOME

A Sun-sign Guide to Home Décor

Just as there are two distinct types of Capricornian, so there will be two distinct types of Capricornian room. One will be spartan in the extreme—although not unattractively so—with much plain, unpolished wood furniture, simple linen fabrics, bare floors with sheepskin rugs and rather thin, economical curtains and drapes. Perhaps, too, there will be simple gingham cushions. There will be no air of luxury or opulence, and the room will be functional and well laid-out, the best possible use being made of available space. The dining-room table, for instance, may have matching benches or forms rather than individual chairs, and the armchairs could be a little too hard for real comfort.

The other type of Capricornian room is very different, and although still not geared to comfort or luxury will be designed manifestly to *impress*. Instead of plain wood, there will be a prevalence of highly-polished oak or mahogany; the chairs are likely to be real leather (very shiny, with plenty of brass studs), and there may well be a kind of nineteenth-century atmosphere (from the earlier period before people's tastes became somewhat overblown and heavy). The carpet will have a traditional Turkish or Chinese design; there will be plenty of expensive pottery, perhaps in black glaze, and many generally agreeable-looking objects about the room—of the sort others may admire but not necessarily have in their own home. There may be lovely traditional cut-glass bowls; and the whole atmosphere will strongly reflect the kind of respectability that Capricornians seek to acquire for themselves.

It is in his own home that the Capricornian will show the world—and constantly remind himself in the process—that he really is a pillar of society. The heavy curtains and drapes will echo this attitude; browns, greys and black are Capricorn's favourite colours. It is, by the way, always advisable when visiting a Capricornian to take an additional sweater; they are chilly creatures and do not like heat. There may be draughts and the heating will be turned low.

The Capricornian's choice of paintings spans both goat-types. While the prosperous, ambitious man will inevitably collect a group of alleged family portraits, the less aspiring members of the sign are inclined to try to do the same! There may be portraits by Dutch artists of grimly respectable citizens, wearing black suits and dresses with impeccable white ruffs, staring down at the room. Eighteenth-century Dutch landscapes will also feature. There may be flower-pieces or, in a more modern style, abstract paintings by Mondrian. The Capricornian will also favour pictures in which castles or cathedrals form part of the composition.

The music greeting the visitor on his arrival will be fairly stark: Beethoven's late string quartets are not an impossibility if the Capricornian in question likes classical music; or he may prefer pop songs which make a social point, or describe the harsh realities of life.

DINNER WITH CAPRICORN

Entertaining with Your Sun-sign

THE HOST

The Capricorn host will probably have spent the whole week planning his dinner party. With great deliberation he will work out precisely what to give his guests and precisely how they will relate to each other; then he will plod determinedly forward, doing all the shopping, preparing the food and cooking it. On the night he will serve the meal methodically and carefully, and be out of his mind with fury and frustration if anything goes wrong. The evening may be a little bit like hard work, for Capricornians are not always easy to communicate with; guests may even begin to worry because it seems as though their host has simply become a sort of waiter-cum-chef, while they are having all the fun. But don't worry: that's Capricorn for you.

THE GUEST

When you invite your Capricornian guest, you should remember that it is sometimes difficult to tell when he is enjoying himself, such is the staid exterior he likes to preserve—even once he has settled and begun to relax and respond to the company around him. He will arrive on time, having worked out his route several weeks in advance. He will expect a methodical evening, starting with sherry and working through an orthodox menu item by item, finishing with coffee. The temptation to worry him by serving the fish after the sweet may wickedly cross your mind; but resist it! And do not worry too much if he spends the evening apparently plunged in depression. The solution is simply that he *is* in a state of depression; and when a Capricornian is depressed, all the dinner parties in the world will not snap him out of it!

THE SETTING

Rather sombre colours appeal to Capricorn: he is not, however, the sort to bother a great deal about table decorations, though an arrangement featuring shades of dark green will probably appeal to him. His kind of music is stark and decidedly not the sort to enliven an evening; if you are the host and Capricorn is your guest, it will probably be best to play what *you* like!

WINES

The host choosing wines for a Capricorn should concentrate on those that are a little dry and uncompromising. Perhaps a bottle of Muscadet, dry to the point of sharpness, would suit his tastes.

An all-star evening for famous Capricornians of past and present would very likely include the illustrious guests in our picture. For details of the dishes on the table—every one a Capricornian favourite—turn to page 180.

Mohammed Ali

Marlene Dietrich

Sir Isaac Newton

RECIPES FOR CAPRICORN

Cooking with Astrology

Instinctively taking his proper place at the table, the Capricorn will approve a meal properly served, in the traditional manner, fish following soup and cheese following sweet. He will be discriminating, elegant, but not over-ostentatious, simple but 'gracious'. Mushroom soup is simple enough, but will appeal to him both because of its grey-brownish colour (just plain dull to the rest of us), and because it originated in a plant springing from the Capricornian element—earth. Lamb chops, generally inexpensive, will frankly appeal to the Capricornian's sense of economy: but he will take trouble in cooking them, for he would not want to be accused of meanness! Fillet of pork, also fairly inexpensive, takes on a notably distinguished air in the recipe given, and with the pineapples and kirsch the Capricornian will, at moderate expense, be able to provide a centrepiece for his dessert table worthy of a royal banquet—and send his guests from his table impressed with the distinction of his taste! You will get a rather formal letter of thanks: 'a few words' acknowledging an enjoyable evening will be all you will receive.

'I eat merely to put food out of my mind.' N. F. Simpson, 1919–.

MUSHROOM SOUP
Simplicity itself, and Capricorn will love it! Simply take $2\frac{1}{2}$ cups sliced mushrooms and drop them into $2\frac{1}{2}$ cups boiling stock. Simmer for 30 minutes. Allow to cool slightly, then blend to a purée. Add $1\frac{1}{4}$ cups milk and/or some cream, salt and pepper to taste. Serve.

STUFFED EGGS
The good thing about eggs is that you can stuff them with almost anything—having, of course, cooked them first, which you do by boiling them for 10 minutes, and peeling them under running cold water. Slice in half lengthwise, remove yolk from white and combine it with, say, chopped anchovy fillets. Replace it in the hollow in the whites. Or you could use, perhaps, a mixture of chopped fried mushrooms and onions, combined with the yolk (in which case, serve hot).

LAMB CHOPS
Why include a recipe for broiling lamb chops? Ah, but they can be improved no end, especially when it is getting on in the season and they are losing that early, succulent flavour. For instance, having seasoned them with salt and pepper, add a couple of finely crumbled bay leaves and some chopped garlic; pour over 6 tablespoons each olive oil and dry white wine or vinegar, and just let them lie there for 2 or 3 hours, turning them when you think of it. Get your broiler really hot before you place chops under it; then broil for about 3 minutes on each side, longer if you prefer meat well done. You can add chopped mint and grated lemon rind to the marinade for additional flavour.

PORK TENDERLOIN WITH SAGE
With a sharp knife, make slits along the length of the pork tenderloin say at 2-inch intervals, and push in little pieces of sage leaf. Season with salt and pepper, and add a little thyme and a small bay leaf. Sprinkle with a little olive oil and allow to stand for a while—in fact, for about 12 hours. Transfer pork to an ovenproof casserole; add 6 tablespoons each olive oil and water, together with some crushed garlic (to taste; but as much as 3 cloves if you like it). Roast in a slow oven until pork is done: say 40 minutes?

PINEAPPLES WITH KIRSCH
A decorative and enjoyable dessert. Cut your pineapple(s) in half lengthwise and scoop out the flesh; a tricky business if you are not to puncture the outside shell, which you are *not* to do! Sprinkle insides of shells with a little confectioners' sugar and leave in the refrigerator until required. Meanwhile, mash up flesh of pineapple(s) with a large fork. Add some canned pineapple juice, a little water, about $1\frac{1}{3}$ cups sugar and the grated rind of 1 lemon. Bring to a boil and boil for 5 minutes; then sieve, pour into ice trays and freeze in the freezing compartment of the refrigerator, turned up to its highest setting, i.e. lowest temperature. (Let it all cool before you put it in the freezing compartment, or the refrigerator will have a nervous breakdown.)

When mixture has frozen to the consistency of wet snow, fold in $1\frac{1}{4}$ cups heavy cream, whipped, and flavour to taste with one or two tablespoons of kirsch. To give a pleasant 'edge', add the juice of $\frac{1}{2}$ lemon to the mixture before freezing. Then complete freezing. Serve this pineapple ice cream in chilled pineapple shells. As an exotic alternative, fill out the scooped pineapple with a pulp of thinly sliced pineapple flesh, strawberries, peaches, apricots, fresh blanched almonds and all kinds of fruit steeped in kirsch and castor sugar. Fruits of the earth for the Capricornian!

AQUARIUS
20 JANUARY–19 FEBRUARY

Aquarius is the eleventh sign of the Zodiac. This is the sign of the independent one, sometimes aloof but also the most humanitarian of all the signs—and the most friendly, too. Although he is represented by the Water Carrier, the Aquarian's element is air. He is attracted to all that is new, scientific and futuristic, and is thus linked with air waves and also with radio waves. His ruling planet is unconventional Uranus. The Aquarian quality is fixed, and although he may be ahead of his time, his opinions, once formed, are adhered to with surprising rigidity. The modern metal of the sign is uranium; and a scientific theme is echoed in the Aquarian colour—electric blue. His stone is the amethyst.

YOUR SUN-SIGN CHARACTER
The Zodiacal Self Revealed

It is true that of all the signs Aquarius ranks as the individualist of the Zodiac, but what pleasant qualities he bestows on his subjects. Aquarians are the world's benefactors in the broadest sense. They have an abundance of humanitarian qualities and often they themselves simply do not realize just how much they are contributing to the general good of the human race.

They are nearly always unconventional people. Although kind, generous and friendly (and always helpful) they never seem really emotionally involved in any of their 'good works'. An Aquarian, on being praised for some act of kindness, may well receive such praise with surprise—almost as though he had had no hand in the matter. His reaction may then be: 'Oh, well, it was the obvious thing to do'. And he will go on to his next charitable act quite unconcernedly, in his usual independent and perhaps rather aloof way.

NEED FOR INDEPENDENCE
The Aquarian must have his independence, and at times he should be careful to guard against becoming lonely. If he is unmarried, for instance, he will tend to live in a small apartment, alone rather than sharing with other people or even with one other person. But if circumstances are such that he *has* to live with others, he will not be all that good at mixing in with the rest of the community. One result may be that he will arrange his life so that he is only ever in the kitchen when the others are out of it! This is part and parcel of the Aquarian's psychological make-up; he is at his best when left alone, and that is the life he often chooses for himself. Others can rely on him if he is needed, however; and probably they will not have to ask for help—he will instinctively know both when to stay clear and when to intervene.

CRANKY AT TIMES
Perhaps the most notable Aquarian failing is eccentricity. In a mild form, this can be endearing and sometimes very amusing; but at times Aquarians can be somewhat excessive, and there may be crankiness and even perversity. This can make an Aquarian difficult to deal with; what is more, he may become extremely unpredictable. His reactions to situations and statements made by others can vary enormously: sometimes he will agree, sometimes he will not only disagree but will come out with opinions of his own that are so wild that his listener may be quite put out and simply not know how he stands with him. Such instances are proof of his need consciously to control his eccentric tendencies. But the Aquarian will not find this easy, because much of it is merely fun to him and helps to make his life interesting: often, indeed, the shocked reactions of others afford him great amusement.

AQUARIUS IN ACTION

Mind and Body: You and Your Life Style

Others may find it difficult to make real contact with the Aquarian, whose independent outlook and natural detachment may create psychological barriers. Aquarians need to establish a sense of 'space' around them and outsiders are thus required to keep their distance. They for their part should respect the Aquarian's wishes and not try to probe too deeply into the recesses of his personality.

The Aquarian can be something of an enigma. Extremely modern in outlook, his is the most far-sighted of signs; but he can at the same time be enormously stubborn and fixed in his views. Once he has formed an opinion, he will not be easily persuaded to change it. It is not that he is irrational; he will listen to other people's arguments. Nevertheless he may have little intention of altering his views. If he is given advice, occasionally he will react in a precisely opposite manner. Those who are canny, and know their Aquarian well, will give advice which is the opposite of what they really feel in the hope that perversity will drive the Aquarian along the desired path. This has its dangers, of course! But perversity is so strong in many Aquarians that it can almost be taken for granted. They, in fact, are often the 'only ones in step'. However, except in extreme cases the excellent humane qualities of Aquarius shine brightly, and while he may show comparatively little real warmth, he has much to offer in terms of natural friendliness and kindness.

AHEAD OF HIS TIME

In some respects, those who live under the aegis of other signs may envy the Aquarian his style of living. In his unconventional way he will dare actually to do things that others may only dream about—and, furthermore, he will do them in an unconventional manner. Many people would like to express themselves in a 'modern' way, have unconventional relationships and live a free, uncluttered life but are simply nervous of doing so. The Aquarian, on the other hand, tends to be ahead of his time; at present, for instance, many are already in spirit living in the twenty-first century!

There is so much talk of the new Age of Aquarius that many Aquarians are inclined to think that they somehow are a chosen people. They are not. The Age of Aquarius is concerned with an astronomical event, which arises because of complexities in the earth's motion. No-one knows precisely when a new 'Age' will start; especially at close range, it is impossible to tell. In astrology each Age is seen as one month in a cycle called the Great Year, and each is thought to confer a particular spirit on the period of time it covers. An Age lasts for approximately 2,500 years, and humanity is currently at the changeover point between the Age of Pisces—in which events on earth have been dominated

by the rise of Christianity—and the Age of Aquarius, heralded as the new dawn of scientific expansion, when humanitarian movements will reach new peaks. But it is, of course, important to remember that the Age of Aquarius is a *universal* phenomenon and will not affect individual Aquarians either more or less than Pisceans, Leos or any other sign.

DISTRUST OF EMOTIONS

The Aquarian thinks clearly and concisely, not caring one jot what other people think, either of himself or his opinions. He will ignore others, and carry on in his own independent way. He is both rational and intuitive, and usually broad-minded—though not broad-minded in the usual mildly permissive yet conformist sense of the word. The Aquarian will have thought out exactly how *he* stands in matters of behaviour, and simply will not care about other people's thoughts or activities. He will be indifferent about local gossip and show little interest in his neighbours' private lives.

Generally speaking, the Aquarian mind is scientific; his approach to his own problems is scientific, too. He will look at them analytically, and he can be quite harsh with himself for misjudging a particular situation. He is often far more stable than he may seem.

Aquarius figures low down on the emotional scale. And even if an Aquarian is uncharacteristically emotional he will probably despise this trait in himself, and try hard to rationalize his feelings: not exactly hiding them, but trying hard to be objective, to stand outside himself and find some reason why he is moved to tears —he, an Aquarian, weeping, how ridiculous! Or so he will think. The contrast between his rational distrust of emotions and his own natural feelings can obviously be a source of conflict.

SCIENCE FICTION MIND

Despite his occasionally clinical attitude, the Aquarian does not lack imagination; indeed, he has it in plenty— but it is a sharp, clear-cut imagination, not woolly or sentimental. If he is a writer—and a great number of Aquarians do write—he will want to deal with pressing humanitarian problems, and will use his imagination to give additional depth to known facts. His imagination should blossom in the realm of science fiction, for instance, where man steps into remote areas of time— either in the future or the past. Both these areas will be a great source of inspiration to him, as will anything savouring of the unusual or the unconventional.

The Aquarian should be wary of nervous tension in himself. This can cause a tendency to be 'brittle', and may be related to his habit of self-analysis. The Aquarian's sense of independence may make it difficult for him to confide in friends.

EMOTIONAL RELATIONSHIPS

Couples: How You Compare in Friendship, Love and Marriage

AQUARIUS IN LOVE

It may be difficult for an Aquarian to fall deeply in love. He is naturally a friendly person, but tends to prefer many ties of friendship—with people of both sexes—to a single deep emotional involvement. However, once he has been charmed to the point of thinking of love in emotional terms, he will concentrate his attentions and will also be extremely faithful.

He is something of an innovator, and will like to experiment in his love-making; but, even when deeply in love, he retains some element of his 'distant' self, holding on to his independence; a sensible partner will recognize his needs.

Aquarians have a great magnetic attraction, and may be surrounded by idolizing admirers prepared to

sacrifice their hearts for the sake of an occasional glance from their admired one. The Aquarian will of course be sublimely unaware of this. He may not in himself be aloof, but he will give that impression through his tendency to be preoccupied. This gives him a kind of film-star glamour, dynamic and with an added air of 'touch me not'.

AQUARIUS THE FRIEND

Of all the signs, Aquarius has the highest reputation for being 'friendly'. And he is, indeed, a very good friend to have—always ready to give a helping hand, and to look at other people's problems. And, what is more, he will probably see them in a totally fresh light, and be able to propose entirely new solutions.

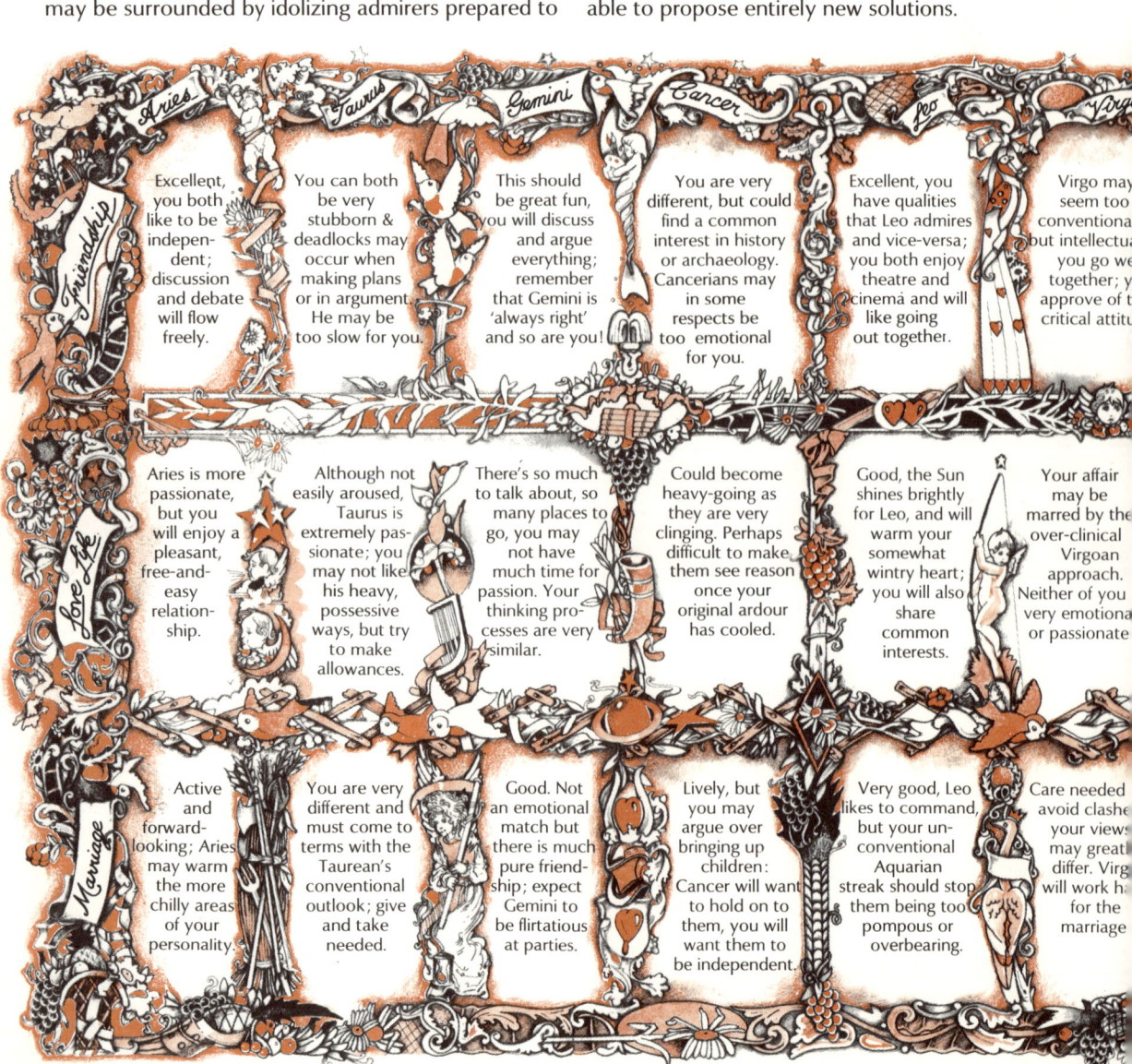

Aries

Friendship: Excellent, you both like to be independent; discussion and debate will flow freely.

Love Life: Aries is more passionate, but you will enjoy a pleasant, free-and-easy relationship.

Marriage: Active and forward-looking; Aries may warm the more chilly areas of your personality.

Taurus

Friendship: You can both be very stubborn & deadlocks may occur when making plans or in argument. He may be too slow for you.

Love Life: Although not easily aroused, Taurus is extremely passionate; you may not like his heavy, possessive ways, but try to make allowances.

Marriage: You are very different and must come to terms with the Taurean's conventional outlook; give and take needed.

Gemini

Friendship: This should be great fun, you will discuss and argue everything; remember that Gemini is 'always right' and so are you!

Love Life: There's so much to talk about, so many places to go, you may not have much time for passion. Your thinking processes are very similar.

Marriage: Good. Not an emotional match but there is much pure friendship; expect Gemini to be flirtatious at parties.

Cancer

Friendship: You are very different, but could find a common interest in history or archaeology. Cancerians may in some respects be too emotional for you.

Love Life: Could become heavy-going as they are very clinging. Perhaps difficult to make them see reason once your original ardour has cooled.

Marriage: Lively, but you may argue over bringing up children; Cancer will want to hold on to them, you will want them to be independent.

Leo

Friendship: Excellent, you have qualities that Leo admires and vice-versa; you both enjoy theatre and cinema and will like going out together.

Love Life: Good, the Sun shines brightly for Leo, and will warm your somewhat wintry heart; you will also share common interests.

Marriage: Very good, Leo likes to command, but your unconventional Aquarian streak should stop them being too pompous or overbearing.

Virgo

Friendship: Virgo may seem too conventional but intellectually you go well together; you approve of their critical attitude.

Love Life: Your affair may be marred by the over-clinical Virgoan approach. Neither of you very emotional or passionate.

Marriage: Care needed to avoid clashes; your views may greatly differ. Virgo will work hard for the marriage.

Aquarians are often the king-pins of clubs and societies, or any gatherings where people are brought together through a mutual interest. They like to be 'friends to all', and are at their best when spreading themselves around, sharing their talents among large groups of acquaintances.

AQUARIUS IN MARRIAGE

It is sometimes the case that marriage, for the Aquarian, is not the easiest sphere of life; he needs, perhaps more than anyone else, a partner who will understand his strongly individual character. It must be recognized that the Aquarian is extremely independent and cannot bear possessiveness. At times he tends to be eccentric and unpredictable – something his partner must learn

to cope with, preferably regarding it as a challenge. These characteristics are very much part of the Aquarian's psychological make-up, and although they can and should be controlled, they cannot be completely quashed. The partner should, in any event, be an understanding type of person. All the same, Aquarians can be great fun and, once committed to a partnership, are extremely loyal and faithful; commitment is likely to be a far more serious matter for them than it is for many others.

Below: Use this Friends and Lovers Sun-sign chart to check how Aquarius is likely to make out with others in friendship, love and marriage. Relationships are listed from left to right, Aquarius to Aries, Aquarius to Taurus, etc., and from top to bottom in friendship, love and marriage.

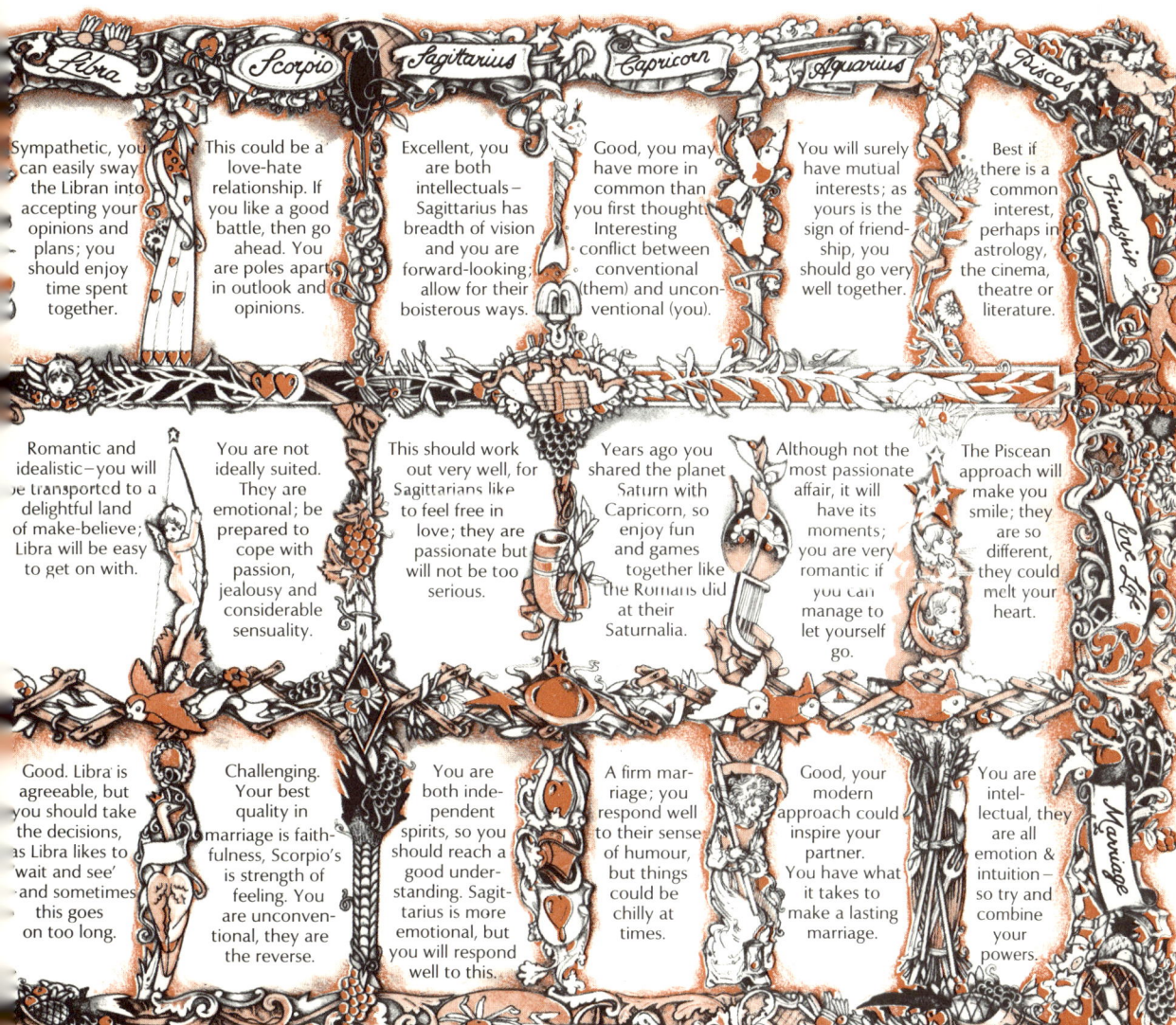

	Libra	Scorpio	Sagittarius	Capricorn	Aquarius	Pisces
Friendship	Sympathetic, you can easily sway the Libran into accepting your opinions and plans; you should enjoy time spent together.	This could be a love-hate relationship. If you like a good battle, then go ahead. You are poles apart in outlook and opinions.	Excellent, you are both intellectuals – Sagittarius has breadth of vision and you are forward-looking; allow for their boisterous ways.	Good, you may have more in common than you first thought. Interesting conflict between conventional (them) and unconventional (you).	You will surely have mutual interests; as yours is the sign of friendship, you should go very well together.	Best if there is a common interest, perhaps in astrology, the cinema, theatre or literature.
Love Life	Romantic and idealistic – you will be transported to a delightful land of make-believe; Libra will be easy to get on with.	You are not ideally suited. They are emotional; be prepared to cope with passion, jealousy and considerable sensuality.	This should work out very well, for Sagittarians like to feel free in love; they are passionate but will not be too serious.	Years ago you shared the planet Saturn with Capricorn, so enjoy fun and games together like the Romans did at their Saturnalia.	Although not the most passionate affair, it will have its moments; you are very romantic if you can manage to let yourself go.	The Piscean approach will make you smile; they are so different, they could melt your heart.
Marriage	Good. Libra is agreeable, but you should take the decisions, as Libra likes to 'wait and see' – and sometimes this goes on too long.	Challenging. Your best quality in marriage is faithfulness, Scorpio's is strength of feeling. You are unconventional, they are the reverse.	You are both independent spirits, so you should reach a good understanding. Sagittarius is more emotional, but you will respond well to this.	A firm marriage; you respond well to their sense of humour, but things could be chilly at times.	Good, your modern approach could inspire your partner. You have what it takes to make a lasting marriage.	You are intellectual, they are all emotion & intuition – so try and combine your powers.

187

PARENTS AND CHILDREN

The Zodiac Family Portrait

THE AQUARIAN FATHER

The Aquarian father will, in his role as parent—as in every sphere of his life—have an advanced outlook. He will want at all times to keep up with, and indeed ahead of his children's ideas, preoccupations and interests. When they are very small he will be fascinated by, for instance, the way they are being taught at school; he will not want to lag behind in his understanding of new teaching techniques. He is the person least likely to say, 'We didn't do it that way when *I* was at school'. It would make him blush even to *think* that way.

As his children grow up, he should have no difficulty in bridging the generation gap; but he will need to be just a little careful, to make sure that he does not at times overstep the mark, and perhaps forget the inhibitions, difficulties and problems of adolescence in his eagerness to appear on the same wavelength. His advanced outlook may also lead him to dictate what he feels his children *should* do. In such cases he may try to make them grow up too quickly—a temptation that he should use his far-sighted powers to recognize and then resist.

THE AQUARIAN MOTHER

The Aquarian mother will be a great friend to her children, and will encourage them to be very independent and to live their own lives in their own individual ways. Her impartial outlook will help her to recognize that their lives may be very different to her own. However, she should in some respects look to herself for, although friendly, she may be just a little cool and not an especially loving or affectionate mother. If she is not careful, she could put a 'distance' between herself and her children.

She is unemotional, but if she has an emotional child, she will have to fight some inner battles. She will probably come to realize that it is not *wrong* to be emotional or to express personal feelings with force; but she will find it difficult to come to terms with any such tendency. However, she will be rational, and must bring this quality into play when dealing with the sort of child who is essentially all smiles one minute and all tears the next. It is possible that she will be inclined to favour a boarding-school education; but she must also

consider this from the children's point of view and not purely because she wants them, like herself, to be independent.

THE AQUARIAN CHILD

The Aquarian child is an individualist. He will hate to conform and will probably loathe discipline—especially the more trivial rules at school. However, he has a logical mind and may well play his part in reforming such rules; indeed, it is essential that he has teachers who will listen to him—he could well teach them a thing or two! It is important for parents to accept that when the Aquarian child is unhappy or unfriendly towards his parents or brothers and sisters, it is more than likely that someone is cramping his style. He himself has such an original style that others may well not feel inclined to fall in with his ideas; this is something he will have to recognize and learn to tolerate. More conventional people may well be irritated or find him unacceptable; and if he comes across a particularly crusty teacher at school a stormy period could well follow.

He can be surprisingly stubborn: this will emerge when he feels he wants to be 'different' (these can be difficult moments for the parents of an Aquarian child). However, in spite of his stubbornness, he has a lively mind which it should not be difficult to stimulate; and the more he can be encouraged to involve himself in activities outside school hours, the better. The Aquarian girl will love dancing lessons, and both sexes will probably enjoy drama classes. Their best subjects may well be scientific, and if they have an opportunity to look through a large telescope or go on a dinosaur dig, they will be completely in their element.

Basically the Aquarian child is unemotional and to some people he may seem a little distant and chilly—indeed he can be so, but he is friendly and can usually overcome any lack of warmth. While considering his low emotional level one should also remember the extremely powerful humanitarian spirit in every Aquarian; it is not difficult to encourage him to be kind to old people, for instance, or to raise money for charity and generally help to make the world a better place.

CAREERS AND PASTIMES

A Sun-sign Guide to Work and Play

It is essential for the Aquarian, in choosing his career, to consider professions where his inventiveness, originality and independence are fully expressed. He is not suited to a dreary, monotonous routine that gives him no scope to express his powerful individual traits.

This does not mean, though, that the Aquarian will not do a dull job; if circumstances compel, he will try his best. But he will have to find plenty of spare-time interests to take himself out of the daily routine and to make his life interesting and adequately balanced. It will be unfortunate if he is forced into restrictive work; too many of his natural talents will lie dormant, and, quite apart from the loss to the community as a whole, such work could become a psychological burden for him, possibly driving him towards eccentricity.

SOCIAL REFORMERS

Many Aquarians feel an instinctive need to try and set right some of the injustices—either social or political—to be found in the world, and will therefore be highly suited to work in such international organizations as UNICEF. Administrative or field work for a big charity will admirably suit their inclinations, too. Many Aquarians are social workers: this is also an excellent choice of career and a positive outlet for their strong reforming spirit.

Aquarians tend to walk off with splendid scientific degrees, and should obviously continue such work in their careers, preferably adhering to the specialist field in which they originally qualified. This will enable them to extend their knowledge and so increase its usefulness for the rest of mankind. The image often conjured up by Aquarius is that of an eccentric scientist, hair on end, glowering over bubbling retorts and their weird contents. This is not in reality too far from the mark. Aquarians really do love things that are strange and different, and if it is possible to incorporate this tendency into a career, so much the better!

The theatre, films and literature seem to be the artistic media for Aquarians, and many do well in these

spheres. Astronomy also fits the Aquarian very well—as indeed does astrology, to which the sign is strongly suited. Aquarians therefore tend to figure prominently in the ranks of astrological groups and societies.

AERIAL SPECIALISTS

The 'element' of Aquarius is air; it is fascinating to see how strongly this element makes its presence felt in the Aquarian's choice of career. Aquarian technicians abound in the professions of broadcasting and television; many, too, become airline pilots and air hostesses.

A good guideline for the Aquarian on the verge of choosing a career or profession is to remember that if he is at all attracted to anything concerned with the deep past or the equally remote future, he should follow this up; both these areas are naturally 'right' for him. Whatever form his particular interest may take, he should settle extremely well if it has connections with either the past or the future.

The twin themes of deep past and remote future are echoed in the possible choice of hobbies and pastimes for the Aquarian. He could well become an enthusiastic amateur astronomer, or an avid reader—or writer—of science fiction. Archaeology, too, is a big favourite among Aquarians. Coming nearer to our own time, we often find that Aquarians develop an interest in machinery—this is perhaps in alignment with their natural imaginative streak, for they often invent gadgets purely for fun. Many Aquarians love veteran cars and, if they can afford to own one, derive enormous pleasure from making spare parts for it. Generally speaking, Aquarians are clever, and usually demand a high standard in whatever they do.

The Aquarian will probably like rather light sports, as opposed to heavy team games. Gliding and flying will be the aim of many; but they may also be excellent at tennis, squash, or any game savouring of the slightly unusual or the archaic; such a game would be croquet.

AT HOME

A Sun-sign Guide to Home Décor

Whatever the style of the Aquarian's room, it will not be ordinary or commonplace. It will inevitably reflect elements of his unusual personality, and more than likely will be very modern indeed. The Aquarian should in fact be careful that he does not choose furniture that is so wildly of the moment that it will look silly all too soon; once having 'set' his room, he may be reluctant to change it. However, he generally has good taste, and should be able to use this when the time comes to make a home for himself.

Very often white, as well as the much-loved turquoise ('Aquarius blue', as it is now often called) will tend to predominate. There is also likely to be a predominance of glass—perhaps a glass table, or some clear perspex chairs. Mirrors will also feature. If the Aquarian is young and cannot afford opulent designs, he may instead choose inexpensive inflatable chairs; or, as decoration, clear plastic cushions. There may well be pleasant, shaggy wool rugs on the floor—in fabric form rather than sheepskins, for the Aquarian will not like the idea of having an animal skin in his own domestic environment.

DRIFTWOOD SCULPTURE
There are also likely to be some unusual ornaments: perhaps a piece of abstract sculpture, if the Aquarian is comfortably off; or some interesting pieces of stone, driftwood, shells or quartz if he is not. The atmosphere will be rather clinical, but easy on the eye. The Aquarian will make a great feature of his lighting arrangements; these will probably be dramatically arranged, so that the sources of light are unobtrusive and are used to the best possible effect. Not for him fussy, frilly table lamps with bits and bobbles on every conceivable corner. He will choose plain, functional, unobtrusive lights which stand quietly in corners and blend with the rest of the extremely modern setting.

TOMORROW'S ART
The visitor to an Aquarian home will tend to be particularly fascinated by his choice of paintings, which will more than likely be as modern as tomorrow. Jackson Pollock will be an Old Master to the Aquarian; he will delight in the work of young, vigorous, probably as yet unknown artists; perhaps he will have an artist friend who will lend his latest works for the walls. However, the past will also be present: we may find reproductions of Egyptian paintings and old star maps alongside more recent works by Léger, Klee and Camille Pissarro (especially the snow scenes) as well as timeless Old Master drawings.

There is no doubt that the visitor will receive a splendid welcome—possibly to the strains of the latest avant-garde music from the record player; the music may be progressive jazz or pop . . . but whatever it is, it will certainly sound *interesting*!

DINNER WITH AQUARIUS

Entertaining with Your Sun-sign

THE AQUARIAN HOST

Aquarian dinner parties may tend to be rather formal, and his passion for originality may perhaps lead him into culinary experiments which you (possibly even he) may regret. If he is involved in one of his 'causes', this may be another complication: being served with a crust of bread and a glass of water, and a note asking for contributions to the latest famine relief fund may be very worthy, but on the whole perhaps does not lead to the most enjoyable of evenings.

If Aquarius is a vegetarian, he will be one to the point of crankiness, having read and completely believed all the latest theories on diet, some of them extremely eccentric: for example, reporting conclusively that cabbages emit an audible squeak of rage at the moment they are placed in boiling water. And if you think that is an exaggeration, you may nevertheless find it worth your while to make inquiries if you are invited out by an Aquarian; then an alternative engagement can be invented if the evening promises to be too much like hard work.

THE AQUARIAN GUEST

Similarly, you may find your Aquarian guest refusing potatoes on the grounds that if the starving peoples of Asia cannot eat them, then he should not. All this will be very kindly and sympathetically conveyed, for the Aquarian will not want to hurt anyone's feelings. He may also tend to arrive half an hour too late for dinner, having forgotten to plan his journey or because he has made some critical miscalculation en route. Absent-mindedness may affect him as cook or consumer.

THE SETTING

The Aquarian probably will not take too much notice of how a dining-table is decorated, except that he will not like anything too luxurious. He himself will favour a quiet kind of elegance, with shades of electric blue featured somewhere about the table, if that can be con-trived. His choice of music may be for something 'up-lifting': perhaps not the *Hallelujah Chorus* but, equally, nothing too 'lightweight' either.

WINES

Something unconventional and unusual in the way of wine may intrigue the Aquarians, perhaps Retsina, or even a home-made wine—though this is an area that calls for a thoughtful choice, rather than a wild or wilfully eccentric stab in the dark.

Right: An all-star evening for famous Aquarians of past and present would very likely include the illustrious guests in our picture. For details of the dishes on the table—every one an Aquarian favourite—turn to page 194.

Franklin D. Roosevelt

Abraham Lincoln

Charles Dickens

Clark Gable

Lord Byron

Jeanne Moreau

RECIPES FOR AQUARIUS

Cooking with Astrology

If an Aquarius looks glum during a meal, it will be because he feels he ought to be eating bread and cheese and sending the money saved to Oxfam; he may feel inhibited from second helpings. Where Aquarius is concerned, something light but also 'different' is essential, so watercress soup is probably excellent; this is one of the air signs, but an air soup would probably be too insubstantial even for a high-minded Aquarian! The trendy Aquarian will sit up at the sight of the delicious chicken and cucumber recipe, which he is unlikely to have tasted before. He will appreciate its elegance and the delicate flavour. By much the same argument, we recommend the veal dish while, for an air sign, a soufflé could scarcely be bettered; and the Aquarian loves citrus fruit, hence the lemon flavour, though orange will do equally well. The Aquarian will go out of his way to find an original little gift to acknowledge his evening: you will be surprised and pleased by the personalised distinction of his choice.

WATERCRESS SOUP

A delightful and unusual chilled soup: slice 2 large leeks and 4 peeled potatoes, and simmer until soft in 2 pints chicken stock. Blend to a purée or rub through a sieve. Add salt and pepper to taste; chill. Meanwhile, clean and chop finely 1 or 2 bunches watercress. Just before serving, stir watercress into soup, together with $\frac{1}{2}$ pint double cream.

SMALL STUFFED ROLLS

More trouble than the soup, but worth it. Buy enough small soft 'bridge' rolls to give your guests two each. Either cut the ends off and hollow out center, or cut them in two and scoop out center, taking care not to break cases. Shred bread center and combine with 2 smoked sausages (garlic if you like), finely chopped, and $\frac{1}{4}$ cup finely chopped ham. Place in a pan, pour over 4 to 5 tablespoons each milk and cream, and stir to a mush over a low heat. Season with salt and pepper, and continue to stir over a low heat until thoroughly warmed through. Fill rolls with this mixture and heat through in a slow oven. A little cognac or sherry may be stirred into the mixture before you stuff the rolls.

CHICKEN AND CUCUMBER

Brown a chicken all over in butter; transfer to a large pan, breast down, with $\frac{1}{4}$ pint each chicken stock and dry white wine, and a bouquet garni. Cover tightly and simmer for 45 minutes, or until tender. Meanwhile, peel a large cucumber, remove seeds and cut flesh into matchstick strips. Drop into boiling water, bring to a boil again, simmer for 1 minute and remove from heat. When chicken is tender, divide into joints and keep warm. Strain stock (no more than $\frac{1}{2}$ pint) back into pan; add 4 oz sliced white mushrooms and simmer for 1 minute. Blend 1 teaspoon flour smoothly with $\frac{1}{4}$ pint single cream. Stir in a little hot stock; season; mix well and blend with remaining stock. Simmer until thickened; add cucumber sticks and simmer for a minute or two longer. Arrange chicken joints on a heated dish; pour over sauce; garnish with chopped chives and serve.

'Alcohol is a food well in advance of modern medical thought.'
P. G. Wodehouse, 1881–.

VEAL ALLA MARSALA

Buy boned veal cutlet or escalopes and pound them out very thinly. Allow about 6 oz per person. Cut veal into little medallions about 2 inches square, and dust with seasoned flour. In a large frying pan, heat plenty of butter and gently fry medallions until golden on both sides, and tender but still moist. Add 1 to 2 tablespoons Marsala and 2 to 4 tablespoons chicken stock to the pan. Simmer, stirring, until this sauce has thickened. Serve at once. (We can now reveal that we have on one or two occasions made this veal dish with sweet sherry and no one noticed the difference. With such relaxing friends a chef can afford to wander somewhat from the straight and narrow columns of the recipe book and improvise a little!)

LEMON SOUFFLÉ

Beat 6 egg yolks thoroghly with 6 oz caster sugar, the juice of 1 or 2 lemons and the finely grated rind of 1 lemon. When mixture is white and fluffy, transfer to the top of a double saucepan (or a bowl which fits snugly over a pan of water) and stir over hot water until thickened. Do not allow it to boil, though, or egg yolks will curdle. Allow to cool to lukewarm before folding in 6 egg whites, stiffly beaten. Add 2 tablespoons gelatine, softened and dissolved in $\frac{1}{4}$ pint water, folding it in lightly but thoroghly. Pour mixture into individual dishes and chill until set. All being well you have made it—the air dish to end them all. Aquarians should fly from miles around just for the thrill of a spoonful!

PISCES
20 FEBRUARY—20 MARCH

Pisces is the sign of the poet, the dreamer, the inspired but
impractical one, whose nature leads him to feel
simultaneously swayed by opposing forces. Piscean's quality is
mutable, which makes him essentially adaptable; his element,
naturally, could be nothing but water. Fishes apart, here is
flexibility; there may be instability and uncertainty.
Pisces offers all or nothing—divine, blessed humility or
confused, deceitful nothingness. The colours of the sign are
all the shades of sea-green, and the Piscean metal is tin—
the metal of Jupiter, from ancient times the sign's ruling planet.
However, we now have the modern planet Neptune (the
sea-god himself) ruling this enigmatic sign. Piscean stones
are the mysterious bloodstone and the beautiful,
diffuse moonstone.

YOUR SUN-SIGN CHARACTER
The Zodiacal Self Revealed

The pure Piscean is the kindest, gentlest and most emotional creature on earth! One look into a pair of Piscean eyes is enough to show that tears—of joy or sorrow—are never very far away. Indeed, it is often possible to recognize a Piscean from this very feature. Other signs are emotional—some in a disruptive, deep and passionate way, others with fiery enthusiasm; but the Piscean emotion tops them all, for it is pure beyond description.

Some astrologers say that Pisces is sensation-seeking, but this could be unjust, for the Piscean is really a bundle of emotion, which simply gushes out quite naturally and without affectation. When this torrent is channelled and used artistically and creatively, the result is talent supreme—the talent of the real artist, whether a dancer, a painter or, perhaps best of all, a poet.

LIQUID EMOTION

His emotional qualities seem to represent the very essence of the Piscean, and even if he has never been positively creative, his nature is deeply imbued with the artistic spirit. It may, alas, only be expressed in flights of fancy, or, because of an all too prevalent sense of inferiority, may not be expressed at all; that would be a great pity. However, if other, stronger and more practical mortals can take a firm hold on their Piscean friend and become a mould for his liquid emotion and creativity, they will be doing him a good turn indeed. The Piscean will then develop into not only a potentially creative and artistic person, but the best 'type' of those that fall under this sign. Other qualities, such as humility and charity will then be positively expressed in a constructive way—rather than in the amorphous and confused fashion of which Pisces is also capable. Otherwise, without such outside guidance, the Piscean, lacking a practical approach and organizing ability, may work all hours of the day and night without achieving hoped-for results.

The worst Piscean fault is his tendency to misread a situation. This tendency may give him great problems if it is not somehow controlled. Self-deception is a dangerous characteristic and it is regrettably easy for the Piscean to convince himself both that he is different from the way he really is, and also that situations are not what they seem. In this the Piscean's motives may be perfectly worthy; he is capable of deluding himself whether he is in a jubilant, optimistic mood or engulfed in gloom. The fault lies not so much with self-interest as with the intensity of his moods. Whatever the truth of his situation, the Piscean is often swayed into errors by the sheer force of his emotions. He would do well in many cases to seek impartial advice—and then to follow it!

PISCES IN ACTION

Mind and Body: You and Your Life Style

The Piscean does not find it easy to obtain a clear-cut perspective on life, and he has to try very hard indeed to develop this quality; he is not, generally speaking, a well-organized person and very often his life, his love affairs and indeed his whole immediate environment are in a state of chaos! At best this may be little more than mild confusion; but often things are not so well arranged and in less happy circumstances his life may completely lack a sense of purpose.

A great Piscean gift is the ability to relieve suffering, and this can be expressed in an almost infinite number of ways, from the purely practical—through such activities as giving a helping hand to a sick neighbour—to the much more serious decision to become a member of a closed religious order, and to spend his days praying, meditating or simply sending positive thoughts to those in trouble.

FANTASY WORLD OF GNOMES

The Piscean way of helping will usually be enormously practical; no job will be too humble, no work too unpleasant or dirty, if it is directed towards the ever-present need to relieve other people's suffering or general discomfort. There is another angle to this: many Pisceans will express this facet of their personalities through entertainment and their ability to 'take people out of themselves'. They will be, for instance, very amusing, with a delicious sense of humour; and through their artistic abilities, too, they will be able to elevate their fellow mortals to their own wonderful fantasy world—the kind of world that might well be inhabited by hobbits, sylphs, gnomes or elves.

The weaker type of Piscean may tend towards escapism: the danger is greater here than in any other sign. The Piscean is one to fall back on the line of least resistance, and he will be inclined to look for easy ways out of problems. So it is important for him to try to realize that he has this proclivity. Then he can guard against it, and perhaps pull himself up sharply before it is too late. Otherwise he may drift into what for him could very well be a disaster area.

ACCENT ON FEET

The Piscean area of the body is the feet, and these are either neat and—as far as the girls are concerned—very pretty, or they are pretty ugly! But all Pisceans either have a passion for shoes or they prefer to slop around in 'canoes'. The Piscean's health can also be affected by worries—usually these are quite irrational—and Pisceans must also be extremely careful about drugs of all kinds, medically administered or otherwise. They can be allergic to drugs, and for the sake of safety they should ask for a test before accepting treatment by some new drug. Tainted water and fish-poisoning are also above-

average hazards for the Piscean to remember.

Many astrologers in the not so distant past had little that was good to say for Pisceans. This is on the whole an insensitive view, for the Piscean is splendid in many ways, and we certainly feel that his fine qualities well outnumber his weaknesses. But perhaps it is weakness itself that sums up the difficulties of Pisces. If he finds himself sunk in the pit of despair, then it is because some inhuman beast has cast him there, and it is more our duty to reclaim him, dust him down and inspire some much-needed confidence in him, than it is to sneer at his misfortune. We, moreover, will be the richer for helping him.

INTUITIVE MENTAL FLOW

It is true to say that all the 'water' signs (Cancer, Scorpio and Pisces) are extremely intuitive, but equally so that the other two fall quite a long way behind Pisces. He must not ignore his natural intuition—it is enormously basic to him and should be used to the fullest. However, Pisceans have to try to balance this quality against their irrationality, which is also very much part of the way their minds work. In some respects the one quality flows from the other, and a common phrase among Pisceans is: 'Well, I know it's quite irrational, but I feel that . . .' Often, too, what they have to say is not far wrong. This quality cuts across the sexes, and men of this sign should not feel embarrassed to admit that they possess it—even though it is often brushed aside as mere feminine intuition!

The Piscean's way of making decisions ignores logic or reason. It is not possible for him to relate A to B in an ordered way, and it is not really necessary for him to do so, for eventually he will work his way around the edge of any problems that have to be solved and will come up with the right answer. But he must guard against a tendency to go back on his word—which can be rather trying for other people. The Piscean is highly imaginative and he will have ideas in plenty; but many of these will be completely impractical. This should be pointed out to him, preferably in time to rescue him from being carried away; but even if it is too late he will eventually return to earth and the lesson will be learned. He must try to use his imagination creatively; maybe it is at this point that the poet and the artist in him should be encouraged to make their appearance.

Sometimes, Pisceans are very attracted to 'cults' and all that is psychic, mystic or just weird. They must develop a sceptical approach to such matters because, generally speaking, they can be rather gullible; so far as the more esoteric interests are concerned, Pisceans are especially vulnerable; by suddenly and perhaps prematurely deciding to embrace one such area, they could be courting disaster!

EMOTIONAL RELATIONSHIPS

Couples: How You Compare in Friendship, Love and Marriage

PISCES IN LOVE

When a Piscean falls in love, he falls extremely hard. His heart will probably be broken many times, and he will experience much pleasure and pain in this sphere of his life—probably much more so than his fellow human beings. In fact, the Piscean's life may well be centred around suffering of one sort or another, and it can be his love life that is hit hardest of all.

He is a great romantic, and his loved one will be greatly charmed, no doubt, by his delightful presents of flowers and perfumes—which he loves—and splendid evenings out; the Piscean loves life and likes to enjoy himself, so meals at intimate restaurants will certainly feature. Because he is emotional, he will both climb to the peaks and plummet to the depths when he is in love. An affair with a Piscean will certainly have its moments! It will be long remembered as a delightful experience—colourful, glamorous and essentially romantic, with a capital R.

THE PISCEAN FRIEND

When the Piscean's life collapses around him, his friends will certainly know about it. However, any help given will be returned a thousandfold, for the Piscean has a good memory and will not forget a kindness shown to him. He is easy to get on with, and—unless he is under powerful emotional stresses—undemanding. He may not be ready on time for an evening out, and it

Aries

Friendship: You will smile at his bright and breezy approach, but his extrovert enthusiasm may frighten you a little.

Love Life: You are both passionate and emotional, but you could find Aries too fast and too self-assertive as a lover.

Marriage: Recognize your wide differences, relax and build a splendidly colourful marriage together.

Taurus

Friendship: This should work out extremely well; you will enjoy discovering the slow Taurean attitude to life and should soon develop mutual interests.

Love Life: Remember that the Taurean is extremely passionate, even if he/she is slow off the mark. You should have a lot of fun and the affair will be spiced with luxury.

Marriage: Excellent, Taurus will give you security and stability which you tend to lack, try to allow for their possessive ways.

Gemini

Friendship: You should have fun, Gemini is amusing, but you may find him puzzling at times; you are likely to share an interest in music or literature.

Love Life: Don't expect a highly emotional affair; Gemini expresses himself well in love, but is very flirtatious.

Marriage: You will probably live through many changes of residence, decoration schemes, etc, look out for deeper restlessness.

Cancer

Friendship: This could be a bit 'milk and water'; pleasant, but may lack a lively rapport because you identify too easily with each other's personalities.

Love Life: Touches of real romance and high passion are both very likely. Cancer is clinging, and you may find this annoying.

Marriage: Could work out very well; you will probably make excellent parents, but the Cancerian tendency to 'snap' when annoyed may be upsetting.

Leo

Friendship: Marvellous. You are both creative, artistic and emotional, but in exactly opposite ways; Leo has much to give you and vice versa.

Love Life: Splendid, let Leo do things in his own rather grand way; this will inspire you with confidence and you should have a lovely time together.

Marriage: Good, you will have many joint interests; Leo makes an excellent 'container' for your liquid, intangible feelings (see also Friendship).

Virgo

Friendship: You are opposites, but are both kind and charitable; you will warm the rather clinical Virgo personality.

Love Life: Virgo can be brittle and difficult in love, you may find this difficult to understand. Expect criticism.

Marriage: Good, if you can blend your opposing characteristics but you are emotional and loving and Virgo tends to be co

is up to more punctual and precise mortals to allow for this. Pisceans often lack aggression and must remember that, like Cinderella, herself a sure Piscean, others may take advantage of them from time to time.

THE FACTS OF MARRIAGE

The Piscean in marriage must be very careful indeed not to let his emotions run away with him. In marriage he can be surprisingly critical, carping at his partner about small, unimportant details—though very likely regretting his rather tense and edgy words as soon as he has spoken. The Piscean is not always as stable in marriage as he might be, and it will be to his advantage if he tries to develop a fairly firm attitude to this sphere

of his life. Otherwise, he may be drawn somewhat more easily than other signs of the Zodiac into emotional relationships outside marriage. This may well be because the Piscean has a high emotional level, and also because he has a great appreciation of sheer romance and beauty. He has, however, an extremely natural gift for keeping the flame of real romance burning in marriage.

Below: Use this Friends and Lovers Sun-sign chart to check how Pisces is likely to make out with others in friendship, love and marriage. Relationships are listed from left to right, Pisces to Aries, Pisces to Taurus, etc., and from top to bottom in friendship, love and marriage.

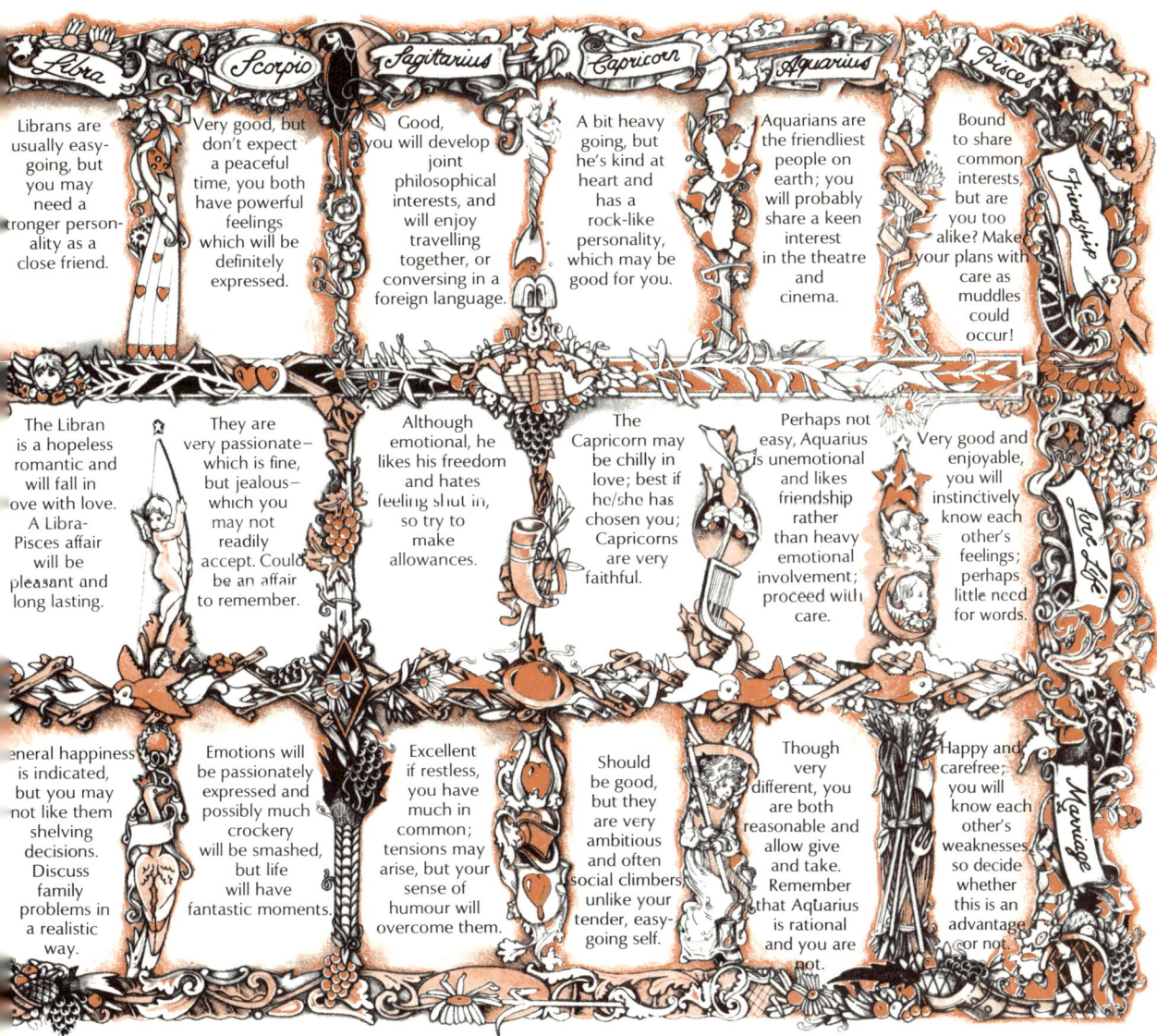

Libra / Friendship
Librans are usually easy-going, but you may need a stronger personality as a close friend.

Scorpio / Friendship
Very good, but don't expect a peaceful time, you both have powerful feelings which will be definitely expressed.

Sagittarius / Friendship
Good, you will develop joint philosophical interests, and will enjoy travelling together, or conversing in a foreign language.

Capricorn / Friendship
A bit heavy going, but he's kind at heart and has a rock-like personality, which may be good for you.

Aquarius / Friendship
Aquarians are the friendliest people on earth; you will probably share a keen interest in the theatre and cinema.

Pisces / Friendship
Bound to share common interests, but are you too alike? Make your plans with care as muddles could occur!

Libra / Love Life
The Libran is a hopeless romantic and will fall in love with love. A Libra-Pisces affair will be pleasant and long lasting.

Scorpio / Love Life
They are very passionate—which is fine, but jealous—which you may not readily accept. Could be an affair to remember.

Sagittarius / Love Life
Although emotional, he likes his freedom and hates feeling shut in, so try to make allowances.

Capricorn / Love Life
The Capricorn may be chilly in love; best if he/she has chosen you; Capricorns are very faithful.

Aquarius / Love Life
Perhaps not easy, Aquarius is unemotional and likes friendship rather than heavy emotional involvement; proceed with care.

Pisces / Love Life
Very good and enjoyable, you will instinctively know each other's feelings; perhaps little need for words.

Libra / Marriage
General happiness is indicated, but you may not like them shelving decisions. Discuss family problems in a realistic way.

Scorpio / Marriage
Emotions will be passionately expressed and possibly much crockery will be smashed, but life will have fantastic moments.

Sagittarius / Marriage
Excellent if restless, you have much in common; tensions may arise, but your sense of humour will overcome them.

Capricorn / Marriage
Should be good, but they are very ambitious and often social climbers, unlike your tender, easy-going self.

Aquarius / Marriage
Though very different, you are both reasonable and allow give and take. Remember that Aquarius is rational and you are not.

Pisces / Marriage
Happy and carefree; you will know each other's weaknesses so decide whether this is an advantage or not.

201

PARENTS AND CHILDREN

The Zodiac Family Portrait

THE PISCEAN FATHER

In many ways, the Piscean father may be an ideal person to encourage and develop his children's interests. He will very likely be involved in some form of artistic activity himself, or at least will be enthusiastic about the arts even if he is not creative, and this he will gently and easily pass on to his children.

He must, however, remember that his children may well be made of much stronger stuff than he, and may tend to take advantage of his easy-going ways. They should not find it too difficult to persuade him to see things their way; and the temptation to exploit his generosity may at times be hard to resist.

The Piscean father will also use his creative imagination in his role as parent, and may well make fine ciné-films or photograph his children with great skill and tenderness; and bedtime will be no problem, because he knows some wonderful bedtime stories.

The Piscean father is likely to be easily hurt and a trifle moody – rather than angry – when his children are naughty; perhaps in essence he recalls that strange professor of fiction who, when his boys did wrong, made them cane him, so that he bore the pain arising from their misdemeanours!

THE PISCEAN MOTHER

It is the easiest thing in the world for the Piscean mother to spoil her children. She is so kind, sensitive and emotional that she too will burst into tears if one of her little ones cries! To enforce any kind of discipline is extremely difficult for her, and she will probably avoid doing so. While this may, in some ways, be admirable, she must realize that, in the long run, the children may well suffer: when they grow up and have to face reality, this may come as a far greater shock than it would have done if they had earlier received the occasional telling-off at home.

The Piscean mother may not think it important to be tidy and systematic; but she should try to train her children to be so, because when they are older they will forever be losing clothes, books, and other possessions at school – which can be expensive as well as annoying!

She will certainly not force her own interests on her children, for that in itself would be a form of discipline;

she will fall in line with whatever direction their tastes seem to follow, and will take her lead from them – which is, of course, excellent for the developing child.

THE PISCEAN CHILD

The Piscean child is delightful in many ways: extremely kind, for instance – you won't catch him pulling the legs off a fly, or being beastly to friends. But, because of their charm, it is easy to spoil Piscean children; and while they cannot take strict discipline, they do need gentle guidance. It is not easy to appeal to them rationally, but parents should persevere – slowly and gently – until one day, perhaps unexpectedly, things will fall into place. A good way to encourage Piscean children to be a little more systematic and disciplined is to make a busy schedule for them outside school hours. Although they won't have too much time to daydream, they will then have a rhythm to their lives which will suit them.

They must be allowed to have plenty of paint and paper, and if ballet lessons, drama classes or perhaps ice-skating lessons can be afforded, the Piscean child will be eternally grateful – for both sexes love this kind of activity. They should also learn to swim early in life, and probably will be attracted to generally rather gentle occupations, perhaps growing small flowers. They will also love to take care of animals, and if at all possible should have some small pet to look after. There is an inherent love of animals in all but a very small minority of Pisceans. Visits to the zoo are obviously appreciated!

The Piscean child's imagination is something very special which must be allowed to develop freely and naturally; but it also needs careful channelling for it must not be allowed to become shapeless or negative. This is not easy for parents, but perhaps the child could be encouraged to write down any stories or even snatches of stories that he knows or has invented.

The Piscean child must be gently moulded: and if he is at all artistic, this quality must be nurtured with the greatest care. Parents should always aim to strengthen his character, and care must be taken that he is not led astray by unsuitable companions who are bullying or cruel to him.

CAREERS AND PASTIMES

A Sun-sign Guide to Work and Play

CAREERS

It is perhaps easiest to begin with the sort of work which is not suitable for Pisceans: this includes any career where there is a great deal of noise, discipline, cruelty or monotony. The Piscean likes a reasonably peaceful working atmosphere, and the din of a factory floor, with giant machines whizzing away, is not really suitable for his sensitive talents! He will of course make the best of such conditions if he is forced into them and will toil away – working extremely hard if need be – but he will not be happy.

The range of suitable careers for Pisceans is wide, and the medical profession comes high on the list. Many Piscean girls make splendid nurses, and both sexes become doctors: they are particularly good and patient with elderly people. In the artistic field, the Piscean makes an excellent specialist in mime, for he has a natural flair for mimicry. Many dancers are Piscean, and also a great many straight actors and film stars. It is perhaps interesting to think of these artistic professions from a financial point of view as well: all too often an actor's income is anything but steady, but the Piscean, being enormously adaptable, is able to cope with these private dramas and can change overnight from, say, riches to rags when his show suddenly closes!

PISCEAN FOOTWORK

If a Piscean has a flair for design, he may like to try his hand at designing shoes. If he works in a store, he may enjoy selling shoes, or, in the medical field – for which he has a positive inclination, as already mentioned – he could become a chiropodist. It is quite remarkable just how many Pisceans are feet-orientated; this is of course the Piscean area of the body!

Pisceans are also very spiritual, and many have been intimately concerned in the establishment of churches of all denominations. Both active and contemplative religious orders appeal to them. In general the Piscean has an extremely powerful sense of vocation, and once he feels that a certain way is right for him – whether this be along Sunset Boulevard or in the steps of St Paul

– he will follow that way with all his heart and soul.

HYPNOTISM AND THE SEA

There have also been many Piscean illusionists and hypnotists, and, less exotically, many Pisceans have taken to the sea as a career. The latter raises an interesting point, for although Pisceans do not like discipline, they love the sea; presumably, in choosing the Navy as a career, they decide to tolerate the discipline in favour of their special feeling for life on the waves!

A splendidly satisfying career for the artistic Piscean who shows flair and an eye for composition – though perhaps no great ability at draughtsmanship – is that of photography. Pisceans excel in every aspect of this work and – provided they can keep the business side under control – make excellent freelance photographers (freelance because they prefer to work at their own pace). Interestingly, too, the quiet side of their work – in the darkroom – does much to restore their energies.

PASTIMES

The Piscean enjoys spending his spare time sailing, perhaps on quiet rivers and inland waterways where he can also fish, sitting quietly meditating for long periods of time. He will certainly at some period of his life write poetry, and the results are likely to be better than he thinks. He, if anyone, will have poetry in him; all too often, however, his verses end up in the waste-paper basket, where many of his more extrovert friends' efforts *ought* to be!

It can be something of a problem for the Piscean really to organize his hobby or interest, but he must simply try to overcome this tendency. If he feels inclined to paint, he really should try watercolour; he may find that he can manage this less complicated – as well as watery! – medium very well. Generally speaking, the Piscean's inclinations are essentially artistic, and art is often the centre of his being. He may not be too keen on sports, but could enjoy the thrills of skiing, skating, ski-jumping and perhaps show-jumping.

AT HOME

A Sun-sign Guide to Home Décor

If the Piscean's room is tidy, it will also be extremely attractive and easy on the eye. The colours are likely to be unobtrusive, and perhaps the whole room will be decorated in a rather low key, so that, on entering, the visitor is not knocked sideways by stunningly bright colours, opulent showy furniture, or a general dazzle. Many Pisceans, liking a quiet life, also like a quiet atmosphere in their apartments and houses; and there should be, overall, a general impression of peacefulness.

The Piscean is inclined to favour pale shades of blue and green, and sometimes soft velvets will feature. He tends usually to have good taste and is unlikely to choose furniture that is vulgar or garish. If he likes modern styling, there may be a bare sanded wood floor with many rugs of muted shades and various textures; inevitably, too, there will be a very large pot of dried grasses, bullrushes or dead seed pods prominently placed in the room. Many Pisceans have small, decorative fish tanks, or they may have a small dish of terrapins lazing in water!

MEANDERING WATER-LILY DESIGNS

For contrast, the colour scheme may include some element of dramatic purple or dark blue—perhaps the handy Piscean will have found a bargain settee or elderly couch in a sale, or been given one, which he has then re-covered himself.

The drapes and curtains will be textured, perhaps in various kinds of linen, and will be of some natural, unbleached colour. The lamp-shades will be large and give out a gentle, diffused light. The walls are more likely to be painted than papered, and again the general scheme will be quiet but imaginative.

If the Piscean does branch out into wallpaper, he can be expected to favour large designs, perhaps with meandering water-lilies or flowers in the Art Nouveau style; but, here again, the design will be unobtrusive and executed in the palest of pastel colours.

Bookshelves will be full to bursting and arranged in a pleasant way, with pottery between the books. The Piscean has excellent taste in pictures, and may also collect original costume or theatre designs, if he can find and afford them; more usually, there will be reproductions of the lovely paintings of Picasso's blue and rose periods, or perhaps some of the less vivacious Dufys, or the peaceful afternoon scenes of Seurat.

A visit to a Piscean will be enjoyable and probably relaxing; the atmosphere will be informal, with the meal perhaps served buffet-style. The food should be both good and satisfying, and the welcome warm. The music, if the Piscean likes pop, could be extremely groovy, but not noisy; perhaps oriental—with hypnotic sitars, for instance. If he has classical tastes, Debussy, Ravel or perhaps Puccini will be heard.

Entertaining with Your Sun-sign Celebrities

THE HOST
The Piscean's delight in escaping from sordid reality is such that, when you are invited to his idea of a 'magnificent feast,' to be held in 'palatial surroundings,' you may find yourself sharing a haddock in a one-room apartment! But for goodness sake, pretend to enjoy yourself, or sensitive Pisces may burst into tears. It won't be difficult to pretend, however. Pisceans are delightful, warm, kindly people, and you will find yourself wanting them to be happy; and indeed, you may be in for a pleasant surprise, for Pisceans do dearly love making people feel at home, and cosseting them a little; so the evening may be splendidly comfortable after all. Nor do Pisceans dine on haddock alone. If the host has done his work there will be a typically Piscean meal of rich and tasty food, more than enough to induce warm sensations of well-being.

THE GUEST
As a guest, the Piscean is very amenable to suggestion, and there can be few who will not react to being wined and dined – if the intention is to soften them up for some proposition! If Piscean guests have anything on their minds when they come to visit you, you may find floods of tears arriving with the sweet (after the wine has been finished) and you will hear all their troubles. In the face of such a rush of confidence, what better hospitality could you offer than simply to listen to them? This is all part of being a friend to Pisces.

THE SETTING
Your Piscean guests will very much appreciate a romantic atmosphere, and the soft sea-greens which are their favourite colours; even if the latter give a rather undersea atmosphere to your dining-room, their appeal to the Piscean will be enormous. The music could well be a little misty and evocative of the sea, too, provided the Piscean at whom it is directed is in one of his quieter moods; we would not advise *The Flying Dutchman* full out, but rather Debussy's *La Mer*; and even that may be a little noisy at its peak.

WINES
As for wines, Pisces is the most watery of all the signs – which does not mean that guests will necessarily appreciate watered-down wines! They will probably, however, not have any strong preferences for particular wines. A good rosé will suit them down to the ground, being mild and not especially demanding.

Right: An all-star evening for famous Pisceans of past and present would very likely include the illustrious guests in our picture. For details of the dishes on the table – every one a Piscean favourite – turn to page 208.

Michelange

Queen Boadicea

RECIPES FOR PISCES

Cooking with Astrology

Arriving late, full of apologies, the Piscean will tuck into his cold, congealed soup and rapidly cooling main course without so much as noticing what he is eating. Pisceans will like rich, tasty food: home-made onion soup will be especially seductive—in fact, anything home-made will delight them. And the host who combines a rather fishy menu with the sharp, pure flavour of a water ice will go as near to the Piscean's heart as possible. Don't expect a 'thank you' note immediately: a very pretty notelet or card will arrive, but probably a week late!

ONION SOUP

If there is anything more pleasant than genuine onion soup on a cold winter's day, a Piscean will certainly never have heard of it. Slice 1 lb good strong Bermuda onions and fry gently in 2 tablespoons fat (ideally pork fat but oil will do) until soft and transparent but not brown. Stir in $\frac{1}{2}$ cup flour and simmer for 5 minutes longer, stirring constantly. Add 7 cups beef stock, season to taste with salt and pepper, bring to a boil and boil for $\frac{1}{2}$ hour. Serve with thick slices of bread, toasted and sprinkled with grated cheese. Arrange these in the bottom of a heated tureen; pour over soup and put under a hot broiler until thoroughly browned. Do not believe that only the French can make good onion soup: the best I ever tasted was made in St Louis!

'Fish, to taste right, must swim three times—in water, in butter and in wine.' Polish proverb.

SEAFOOD COCKTAIL

Of course, everyone assumes that Pisceans love fish: not all of them do, so ask first. If the answer is yes, this is a fine starter. Take 1 lb any white fish and, having diced the flesh, marinate for 2 hours in the juice of 2 large lemons. Add to this sliced tomatoes, shredded green pepper, some parsley, some Worcester sauce, to taste, and a dressing of olive oil and wine vinegar in the proportion of 3:2. Serve garnished with olives.

TROUT AU VIN ROSÉ

Trout is a delicious fish, however you cook it. This way is fairly simple: place 1 trout per person in a baking pan and just cover with vin rosé. Scatter $\frac{1}{2}$ small onion, finely chopped, over the top; cover with buttered paper, and bake gently in a 325°F oven until flesh flakes easily, with a fork. Drain off cooking juices into a pan and boil briskly until only about an eggcupful remains. Stir in 4 or 5 tablespoons heavy cream and thicken with a little cornstarch. Skin trout; arrange on a heated serving dish and spoon over prepared sauce. Serve immediately.

COQ-AU-VIN

There are many recipes for coq-au-vin. Beware of any that simply consist of pouring some kind of wine sauce over a precooked chicken. Here is an elaborate one, the splendour of which has to be tasted to be believed. Joint chicken. Melt $\frac{1}{4}$ cup butter in a skillet. Add 1 onion, chopped, and $\frac{1}{2}$ cup unsalted bacon, cut into strips, and simmer until onion is transparent. Add 12 small white mushrooms; continue to stir for a minute or two longer, and remove from heat. With a slotted spoon, transfer onion, bacon and mushrooms to a flameproof casserole. Cover and keep hot in a moderate oven (350°F). In fat remaining in skillet, brown chicken joints lightly all over, two or three at a time, transferring them to casserole as they are done, together with pan juices. Stir in some garlic, 2 bay leaves and a little parsley. Cover casserole and return to oven. When chicken is tender, remove joints and vegetables, and keep hot. Skim cooking juices of excess fat. Place casserole over heat. Warm 4 tablespoons brandy in a ladle; carefully set it alight and pour over pan juices. If you boil the juices, this will blaze away happily for a couple of minutes. Put out flames with $\frac{1}{2}$ bottle red wine. Add a lump of sugar and boil briskly until liquid is reduced by half. Season to taste with salt and pepper. Thicken with cornstarch or a beurre manié (2 tablespoons each butter and flour mashed to a smooth paste, and added in tiny bits). Return chicken and vegetables to casserole; spoon sauce over them and keep hot until ready to serve.

WATER ICE

After a heavy meal—certainly after coq-au-vin—the only sweet. For an orange ice, dissolve 2 cups sugar in 4 cups water. Boil for 4 to 6 minutes; cool slightly. Add 2 cups orange juice, $\frac{2}{3}$ cup lemon juice, and the grated rinds of 1 orange and 1 lemon. Leave until cold; strain through a sieve into ice trays and freeze until firm. Texture of ice will be improved if you beat it up several times with a fork while it is freezing.

SIGN-SEEING

The Sun-sign gives us our 'image', affects the way we dress, and contributes certain physical characteristics. Here are some ways in which you reflect your own Sun-sign, and by which you can recognize your friends' places in the Zodiac.

ARIES

Arians dislike clutter and fussy detail in their clothes. It is essential for them to 'stride out'—usually in front of everyone else—so clothes that hamper movement are not for them. The girls usually favour bright, clear colours, especially reds. The men can never wait to get into a favourite old tweed jacket, battle-scarred though it may be, ready to enjoy the Arian's spare-time work with sharp tools and messy jobs.

GIVE-AWAY

The Aries 'glyph' is often seen on the Arian face, following the line of well-arched eyebrows and the sides of the nose.

TAURUS

Venus, the ruling planet of Taurus, makes her presence strongly felt in the Taurean girls' image: they love floral prints, often in soft, floaty fabrics, and in delicious shades of blue and pink – in fact they can look a bit too 'pretty-pretty' at times. The men are usually conventional in dress, but may well sport a collection of interesting (though not outrageous) ties. They look their best in well-cut conventional suits.

GIVE-AWAY

Taureans are recognizable by their thick necks and shoulders. Often they will have curly hair growing low on the forehead. Taurus is considered to be the best-looking of all the signs!

GEMINI

It's separates all the way for Gemini girls!—lively two- or three-piece suits, blouses and skirts, or dresses that look like them, in a great variety of colours (though bright yellow is as near a favourite colour as a Gemini will have). The men, too, like to mix colours and textures in their clothes, and usually do this very well. Both sexes need to take care that their fashion image doesn't become too 'bitty'.

GIVE-AWAY
It's easy to recognize a Gemini by his springy walk: he seems to move up and down as much as he moves forward! The hands will be used expressively but sometimes restlessly.

CANCER

Many Cancerians have a pale complexion and round faces, reflecting the Moon, their ruling planet! All will have a vertical line that frequently appears between the eyes.

Cancerian girls look their best in soft fabrics such as crêpe, but need to be careful that slight untidiness does not mar their appearance. The men may make mistakes in their dress, wearing ill-matching shirts or socks; the sentimental Cancerian man may well take a favourite jacket or blazer back to the tailor's to get it copied. Both sexes will buy fashionable clothes, but hang on to them too long! Favourite colours are pale grey and green.

LEO

If the Leo girl is worth her salt she will soon convert junk jewellery to real rocks, rabbit to mink! There will be more than a touch of glamour and drama to her appearance, but all too easily she can get carried away and become too showy. She will like clothes with back interest, and look her best in the colours of the Sun (her ruling planet)—from the pink of early sunrise right through the gamut of oranges and yellows, to the flame of sunset. The Leo man, like his mate, will buy the best in town, even if he can't afford it; and will pay great attention to cut, and the set of his clothes, which will display to the best advantage his lionesque figure!

GIVE-AWAY
Most Leos walk extremely well, and tend to look down their long, prominent noses at their 'subjects'! Both sexes have long, straight backs and small waists.

VIRGO

GIVE-AWAY

Nearly all Virgoans have a delightful 'widow's peak' to their hair-line; their movement is usually very quick and rather restless, and they find it difficult to sit really still.

Neatness and cleanliness are the keys to the Virgo image. Here is the perfect secretary, in businesslike, neat clothes, perhaps with small floral patterns or spots—interesting clothes, however, and with white collars and cuffs that never get dirty. Navy blue, dark greens and some browns are often favourite colours. The Virgoan girl has taste, but may play a little too safe at times. Virgo men will love the same small patterns in their shirts and ties, and will never attempt to 'casualize' business clothes.

LIBRA

Librans are undoubtedly romantics, and this will be echoed in their dress, on every conceivable occasion! They will look their best in light, perhaps see-through fabrics in pale blues and pinks. Frills and bows are much favoured. The men want to show themselves off to advantage, too, and may wear see-through shirts open to the waist. Both sexes like a touch of red as a change from their favourite pale colours.

GIVE-AWAY
As they speak or listen, Librans will hold their heads first on one side and then another, almost dog-like! Their features are not generally speaking very clearcut, and often there is a certain feyness in appearance.

SCORPIO

GIVE-AWAY

Scorpio eyes are deep-set and penetrating, the forehead and brows heavy. Sometimes the whole face has something eagle-like about it, giving the impression that absolutely nothing is missed!

Both men and women of this sign usually love the 'leather' look, and know very well that it will enhance their naturally sexy image. Very soft black leather seems to be their top favourite. However, as a welcome change the girls will also favour dusky gypsy-style dresses—often with low-cut neck-lines. Both sexes look good in conventional 'city' clothes; but the Scorpio will somehow, even when formally dressed for the bank or Wall Street, manage to add a touch of mystery to their image. Their colours reflect Mars and Pluto (joint ruling planets), in shades of red to the deepest crimson and maroon.

SAGITTARIUS

Most Sagittarians hate to dress up—in fact, they very often dress down, even if the occasion demands otherwise. The Sagittarian image is often that of the eternal student or sportsman; both sexes will love polo-necked sweaters, anoraks and long university scarves. Dark blue and purple are good colours. The Sagittarian man will probably hate ties, and will wear (and look good in) a cravat or scarf inside his shirt. If Sagittarians play a little additional attention to their appearance, they will look terrific without ever becoming formal; but they often don't bother, which is a pity.

GIVE-AWAY

The Sagittarian is usually an open book, and this will show in the face; a wide, 'intelligent' forehead, rather straight eyebrows, and a very open, lively expression are characteristic.

218

CAPRICORN

GIVE-AWAY
There are usually prominent lines from the sides of the nose to the corners of the mouth, and Capricorns often smile 'in reverse', turning *down* the corners of their mouth!

Capricorns either look ultra-smart and slick, or dowdy and giving the impression that they have the cares of the world on their shoulders. Black, dark clerical grey, and dark browns are their colours. The girls look their best in well-cut rather businesslike suits and smart, conventional dark town clothing. They need to be very careful, however, that their image 'does something' for them; sometimes, it doesn't! The men are at their best in really dark, conventional suits; if they are 'trendy' when young, they will soon break away from this as they rise up the social scale. Both sexes should consider a little light relief in their appearance, which can be too dark all the time if they are not careful.

AQUARIUS

The most original and 'different' of the signs, which very often shows in the Aquarian image, for they are 'out on a limb' in their appearance, and love to look as different as they actually are. Both sexes can be very elegant, but sometimes the overall effect is spoiled by the need to be different. A fairly bright turquoise blue is their best colour, and they like expensive originals. Both sexes need to be careful that they do not hang on to styles for too long. Aquarius resists change, and can become 'set' in an image.

GIVE-AWAY

The 'crazy scientist' look, hair standing on end, long bushy eyebrows, tiny metal-framed spectacles! Otherwise, tall and elegant, trying to be like their opposites in the Zodiac, the Leos; but less conventional.

PISCES

GIVE-AWAY

Pisceans very often stand with feet crossed, like a fish's tail; and their eyes look as if permanently on the brink of tears.

The Piscean girl can, Cinderella-like, look marvellous either in rags or a Paris model. She will look her best in greens, watery colours and fabrics, or fine wool. Overall, the image will be slightly way-out and 'artistic'. The man often looks good in his oldest jeans (perhaps with frayed trouser-bottoms and bare feet). If he has to dress more conventionally, small patterns will appear in his choice of shirt. Both sexes will either be very well-shod, or wear terribly sloppy sandals until they fall to pieces!

YOUTHFUL IMAGES

GEMINI: Always active with many irons in the fire, but needs encouragement to complete tasks.

LIBRA: Finds decision-making difficult. Help to combat this weakness during early years, or life may be difficult later.

PISCES: Needs help to develop strength of character. Powerful emotions and imagination seek positive outlet, perhaps through art.

SAGITTARIUS: Needs freedom, open air, dislikes restrictive discipline, cramped surroundings. Excellent mental powers, open to reason.

CAPRICORN: Tends to be a loner, loves reading, can do well in athletics, climbing. Encourage to realise ambitions.

CANCER: Naturally protective especially towards younger brothers and sisters; should try to broaden horizons.

TAURUS: Has a sweet tooth, parents should control candy intake; likely to put on weight.

VIRGO: Always ready to help clean and tidy; school problems may cause digestive upsets, encourage open discussion.

SCORPIO: May be secretive. Help to develop this positively by letting him plan surprises for the family.

AQUARIUS: Naturally independent, can seem eccentric at times, but has a deeply humanitarian spirit. Friendly though unemotional.

LEO: Good organizer, likes to be in charge. Tends to show off, but natural spirit must not be crushed.

ARIES: Enjoys sport, keen to take the lead, but accident-prone and suffers cuts and bruises.

INDEX

INDEX TO THE RECIPES